## Praise for Antidisestablishmentarianism

"...Great book if you want to know the truth about the Christian foundation our country was built ... "

" ... Great overview of the religious nature of the State Constitutions which were never barred from establishing religion by the U.S. Constitution."

"I enjoyed it!"

"Must Read!"

# What Is Secular Humanism?
## (Serial Antidisestablishmentarianism Part Two)

**by**

**Michael J. and Mary C. Findley**



Findley Family Video Publications

*What Is Secular Humanism?*

*(Serial Antidisestablishmentarianism Part Two)*

by Michael J. and Mary C. Findley



"Speaking the truth in love. "

## Table of Contents

# Preface: Disestablishmentarianism

*... When they knew God, they glorified him not as God, neither were thankful; but became vain in their imaginations, and their foolish heart was darkened. Professing themselves to be wise, they became fools...*
Romans 1:21,22

## The Most Religious People on Earth

The most religious people on earth are those who claim not to have any religion. Dogmatic, intolerant, and bigoted, they refuse to allow anyone to so much as speak their opposition. Yet these same people demand political power and tax support. The mildest opposition, such as the mere mention of Intelligent Design (not God), has blacklisted tenured professors. Just two parents in a middle school in Texas made the national news by objecting to Gideon Bibles placed, without comment, on a table outside the school office.[1] Such people dishonestly claim that they are not religious and "religion" is a group of mythologies. The truth is that they are the ones promoting mythology. In every aspect of life they promote this mythology with unproven dogmatic assertions under the guise of "Science" vocabulary. After hijacking the word "Science," they use the courts to elevate their misuse of the term to an established religion.

## What Science Is, and What it Isn't

Science is the study of the world around us, the use of the experimental method and the improvement of our lives through the application of technology. It is divided into various academic disciplines such as Chemistry,

Physics, Mathematics and Biology. However, what the federal courts, the Academic community and the mainstream Western media mean by science is uniformitarianism. It is the cosmological foundation of the religion of Secular Humanism. "Since the fathers fell asleep, all things continue as they were from the beginning of the creation" (II Peter 3:4). This concise description of Uniformitarianism clearly shows that it is completely and entirely a religious belief in antiscientific myths.

Secular Humanists use words which have been in the English language for hundreds of years but give them "new" meanings. However, "there is no new thing under the sun" (Ecclesiastes 1:9, KJV). The words believe, faith and trust are all historic judicial terms and they also form the foundation of the true scientific method. What Secular Humanists promote as their version of the scientific method consists of preconceptions, presuppositions and assumptions. It is the opposite of an open mind.

## Redefining or Restoring? – The True Meanings of Belief, Faith, and Trust

A true open mind is founded in belief, faith and trust. The historic meaning of believe is to perceive or understand with the mind and then make an informed decision.[2] The most basic use of the word believe which the average American would understand is that of a juror in court. Which witness do you believe? Which piece of evidence is believable? A synonym would be the word credible. When we believe something or someone and then act on that belief, that is faith. The active part of belief is faith. The passive part of belief is trust. Suppose your brother says that he will drive you to the doctor. If you believe him, then you understand what he says and you make a decision to get ready. If you get in the vehicle with him, that is faith. You act on your belief. When you sit in the vehicle as he drives, that is trust, a passive reliance on what you have proven true. You trust in his driving skills. You trust in the vehicle. You trust the roads, etc. Everything we do is a combination of belief, faith or trust. By restoring their historic definitions, belief, faith and trust re-emerge as the clear language of true experimental science. These terms were deliberately segregated from science to deceive people into believing Secular Humanism.

Liberals, Secular Humanists and materialists, however, use the word "belief" as a synonym for a philosophical position, just an opinion. Faith and trust to them are metaphysical words which mean different things to different people. And this is just the tip of an enormous iceberg. Secular Humanists have redefined hundreds of words to support their religion, such as sin, judgment and anthropology. A conversation with them can be very difficult since they use historical English words but mean something entirely different.

## Establishment of Religion – The Church/State Power Grab

The traditional role of religion is to place priesthood as intermediary between God and man. The traditional role of an establishment of religion places the government in that intermediary role between God and man. In the Middle Ages the Roman Catholic Church put itself between man and God, as other religions have in the past. Johann Tetzel, a "professional pardoner," sold indulgences representing forgiveness for sins in Germany. Indulgences were based on the "storehouse" of good works believed to exist because of the sacrifice of Christ and the good deeds and prayers of past saints. Tetzel was said to promise that, "As soon as a coin in the coffer rings, a soul from purgatory springs."[3]

Selling indulgences was the final act of many which brought on the Reformation. People wouldn't have bought them if they hadn't believed the Catholic Church alone could placate God on their behalf. Martin Luther convinced the princes of Germany that they did not need to send their money to Rome because they could go to God directly. Rome sent armies to collect the money. Even Modern Roman Catholics who do not believe that their church today claims to stand between them and God have to admit that the medieval Roman Catholic Church did.

The combined power of Church and State restricted personal worship, scientific study and access to historical truth. Today Secular Humanism has done the same by removing foundational truths from education. It excludes study and discovery that contradicts uniformitarianism. It rewrites history to undermine morality and freedom of expression.

## Scriptural Authority and Freedom

The union between the medieval Romanist church and the state came to an end in two ways. In Southern Europe during the Renaissance, art, architecture, literature, and learning opened up to all men, not just those who were part of the church and state system. The Renaissance left the power intact, however. In Northern Europe, the Reformation abolished the need for a church like Rome through the great affirmations of the Reformation: The Scriptures are the absolute authority; Justification is by faith alone apart from works; and every believer is his own priest with direct access to God. The Reformation made a special priesthood class unnecessary because men could pray directly to God and read His Word on their own.

The medieval Roman Catholic Church kept the Scriptures almost exclusively in Latin to prevent ordinary people from studying them, forcing people to come to the priest. The priest would not only tell them what the Scriptures said, but he also mingled that with the church's interpretation. In order for ordinary people who did not know Latin to read the Bible for themselves, the Scriptures had to be translated into the language of the ordinary people. Translation work by Reformers was essential to enable ordinary men to read the Scriptures for themselves, even though it was punishable by death under the Church-State system. The Renaissance and the Reformation worked together in the development of moveable type to make printing and distribution of translations of the Scriptures easier. Renaissance scholars revived interest in studying forgotten manuscripts and making translations into the vernacular. Erasmus's Greek New Testament provided a basis for more accurate translations of the Scriptures.

The Medieval Romanist Church-State system took away freedom by forcing man to rely on and accept its teachings. The Renaissance and the Reformation restored freedom by returning art, science, and all forms of learning to ordinary people. In particular the people were able to worship God as the Scriptures taught, without Church-State control. Modern western culture, and American culture in particular, was founded on this religious freedom. American culture is more Christian than European cultures, but neither of these cultures can survive if the foundation of religious freedom is destroyed.

## Natural Law

It is this Christian foundation of religious freedom which is the real target of Secular Humanists. These Secular Humanists have taken outrageous liberties in their unrelenting quest to replace religious freedom with their established religion of Secular Humanism, which they incorrectly call science or Natural Law. Their major tool is the US court system. Sympathetic US courts have consistently supported Secular Humanism by using every possible opportunity to replace the word religion with the ancient concept of Natural Law. However, since Natural Law has been used so many different ways, the courts had to standardize the term Natural Law. Their version of Natural Law goes back to Plato's *Republic.* Though Plato never used the phrase "natural law" in his *Republic,* translator Benjamin Jowett's notes state that, "Plato among the Greeks, like Bacon among the moderns, was the first who conceived a method of knowledge... "[4] Plato's *Republic* is at least the foundation of modern Natural Law, if not the detailed finished product. Together with Aristotle, Plato is supposed by secularists to have laid the foundation for learning and development of the Sciences. This is really is essence of Natural Law.

## Plato's Ideal State

Jowett goes on to say that Plato provided for a means to spread his method of acquiring knowledge. "In the ideal State which is constructed by Socrates, the first care of the rulers is to be education."[4] Jowett makes it clear that Socrates meant to impart much more than mere academic knowledge, just as Natural Law means to teach more than mere Science. Socrates promoted "the conception of a higher State, in which 'no man calls anything his own,' and in which there is neither 'marrying nor giving in marriage,' and 'kings are philosophers' and 'philosophers are kings;' and there is another and higher education, intellectual as well as moral and religious, of science as well as of art, and not of youth only but of the whole of life."[4]

Many know that Plato in his *Republic* based his state on a philosopher/king. Few, however, are aware that he believed in communism and free love and that these two "natural" principles were to be foundational principles of the state.

Though the preceding condensation by Benjamin Jowett is an excellent job, as you can read for yourself, the actual words of Socrates, as quoted by Plato, are much longer and more difficult to understand. "None of them will have anything specially his or her own." "... Their legislator, having selected the men, will now select the women and give them to them [the legislator gives selected women to selected men]... they must live in common houses and meet at common meals ... they will be together ... And so they will be drawn by a necessity of their natures to have intercourse with each other... " "... Until philosophers are kings, or the kings and princes ... have the spirit and power of philosophy, and political greatness and wisdom meet in one ... cities will never have rest from their evils."[5]

The philosopher/king, according to Socrates, was to lay these foundational ideas through education. Though he did not use the phrase "establishment of religion," Plato clearly advocated an established religion. It was to be put in place by a philosopher/king through education based on a state where "no man calls anything his own" and where there is neither "marrying nor giving in marriage." Though this education would begin with children, it would continue throughout a person's entire life. This is the Natural Law which the US Court system has imposed.

## Disestablishmentarians

The US needs to disestablish its Establishment of Religion and reestablish religious freedom. In the 1800's churches which tried to break away from the Church of England were called disestablishmentarians. The people who fought against the disestablishment of those churches within the Church of England in the 1800s were called Antidisestablishmentarians. Today, the mainstream media, liberal politicians, the academic community, the liberal courts and all others who file lawsuits, blacklist, fire, refuse to hire, tax, legislate against, libel, slander and do whatever is necessary to maintain their positions of privilege and power are modern Antidisestablishmentarians.

---

1 (No author) "Parents Fuming as Texas Schools Let Gideons Provide Bibles to Students," Tuesday, May 19, 2009, *Fox News.com.* "A spokeswoman for the school district said that a number of materials are made available to students this way, including newspapers, camp brochures and tutoring pamphlets. College and military recruitment information is available all year long. The Gideon Bibles were made available for just one day. 'We have to handle this request in the same manner as other requests to distribute non-school literature — in a view-point neutral manner,' Shana Wortham, director of communications for the district, wrote in an e-mail to *FoxNews.com.*

2 Alexander Hamilton, in an 1802 letter to James Bayard. "I have carefully examined the evidences of the Christian religion, and if I was sitting as a juror upon its authenticity I would un-hesitatingly give my verdict in its favor. I can prove its truth as clearly as any proposition ever submitted to the mind of man."

3 Philip Schaff, *History of the Christian Church,* Volume 7, "The Reformation," Charles Scribner's Sons, 1910.

4 Plato, *The Republic* (c. 360 B.C.), translated by Benjamin Jowett over a period of 30 years until his death in 1893, completed posthumously by Lewis Campbell. (Introductory material (in double quotes) and paraphrases of Plato's ideas (in single quotes) were written by Jowett.)

5 Plato, *The Republic,* Book Five Dialogue excerpts among Socrates, Adeimantus, Glaucon and Thrasymachus have been placed in parentheses within Jowett's introductory material.

# Introduction

*Facts are stubborn things; and whatever may be our wishes, our inclinations, or the dictates of our passion, they cannot alter the state of facts and evidence.*[1]
John Adams

Sometime in the early twentieth century, Secular Humanist indoctrination convinced almost everyone in the United States that "an establishment of religion" in the first phrase of the first amendment of the United States Constitution is vague and can mean just about anything. "The state of the facts and evidence," as John Adams so eloquently put it, is the exact opposite.

**Section One** of this work documents what the founders meant by the phrase "an establishment of religion. " The Founding Fathers made as clear a statement as the English language permitted. The Constitution of the United States is founded on English law and to a lesser extent, various European laws, especially German and Dutch. In each of these countries, an Establishment of Religion was the collection of taxes to support education, welfare and public worship. The various governments appointed the teachers, welfare workers and pastors and expected these people to support the government in turn.

The original state constitutions not only permitted, but openly encouraged establishments of religion, especially in the areas of welfare and education. The foundation of the US Constitution is the fact that federal government was to have no control whatsoever in these areas. Their concept of a separation of Church and State was the exact opposite of what the courts have rammed down our throats for the past hundred years. The church should have the right to pray and teach without any federal intervention whatsoever. Judges should have the right to post any Scriptures they want. The courts should have no authority whatsoever to comment. Removing a state judge from office for posting the Ten Commandments is not merely an Establishment of Religion. It is the Inquisition.

**Section Two** documents the foundations of Secular Humanism and how it grew to become America's Establishment of Religion. The words "Secular Humanism " come from various groups in the 1950's. The phrase "Secular Humanist " is found in court documents to describe this set of beliefs. Secular Humanism is as old as civilization, but the primary foundation of twenty first century Secular Humanism is Plato's *Republic*. In America, Secular Humanism can be said to have originated with Thomas Paine. Secular Humanism has specific beliefs which are written down in various manifestos. Like Christianity, Islam and Judaism, Secular Humanism has many variations. Though Secular Humanists do not like the term, the most accurate words to describe these variants are "sects " or "denominations. " Like Christians, Muslims and Jews, many Secular Humanist denominations do not get along with one another. Therefore, we have attempted to point out the beliefs which have the greatest agreement.

**Section Three** defines science, since Secular Humanists claim that science separates them from all other religions. Since true science is founded in the belief, faith and trust of the Bible, all of these words are defined carefully and in detail. In the Bible, belief, faith and trust are legal terms. Believe means to examine the evidence and come to a reasoned conclusion. Action taken on that belief is faith. Trust is the passive version of faith.

The Scientific Method is the biblical version of belief, faith and trust applied to the material world which God created for us. In the Bible, the Scientific Method recognizes that God is the creator, that we are required to be responsible managers of the material world God has given us and that there is a final judgment after death which will include how well we managed the gifts God allowed us to use.

Our book concludes with **Section Four,** the results of having Secular Humanism as an Establishment of Religion. With the exception of America's founding documents and the ancient documents such as Plato, Plutarch and Genesis, hundreds of other quotes could easily be substituted for the quotes that appear here. There is nothing new or unique in this book. It is a combination of what used to be common knowledge in America before Secular Humanism took over and destroyed the education system and current events. If we were to start over today, we would pull different stories from the daily news. Though the individual stories would be different, the points would be the same. "There is nothing new under the sun " (Ecclesiastes 1:9). Or to state the same thing another way, the more things change, the more they stay the same.

America's Established Religion is Secular Humanism. This work is dedicated to exposing, defining and disestablishing it.

---

1 John Adams, "Argument in defence of the [English] soldiers in the Boston Massacre trial," December 1770.

2 "Alabama's Judicial Ethics Panel removed Chief Justice Roy Moore from office Thursday for defying a Federal judge's order to move a ten commandments monument from the State Supreme Court building. " Friday, November 14, 2003. Posted 6:56 AM Eastern time. *CNN.com*

# 1. What Is Secular Humanism?

*"The United States Supreme Court has held that secular humanism is a religion. Belief in evolution is a central tenet of that religion."*[1]
Antonin Scalia, in the case McLean v. Arkansas Board of Education, 1982

Almost every American colony had some form of establishment of religion. This was because their religion consisted of proven and necessary facts of existence. Religion was reliable, logical and rational to them. The modern established religion of Secular Humanism teaches that it is the only scientifically-based belief system in existence. It claims that all other religions are not scientifically-based, but the opposite is true. The Bible, upon which true religion is based, is a book of Science, and Secular Humanism is a religion of mythology.

*... Scientific history ... is that the method that we use is something akin to the scientific method. It is based on at least three characteristics .... The first is to establish that the evidence is reliable. The second is making certain that the analysis being made is logical. And third, the analysis must lead to a generalisation that is based on rational argument.*[2]

Since time began man has only been able to take one of three positions toward a scientific fact. The first is belief, which means to accept the fact as it is and interpret its significance correctly. The second is unbelief, which means to reject a fact or give it the wrong interpretation. The third position is some degree of compromise between the other two, such as accepting a fact but wrongly interpreting its significance. It is also possible to misinterpret the true nature of the fact and misapply it to come to other wrong conclusions.

Belief does not mean mere opinion, as modern culture has degraded the word. The legal term belief means to accept something as true based on the facts available. Facts are true whether or not you choose to believe them. The Scriptures are the basis of scientific facts. This is the standard the founding fathers began with and also the colonials before them. All scientific facts are based on the Scriptures. "Facts are stubborn things;" said John Adams, "and whatever may be our wishes, our inclinations, or the dictates of our passion, they cannot alter the state of facts and evidence."[3]

Since the opposite is drilled into everyone through western culture and western education, we need to think the following example through slowly and carefully. The Exodus of the children of Israel from Egypt is told in the Bible as a straightforward, factual, historic event. Charlton Heston, in his narration of the picturesque Bible video series, presents the Bible as part of the "oral tradition in storytelling" as if teachings passed on orally were understood to be less accurate or reliable and therefore merely legends and myths. Socrates, in Plato's Dialogue *Phaedrus,* addresses the subject of oral versus written history.

> *Theuth [Thoth] ... was the inventor of many arts, ... but his great discovery was the use of letters. ... Thammus [the god Amun] was the king of ... Egypt; ...To him came Theuth ... desiring that the other Egyptians might be allowed to have the benefit of [his inventions]; ... when they came to letters, "This," said Theuth, "will make the Egyptians wiser and give them better memories;" ... Thamus replied: ... "You ... attribute to them a quality*

> *which they cannot have; for this ... will create forgetfulness in the learners' souls, ... they will trust to the external written characters ... This is an aid not to memory, but to reminiscence, ... not truth, but only the semblance of truth; they will be hearers of many things and will have learned nothing; they will appear to be omniscient and will generally know nothing; they will be tiresome company, having the show of wisdom without the reality."*[4]

Plutarch, in his discourse on the life of Lycurgus and his rule in ancient Greece, expresses the belief that oral tradition is a way of making the law more firmly fixed in the mind.

> *None of his laws were put into writing by Lycurgus, indeed, one of the so-called "rhetras" forbids it. For he thought that if the most important and binding principles which conduce to the prosperity and virtue of a city were implanted in the habits and training of its citizens, they would remain unchanged and secure, having a stronger bond than compulsion in the fixed purposes imparted to the young by education, which performs the office of a law-giver for every one of them.*[5]

There is considerable disagreement about whether the Scriptures were in some part orally communicated before being written down. The point is that even if they were it does not make them less authoritative or reliable. Socrates may not be entirely justified in discounting the value of written records but he reinforces the point that oral communication of history does not make it unreliable or inaccurate. Memorizing and passing on history demands great discipline and does not result in a form of the child's game "gossip."

Gossip, sometimes called Telephone or other names, consists of a group made to stand in a line. The first person in line is given a piece of paper on which is written a phrase to whisper into the ear of the second person. Frequently there is only one opportunity to whisper the message. The second person whispers what he heard to the third, and so on down the line. The last person is to write down or speak aloud what he heard the person before him say. When the final form of the "gossip" message is made public, frequently it bears little resemblance to the original phrase. The distortion of the oral message in the game gossip is simply due to the indifference of the people playing the game. In fact, one simple change in the rules of the game of gossip produces correct transmission of the message even by children. Simply offer everyone who is playing a large enough reward, or punishment, if the final message is correct.

Modern prisoners of war, inmates in prison, gang members, spies and others today pass on important information without writing it down and without changing the message. Most American Indian tribes had no written language and saw no need for one, until Europeans demonstrated the ability to talk to people far away. In the popular TV series Mission: Impossible, the leader of the team received his orders on a recording that self-destructed after he had heard it one time. He was forced to memorize the mission immediately or he would be unable to complete it.

In the Scriptures, the Exodus is not recorded as a "story" which only "contains" truth. The Exodus is recorded as an historic event like WWII, Benjamin Franklin hearing George Whitfield preach or the invention of the steam engine.

The established religion of secular humanism would single out the invention of the steam engine as the only scientific fact included in these historic events. The word science, however, means something has been correctly observed and accurately recorded under controlled circumstances. For an event or experiment to be a scientific fact it must normally be reproducible. There are exceptions to this, however. The explosion of a supernova is a scientific fact, though no one on earth knows of any way to reproduce that explosion. And even though some of the information recorded about WWII is incorrect information, the historic fact of WWII is also a scientific fact. In fact, WWII is probably the most well recorded fact of history. The abundance of evidence allows modern observers to cross reference records to make a true scientific picture of WWII. Benjamin Franklin's observations are just as scientific.

> *He [Whitefield] ... preach'd one evening from the top of the Court-house steps, which are in the middle of Market-street, ... I had the curiosity to learn how far he could be heard, ... I found his voice distinct till I came near Front-street... Imagining then a semi-circle, ... fill'd with auditors, to each of whom I allow'd two square feet, I computed that he might well be heard by more than thirty thousand. This reconcil'd me to the newspaper accounts of his having preach'd to twenty-five thousand people ... and to the antient histories of generals haranguing whole armies, of which I had sometimes doubted.*[6]

On the other hand, Benjamin Franklin's observations of George Whitfield's preaching were the scientific measurements of a single observer. Though a single observer, even a careful one like Benjamin Franklin, might be more prone to error than a large number of observers, Franklin's measurements were still scientific. Franklin used a step-by-step process of investigation. He physically walked off the distance to determine the range of Whitfield's voice. Next he compared his observation with previous witnesses of Whitfield's audiences and range. Finally he adds similar established historic accounts of commanders addressing troops (adding that he previously doubted their truth).

In the following paragraph the Bible presents step-by step scientific proofs of the accuracy of the historical event of the Exodus. Three hundred years after the event Jephthah confirms its occurrence (Judges 11:26). At the time of the beginning of Solomon's temple construction the official historical record of the event (I Kings 6:1) confirms that 480 years have passed. If someone falsely claims that the Biblical record of the Exodus is not scientific, that is an issue of his unbelief, not an issue of science.

In the book of Judges, part of Jephthah's speech to the Ammonites includes an approximate date for the Exodus. "...Israel dwelt in Heshbon and her towns, and in Aroer and her towns, and in all the cities that be along by the coasts of Arnon, three hundred years? Why therefore did ye not recover them within that time?" (Judges 11:26, KJV) By the time of Solomon, the date of the Exodus was the foundational date for the kingdom. "And it came to pass in the four hundred and eightieth year after the children of Israel were come out of the land of Egypt, in the fourth year of Solomon's reign over Israel, in the month Zif, which is the second month, that he began to build the house of the LORD." (I Kings 6:1, KJV) Though the comparison of modern calendars with ancient calendars is very difficult and it is easy to be a few years off, I Kings 6:1 gives a precise date to the Exodus. Anyone who understands that Solomon began to build the house of the LORD in 966 BC of our Gregorian calendar knows that the Exodus took place in 1446 BC according to our Gregorian calendar. If you are interested in understanding these discrepancies, please see the Section Two Appendix on Calendars. Anyone who uses a slightly different date, such as 1444 BC or 1447 BC is not disagreeing about the date of the Exodus. He is simply disagreeing about the proper method of scientifically reconciling ancient calendars to our modern Gregorian calendar. Clearly this documentation of the Exodus is scientific history, actual events recorded and verified by scientific methods.

The believer understands that the Exodus took place in 1446 BC. In this case the word believer does not mean someone who has put his faith and trust in Jesus Christ. It simply means that he has examined the evidence and chosen to accept the facts. For example, Immanuel Velikovsky, author of numerous works on errors in the currently accepted dating methods of mainstream archaeology, believes the Exodus took place at the time recorded in the Bible, even though he rejects everything supernatural.

The unbeliever, however, does not understand that an Exodus ever took place. He simply rejects anything like the biblical record. In other aspects of his life he may be a Hindu, a Muslim, an atheist or almost anything else. He looks at the work of Egyptologists since James Breasted's *Ancient Records of Egypt* and concludes that nothing like the Exodus recorded in the Bible ever happened. Mainstream history has no room for anything like the Exodus. A belief in the Exodus will keep doctoral candidates from receiving their doctorates, PhDs from getting a job, prevent professors from achieving tenure and will blacklist tenured professors. A brief look at a few people who have experienced some of this prejudice is documented in Ben Stein's movie *Expelled*.[7]

The compromiser examines the Exodus recorded in the Bible and the massive works of mainstream historians and attempts to reconcile them. Though it is possible for as many reconciled dates as there are individuals doing the reconciling, the most common date compromisers arrive at is 1295 BC. The 1295 BC date often makes Rameses II the pharaoh of the Exodus, as in the Stephen Spielberg movie, *Prince of Egypt* and the 1956 classic Cecil DeMille's *The Ten Commandments*. The 1295 BC date is a poor fit and is often ridiculed by mainstream historians who completely reject anything like an Exodus. Though it is the best fit these men can come up with, it is still wrong. As Charles Haddon Spurgeon said:

> *A chasm is opening between the men who believe their Bibles and the men who are prepared for an advance upon Scripture. Inspiration and speculation cannot long abide in peace. Compromise there can be none. We cannot hold the inspiration of the Word, and yet reject it; we cannot believe in the atonement and deny it; we cannot hold the doctrine of the fall and yet talk of the evolution of spiritual life from human nature; we cannot recognize the punishment of the impenitent and yet indulge the "larger hope." One way or the other we must go. Decision is the virtue of the hour.*[8]

Compromisers want to "get along," to make allowances for other views, to be tolerant. They won't stand up for the truth because it doesn't matter enough to them. These are people who believe that "getting along" is more important than honesty. Dorothy Sayers said, "In the world it is called Tolerance, but in hell it is called Despair, the sin that believes in nothing, cares for nothing, seeks to know nothing, interferes with nothing, enjoys nothing, hates nothing, finds purpose in nothing, lives for nothing, and remains alive because there is nothing for which it will die."[9]

Though massive tomes have been written on date of the Exodus, that is not the purpose of this work. The Exodus is but one example of the three possible positions of belief, unbelief and compromise. A juror for an automobile accident can be a believer, an unbeliever or a compromiser. A juror who makes a decision based on the evidence of the case alone is a believer. A juror who rejects the evidence and draws conclusions based on some other preconception is an unbeliever. A juror who combines evidence with preconceptions and jumbles it all together into a mess is a compromiser. We are all compromisers on issues where we fail to stand firmly on principle. Compromise is the most destructive thing we can do to our character. Yet as destructive as compromise is, it is an area in each of our lives that we have difficulty seeing clearly.

Throughout history, unbelief has taken many forms. In the Roman Empire the main form of unbelief was polytheism and Christians were viewed as atheists because they believed in only one God. Christianity was dangerous as a "foreign superstition," and its followers "notoriously depraved," said Tacitus, first and second century Roman historian.[10] Suetonius, a second century Roman historian, called Christianity a "new and mischievous religious belief,"[11] in his work *The Twelve Caesars*. In Marcus Aurelius's *Meditations* Christians are called a "gang... of ignorant men and credulous women." He believed they were guilty of lawlessness, or "mere contumacy."[12] Athenagoras, an Athenian who wrote to the Emperor Marcus Aurelius, said that Romans accused Christians of "atheism, Thyestean feasts [cannibalism], [and] Oedipodean intercourse [incest]."[13]

Justin Martyr, a second century Christian apologist, acknowledged the Roman perspective but made the Christian position clear to those who ignorantly or willfully misinterpreted it. "Hence are we called atheists. And we confess that we are atheists, so far as gods of this sort [the Roman pantheon] are concerned, but not with respect to the most true God..."[14] Athenagoras pleaded with Marcus Aurelius to recall that every nation under Roman control was allowed to worship its own gods. Romans believed their vassal states were made better by religious practice, but Athenagoras said that Christians were "harassed, plundered, and persecuted, the multitude making war upon us for our name alone."[13]

The Romans founded this empire-wide persecution of Christians upon the charge of Atheism, since Christians were not pantheists like the Romans. But beneath the mask of the worship of many gods, the Romans held the same beliefs Secular Humanists hold today.

Unbelief can take different forms in different cultures. In Japan it was emperor worship; other cultures have even degenerated into cannibalism. But the predominant form of unbelief in the world today is Secular Humanism. We use the term "Secular Humanist" or "Secular Humanism" because that is what they called themselves. *The Humanist Manifesto I* is a religious document, written by a Unitarian Minister, Raymond B. Bragg, in 1933. Thirty men who believed themselves to be representative of a vast multitude "forging a new philosophy" signed it. "... There is no new thing under the sun." (Ecclesiastes 1:9, KJV)

*The Humanist Manifestos I, II* and *III* can be viewed on the website *americanhumanist.org*. They cannot be reprinted here because of the following notice on the site:

> *Copyright renewed 1973 by the American Humanist Association. Permission to reproduce this material, complete and unmodified, in electronic or printout form is hereby granted free of charge by the copyright holder to nonprofit humanist and freethought publications. All other uses, and uses by all others, requires that requests for permission be made through the American Humanist Association.*[15]

These men quickly learned that using the word "religion" actually hampered their cause. If they could deceive people into believing that secular humanism was not a religion and that religion was bad, then they could get state funding (follow the money trail) and political power while putting ungodly restrictions on those who actually dared to call themselves religious. Humanist Manifestos II and III call traditional religions "traditional theism" and describe them as "obstacles to human progress." Many have also dropped the word "secular" and simply call themselves "humanists."

This is an effective propaganda technique, since they are now denying that they are a religion. The 1973 *Humanist Manifesto II* is lengthy and filled with doublespeak. It is exactly what George Orwell in 1984 and Aldous Huxley in *Brave New World* warned us about. It is important because it was signed by more than one hundred influential people, including doctors, university professors, and others like Isaac Asimov, scientist and writer, B. F. Skinner, Prof. of Psychology, Harvard University, Betty Friedan, Founder of *N.O.W*, and Sir Julian Huxley, former head, *UNESCO,* Great Britain. All the manifesto texts can be viewed online. *Humanist Manifesto III* is the most seductive. True intentions are cleverly obscured and it sounds very good. As commentator Bill O'Reilly points out, the term Secular Humanist is not very accurate. It is, however, the oldest and most accurate of the labels they have chosen for themselves.

It is also the term used in court documents, including the US Supreme Court, so we will continue to use it. "Among religions in this country which do not teach what would generally be considered a belief in the existence of God are Buddhism, Taoism, Ethical Culture, Secular Humanism, and others."[16] Justice Black based his comments on the 1957 case of *Fellowship of Humanity v. County of Alameda.* In this case an organization of humanists sought a tax exemption on the ground that they used their property "solely and exclusively for religious worship." The court ruled that the activities of *Fellowship of Humanity* entitled it to an exemption. These activities included weekly Sunday meetings. The *Fellowship of Humanity* case used the word humanism, not secular humanism.[16]

Secular Humanism also made a separate manifesto, first published in 1980 as *A Secular Humanist Declaration* by *CODESH (Council for Democratic Secular Humanism)* co-authored by Paul Kurtz and Edwin H. Wilson, both editors of *The Humanist* magazine. Its principle purpose was to declare its compatibility with democracy and how enlightened man should view traditional religions as inferior to secular humanism.

Still," ...There is nothing new under the sun." (Ecclesiastes 1:9, NIV). Plato praised many of these same follies in his dialogue *The Republic.* Since Plato is so verbose, few study him in detail today, which is good. Where Aldous Huxley in *Brave New World* and George Orwell in 1984 viewed the following principles as deplorable, Plato praised them as necessary. His philosopher king would use thugs he called guardians to enforce the will of the legislators on a hapless society divided into classes. Plato's philosopher/king together with legislators and guardians would determine what the classes would be and who would belong to which class. The class you belonged to would determine every aspect of your life.

But Secular Humanism is older than Plato. It is older than anything written which is still in existence. "What has been will be again, what has been done will be done again; there is nothing new under the sun." (Ecclesiastes 1:9, NIV). Contrary to scientific facts, the modern version of the religion of Secular Humanism believes that a simple, chaotic universe evolved into a complex, ordered universe. To oversimplify, everything came from nothing. Secular Humanists deny that they are a religion for the express purpose of attacking all other religions, collecting tax money and obtaining political power. They also deny that same political power to anyone who disagrees with them. As no two Christians, Jews, Taoists, etc. believe exactly the same way, so no two Secular Humanists believe the same thing. Despite their differences, Secular Humanists hold many beliefs in common.

People who hold beliefs in common can be labeled by those common beliefs. For example, the *Niagara Bible Conference* is where the term Fundamentalism first began to be used. The term was also used to describe "The Fundamentals," a collection of twelve books funded by Milton and Lyman Stewart. These men collected as many addresses of Christian teachers, preachers and other leaders as they could find. They published the books and sent them to these addresses over a period of time ending around 1910. This group of beliefs became known as Fundamentalism.

Fundamentalists defined their beliefs so clearly that anyone willing to be called a Fundamentalist told others something about what they believe.[17] The term Fundamentalist, however, applies to every aspect of life. A football coach who emphasizes the basics of blocking and tackling as opposed to trick plays or a wide open offence like the West Coast offence is known as a Fundamentalist. An architect who designs simple, inexpensive buildings using the basics of engineering is a Fundamentalist. And a believer in the following list of fundamentals for Secular Humanism makes a person a Fundamentalist in Secular Humanism.

*The Fundamentals of Secular Humanism*

1. Secular Humanism is a religion based on feelings and emotion, not reason.

2. Secular Humanism denies anything non-material. Anything spiritual is redefined as "energy." Various humanists use terms such as "Life Energy," "Life-Force," "Interdimensional Energy," etc. The source of the energy is always material or natural, not supernatural.

3. Secular Humanism denies the existence of a supreme being including Intelligent Design.

4. While acknowledging the existence of evil it denies the concept of original sin. It believes in the perfectibility of man.

5. Though Secular Humanism is open to things not yet discovered, at this time there is no scientific evidence for life after death.

6. Man's existence on the Earth, like everything else in the universe, is a result of chance and not a plan. The most likely explanation for this chance is evolution, which is based on uniformitarianism.

7. Secular Humanism demands that science include only what is within the scope of "natural law" but does not allow for any explanation for the origin of natural law, and therefore the origins of matter or energy; nor is there any reliable information on a possible end to the universe.

8. Only secular humanist beliefs are reasonable; all other religions raise false hopes, restrict personal fulfillment, or both.

9. The purpose of life is to make you a better person. This is accomplished by service to others and seeking fulfillment in this life. Though each person might have a different concept of fulfillment, no one has the right to tell another person that what he is doing is wrong, unless it harms someone else. This is especially true with sexual gratification.

10. The accumulated improvements of many individuals will drive the evolution of the human race.

11. The best way for society to survive and thrive is to allow enlightened leaders complete freedom to guide all institutions and organizations that serve all people from the beginning to the end of life.

12. Man exists only as a member of the world community. The world community is responsible to provide for the protection and guidance of the

enlightened society from the earliest age. Children must not be separated from the world community. Any persons of majority age who oppose the ideals of the world community must be forced into conformity through employment sanctions or reeducation. Opposition must be suppressed by any necessary means.

13. Improvement of society is the essential duty of the enlightened guardians and includes guidance to prevent nonproductive, undesirable or inferior types.

14. Enlightened leaders guide others to fulfillment in this life. The community chooses the values of these enlightened leaders. The enlightened leaders help to guide the community in developing their values system.

15. Compulsory education indoctrinates the citizen of the world community. It is the catechism of the new society.

16. Personal property is evil. This includes any type of marriage since marriage is a property arrangement. Since Secular Humanists recognize evil, it is the responsibility of the guardians to supervise the distribution of material possessions, including social contracts. Individuals corrupt material possessions by unnecessarily hoarding them.

17. National sovereignty is the cause of war, poverty, overpopulation, and waste or destruction of resources. A unified world government is essential to stable economics and freedom in the areas of communication, travel, arts, sciences and education.

18. Unity means eradication of opposition. Secular Humanists characterize anyone who differs from them on these fundamentals as opponents. Opponents are characterized as being oppressive, divisive, fearful of change, bigoted or guilty of hatred.

Some of these items may seem extreme, even to those who claim to be humanists. Some will protest, “I don’t believe that!” As was said before, not all humanists believe all these points exactly in these words. The position of the Secular Humanists has been evolving over millennia, not just centuries, and in the next chapters some surprising adherents will come to light. Prepare to hear from people who lived in times when they could see and touch the gods the state demanded they worship, yet their words produced the echoes secularists proclaim today as "new ideas for new times." Look for parallels of these "modern" beliefs in the words of ancient writers who were required by law to believe in the gods of Sumeria, Babylonia, Egypt, India, Meso-America, Greece and Rome. They still spoke clearly about how they had already forged their own beliefs with man as his own prophet, priest and object of worship. Moving closer to modern times, hundreds of well-known humanists will make it clear that those who are influencing every aspect of our culture have believed these concepts for centuries and do, in fact, believe them and work for their realization today.

---

1 *Edwards v. Aguillard, U.S. Supreme Court,* 1987. Justice Antonin Scalia's dissenting opinion Chief Justice William Rehnquist concurring with Scalia.

2 Professor Romila Thapar, *Frontline* magazine Volume 18 - Issue 19, Sep. 15 - 28, 2001 India's National Magazine from the publishers of *THE HINDU.*

3 John Adams, "Argument in defence of the soldiers in the Boston Massacre trial," December 1770.

4 From Plato's Dialogue *Phaedrus,* Translated by Benjamin Jowett, 1871.

5 Plutarch, from his *Life of Lycurgus,* translated by John Dryden and others, 1683.

6 Franklin, Benjamin. *Autobiography.* First English version published London, 1793. (The Appendix of the

Great Awakening includes the publication history of this work.)

7 *Expelled: No Intelligence Allowed.* Producers Logan Craft, Walt Ruloff and John Sullivan. Director Nathan Frankowski. Writers Kevin Miller and Ben Stein. Associate Producer Mark Mathis. Editor Simon Tondeur. copyright 2008 Premise Media Corporation, Rampart Films Production.

8 Charles Haddon Spurgeon, "Our Reply to Sundry Critics and Enquirers," *The Sword and Trowel*, Metropolitan Tabernacle, Elephant and Castle, London, Sept. 1887.

9 Dorothy L. Sayers, "The Other Six Deadly Sins," *Creed or Chaos,* Harcourt, Brace and Company, New York: NY, 1994, p. 81.

10 Tacitus, *The Annals of Imperial Rome,* 109 AD, XIII. 32, Translated by Alfred John Church and William Jackson Brodribb, 1876.

11 Gaius Suetonius Tranquillus, *The Twelve Caesars,* written c. 117 138 AD, translation J. C. Rolfe, 1913-1914.

12 Marcus Aurelius, *Meditations,* XI.3, 167 AD, translated by George Long, 1862.

13 Athenagoras of Athens, *Legatio pro Christianis* [translated "Supplication for the Christians"], a letter to Marcus Aurelius written in 177 A.D. Translated by B. P. Pratten in "Athenagoras." *The Ante-Nicene Fathers,* vol. 2, Wm. B. Eerdmans, Grand Rapids: Michigan, 1954.

14 Justin Martyr, *First Apology,* Chapter 6, "The Charge of Atheism Refuted," Alexander Roberts and James Donaldson, Translators, 1867.

15 Humanist Manifestos I, II, III, *http://www.americanhumanist .org/ Who_We_Are/About_Humanism/Humanist_Manifest o_I (II or III).*

16 *Torcaso v. Watkins, United States Supreme Court,* 1961, Justice Hugo Black in a footnote. Justice Black based his comments on the 1957 case of *Fellowship of Humanity v. County of Alameda.* Where an organization of humanists sought a tax exemption on the ground that they used their property "solely and exclusively for religious worship."

17 More detailed information on the Niagara Bible Conference and the Fundamentals can be found in the following sources: Ahlstrom, Sydney F. *A Religious History of the American People.* New Haven: Yale University Press, 1972; Beale, David O. *In Pursuit of Purity.* Bob Jones University Press: Greenville, SC, 1986; Dollar, George W. *A History of Fundamentalism in America.* Greenville, SC: Bob Jones University Press, 1973.

## 2. When Did Establishments of Religion Begin?

*We have gone back to ancient history for models of Government, and examined the different forms of those Republics which, having been formed with the seeds of their own dissolution, now no longer exist.*[1]
Benjamin Franklin, from his speech at the Constitutional Convention

*He[Nimrod] persuaded them not to ascribe it [success] to God ... but to believe that it was their own courage.... He ... changed the government into tyranny-seeing no other way of turning men from the fear of God, but to bring them into a constant dependence upon his own power. He also said he would be revenged on God ... that he would build a tower too high for the waters [of another flood] to be able to reach!*

From Josephus' *Antiquities of the Jews*[2]

*Cush begat Nimrod; he began to be a tyrant in the earth. He was a tyrannical hunter in opposition to the Lord. Thus it is said,"Nimrod the tyrannical opponent of YHWH. "*

Genesis 10:8-9, as translated by Dr. David P. Livingston.[3]

Various scholars identify Nimrod with the Akkadian/Sumerian/ Assyrian/Babylonian part-god/part-human Gilgamesh, the Akkadian human king Sargon, Babylon's King Hammurabi, the son of a god Hercules (Roman), or Herakles (Greek), the "king of the Indus Valley" Erekles (India) and the predynastic pharaoh and god of Egypt Osiris. Perhaps Nimrod was one of these figures, perhaps he was none of them or perhaps he was all of them. However he is identified, all other ancient kings built on the foundation for an establishment of religion laid down by Nimrod. Each of these names represents a foundation for an establishment of religion in different cultures.

The story of Gilgamesh is supposedly the oldest written story in the world. There are fragments of the Gilgamesh story in Akkadian, Sumerian, Hittite, Assyrian and Babylonian. The most complete extant copy, however, only goes back to the eighth century BC. Though there are some differences, there are some identical elements in all the versions. Gilgamesh is a powerful tyrant whose people complain to the gods that he oppresses them, taking every woman he wants and killing any man who opposes him. Key to the Gilgamesh story is his quest for immortality, to continue as a tyrant forever. Whatever else there is in the true identity of Gilgamesh, he is the first tyrant.

Hercules, Herakles, Erekles and Osiris are tyrants, but not like Gilgamesh. Still, these names are key to founding national establishments of religion. Though regarded as completely mythical by today's established religion of Secular Humanism, the stories of these men are also the stories of tyrants. Each one is credited with godlike powers. Each one allows their followers to develop a powerful priesthood, which includes a potential for control of life after death.

By contrast, the kings Sargon of Akkadia and Hammurabi of Babylon were entirely human tyrants. Though the basalt stele law code testifies that at least Hammurabi was a real person, we know little about either of their historic accomplishments. We do know that the records of ancient kings depict them as tyrants who used an establishment of religion to help control their people. There is no reason to assume that Sargon of Akkadia or Hammurabi were any different.

Genesis 10:8-12 KJV

> *Cush begat Nimrod: he began to be a mighty one in the earth. He was a mighty hunter before the LORD: wherefore it is said, Even as Nimrod the mighty hunter before the LORD. And the beginning of his kingdom was Babel, and Erech, and Accad, and Calneh, in the land of Shinar. Out of that land went forth Asshur, and builded Nineveh, and the city Rehoboth, and Calah, And Resen between Nineveh and Calah: the same is a great city.*

*From the Li Ki, a Confucian compilation of ancient Chinese manners and customs:*

> *If to any of the younger cousins there have been given vessels, robes, furs, coverlets, carriages and horses, he must offer the best of them (to his chief), and then use those that are inferior to this himself. If what he should thus offer be not proper for the chief, he will not presume to enter with it at his gate, not daring to appear with his wealth and dignity, to be above him who is the head of all the clan with its uncles and elder cousins.*[4]
>
> *"How The Great Kaan Enjoineth His People To Supply Him With Game."*
>
> *The three months of December, January and February, during which the Emperor resides at his Capital City, are assigned for hunting and fowling, to the extent of some 40 days' journey round the city; and it is ordained that the larger game taken be sent to the Court. To be more particular: of all the larger beasts of the chase, such as boars, roebucks, bucks, stags, lions, bears, etc., the greater part of what is*

> *taken has to be sent, and feathered game likewise. The animals are gutted and dispatched to the Court on carts. This is done by all the people within 20 or 30 days' journey, and the quantity so dispatched is immense. Those at a greater distance cannot send the game, but they have to send the skins after tanning them, and these are employed in making of equipments for the Emperor's army.*[5]

Like The Great Khan and thousands of other rulers, Nimrod used his hunting skills to first impoverish, then control and finally enslave people. As Xenophon points out, hunting is the ideal way to learn military skills. "Therefore I charge the young not to despise hunting or any other schooling. For these are the means by which men become good in war and in all things out of which must come excellence in thought and word and deed."[6] It was easy for Nimrod to apply his successful hunting skills to war. He then made cities for the conquered people along with an establishment of religion to control them.

The establishment of religion completed government's control of every aspect of life. That control has continued in the unholy Church-State alliances throughout the millennia. Today we have governments within governments. Gang lords, drug lords, terrorist organizations, perhaps a less-refined version of a mafia don's domination all function this way. For each layer of government, control is essential in both positive and negative senses. Sun Tzu examined military principles for keys to success. He asked,"In which army is there the greater constancy, both in reward and punishment?"[7] Consistency is essential to control.

Perhaps the best modern example is radical Islam. Radical Islam shows how constant vigilance maintains control, and includes intimate areas of the underlings' lives.

> *In reality Islam is a revolutionary ideology and programme which seeks to alter the social order of the whole world and rebuild it in conformity with its own tenets and ideals. 'Muslim' is the title of that International Revolutionary Party organized by Islam to carry into effect its revolutionary programme. And 'Jihad' refers to that revolutionary struggle and utmost exertion ... to achieve this objective.*[8]

These leaders, beginning with Nimrod to the Khan to the Jihadist, demand that their followers live according to strict guidelines covering religion, politics, sex and socializing. The leader also promises great rewards or threatens his people with dire consequences, even into afterlife, because he controls access to the god who determines their fates. The underlings have to be kept in line with rewards and punishments in this life and the next or they become distracted at the very least, and disloyal at the worst.

By contrast, Lycurgus, legendary king of Sparta (or Laconia or Lacedaemonia or Lacedaemon), only remade Sparta. He had no designs on conquering the entire world and remaking it into his image. Plutarch, a historian and biographer living in the first and second centuries AD, wrote about Lycurgus in *his Parallel Lives of Famous Greeks and Romans*, a work usually called simply *Lives* today. At the beginning of his biographical account Plutarch says, "There is so much uncertainty in the accounts which historians have left us of Lycurgus, the lawgiver of Sparta, that scarcely anything is asserted by one of them which is not called into question or contradicted by the rest."[9] Plutarch notes the multitude of ancient sources who acknowledge that Lycurgus' laws were a reality, whatever may be true about when and how he lived. He wrote down what was traditionally believed about Lycurgus and his Spartan society. Ancients and moderns who refer to him place him as early as the 9th century or as late as the 7th century BC.

Though Lycurgus is presented in histories as a kind, selfless and beloved ruler, he clearly follows the pattern of the tyrant. Unlike most tyrants though, he believed that his actions were the best for Sparta and the future of Sparta. He did not personally gain from his system. Before Lycurgus "anarchy and confusion long prevailed in Sparta."[9] This anarchy even took the life of the father of Lycurgus. Lycurgus did not rule by force. The people of Sparta "obeyed him because of his eminent virtues."[9] By all accounts, Lycurgus believed that his actions were the best for the Spartan people, even at great personal cost. He certainly never profited from his actions, either financially or politically.

However much Lycurgus believed in his laws, they were not virtuous. What he actually did was to strip the Spartans of all personal liberty, money and possessions, and cut them off from outside trade or commerce. These changes caused them to become arrogant and contemptuous of the world, and removed any hint of true morality. His principles resulted in soldiers who could defend the kingdom against all comers but who came to consider all non-Spartans enemies, cultural as well as physical. "The city is well fortified which hath a wall of men instead of brick."[9] Spartans boasted about their superiority to other Greeks and to the entire world. They were completely self-sufficient and believed they had achieved perfection as men and citizens. Though Lycurgus comes across in histories as humble and selfless, "beloved of God"[9] and reportedly getting sanction for his laws directly from Apollo (see below), he made Spartans the most man-centered, and therefore self-centered, state in the ancient world.

The common thread which Nimrod started and which runs through Sun Tzu, Lycurgus and Plato into modern Secular Humanist thought is the emphasis on self. Lycurgus, like Plato, is not as blatant and open as Walt Whitman in his *Leaves of Grass*; "Song of Myself" ( "I celebrate myself, I sing myself")[10] The expression of their beliefs would be more like Shakespeare's *Hamlet* when Polonius advised his son, "to thine own self by true."[11] This was most obvious in Sparta's "solemn festivals."[9] Spartan religious devotion became legendary through the battle of Thermopylae in 480 B.C., where they refused to send a full force to repel the Persian invasion because it conflicted with the nine-day Carneian festival honoring Apollo. However, for the most part these Spartan festivals "were vaunts of what they would do, and boasts of what they had done, varying with the various ages."[9]

All the Spartans had to be willing to do to create the perfect religious state was to sacrifice personal freedom. Before Lycurgus "their state was overloaded with a multitude of indigent ... while its whole wealth had centred upon a very few. ...he [sought to] expel from the state arrogance and envy, luxury and crime, and ... want and superfluity..."[9] Lycurgus promised that he could eradicate these evils, and all evil, from society simply by a three-part plan. The first was an equal redistribution of the land. "They should live all together on an equal footing; merit to be their only road to eminence, and the disgrace of evil, and credit of worthy acts, their one measure of difference between man and man."[9]

The second step of replacing their money with worthless iron currency, Lycurgus believed, would make them even more virtuous. "With the diffusion of this money, at once a number of vices were banished from Lacedaemon; for who would rob another of such a coin? Who would unjustly detain or take by force, or accept as a bribe, a thing which it was not easy to hide, nor a credit to have?"[9] The third of Lycurgus's reforms, which Plutarch calls, "The most masterly stroke of this great lawgiver,"[9] was communal dining. "That they should all eat in common, of the same bread and same meat, and of kinds that were specified, and should not spend their lives at home... to fatten them in corners, like greedy brutes, and to ruin not their minds only but their very bodies ...[needing] as much care and attendance as if they were continually sick..."[9]

Lycurgus made prosperity synonymous with evil, and by doing so made most personal ownership a sin. He created a religion of equality supervised by the state and made every citizen a spy and an enforcer upon his fellows. "Every one had an eye upon those who did not eat and drink like the rest, and reproached them with being dainty and effeminate."[9] Lycurgus called it brotherhood. "Methinks all Laconia looks like one family estate just divided among a number of brothers."[9] His use of religious terminology, "virtue," "solemnity," "zeal," reveals his intent to forge a state religion without which the people could not function. "To conclude, he bred up his citizens in such a way that they neither would nor could live by themselves; they were to make themselves one with the public good, and, clustering like bees around their commander, be by their zeal and public spirit carried all but out of themselves, and devoted wholly to their country."[9]

At least part of Lycurgus's desire for reform was a desire for true justice, which he sought to achieve through good laws. He was said to have received the Oracle of Delphi's promise that "he is called beloved of God, and rather God than man; that his prayers were heard, that his laws should be the best, and the commonwealth which observed them the most famous in the world."[9] Justice was worshipped in ancient times. From the name *Ma'at*, the Egyptian goddess who assisted Osiris in judging the dead, comes the word Magistrate. *Themis* was a Greek woman who was known for organizing community affairs and assemblies. She later became one of the

Oracles at Delphi and was "promoted" to represent divine justice. *Justitia* was the Roman goddess familiarly portrayed in modern courts with a blindfold, sword and scales. Some statues depicted her as carrying a flame, representing truth, or a bundle of sticks surrounding an ax, the faces symbolizing Rome's unified national law.[2]

Lycurgus's perfect state corresponds closely with another that never came into reality as his did. Plato's *Republic* consists of dialogues where Socrates begins by discussing with his students the meaning of justice. Various definitions fail to satisfy Socrates and they find they must create true justice by creating a perfect state. Though his state differs in some respects from Lycurgus's, Plato's intent was to forge unity between government and religion. Note that the Republic begins with attendances upon religious duties and festivals in honor of "the goddess," just as Plutarch early on relates Lycurgus's visit to the oracle. Both Plutarch and Plato clearly wanted to set a religious tone for the discussion to follow. Near the end of the *Republic* Plato relates a story about a man who recounted a visit to the Underworld. The goddess *Lachesis* is one of the three Fates. She traditionally measures the length of a man's life. Here she has a different function. (Note that *genius* to the ancient Greeks meant a mental or animating force, similar to the soul, and that *Virtue* was also worshiped as a goddess.)

> *Hear the word of Lachesis, the daughter of Necessity. Mortal souls, behold a new cycle of life and mortality. Your genius will not be allotted to you, but you choose your genius; and let him who draws the first lot have the first choice, and the life which he chooses shall be his destiny. Virtue is free, and as a man honours or dishonours her he will have more or less of her; the responsibility is with the chooser --God is justified.*[13]

Plato, through Socrates, claims that a man can choose his animating and driving force, and that he has the power to choose virtue, and grow in virtue by choice. He puts the power and the responsibility on man and proclaims that man cannot blame the gods for a bad life. Therefore the gods are just. This negates the possibility of original sin as taught in the Scriptures and also supports the perfectibility of man. Lycurgus practiced the same belief by claiming that his removing external temptations to vice made men virtuous, since they willingly submitted to his system. The truth is that man is bound by his sin nature, a product of the original sin by Adam and Eve. The freedom of the will is to yield to the Spirit of God, not to choose good or evil. We cannot choose to good as Socrates/Plato claims. "For I know that in me (that is, in my flesh,) dwelleth no good thing: for to will is present with me; but how to perform that which is good I find not. For the good that I would I do not: but the evil which I would not, that I do." (Romans 7:18-19, KJV).

Plato first gets his audience to stipulate that the perfect state must have as its ruling class those who are both guardians and philosophers. Plato sets up a parable of sorts, making an analogy between physical police power and political defenders of the ideal state. A definition of a guardian is simple to agree upon. He must possess swiftness and strength to pursue enemies and to fight them if necessary. Plato next takes pains to sets up a disarmingly humorous scenario to define a philosopher. Socrates at first allows his students to conclude that it may not be possible to find the perfect guardian-philosopher in nature. To find it in nature is essential because they are creating a State where man and his efforts will be exalted and the gods have already made it man's responsibility to succeed by his own abilities, given before birth. Then Socrates brings up the example of the dog, saying that he is a "true philosopher."

*Socrates: He distinguishes the face of a friend and of an enemy only by the criterion of knowing and not knowing. And must not an animal be a lover of learning who determines what he likes and dislikes by the test of knowledge and ignorance?*
*Glaucon: Most assuredly.*
*Socrates: And is not the love of learning the love of wisdom, which is philosophy?*
*Glaucon: They are the same, he replied.*
*Socrates: And may we not say confidently of man also, that he who is likely to be gentle to his friends and acquaintances, must by nature be a lover of wisdom and knowledge?*
*Glaucon: That we may safely affirm.*
*Socrates: Then he who is to be a really good and noble guardian of the State will require to unite in himself philosophy and spirit and swiftness and strength?*
*Glaucon: Undoubtedly.*
*Socrates: Then we have found the desired natures; and now that we have found them, how are they to be reared and educated?*[13]

So Socrates has found in nature his future philosopher-king, since characteristics in dogs must surely exist in humans. This is part of his Natural Law formula. He clearly he means to begin at the beginning, since he mentions rearing and education.

Lycurgus also wanted to condition the people from birth forward to be perfect citizens. Both Socrates and Lycurgus placed strong emphasis on education as the foundation for creating their states. Plutarch credits Lycurgus with desiring, "the good education of their youth (which,...he thought the most important and noblest work of a lawgiver), he went so far back as to take into consideration their very conception... and birth, by regulating their marriages."[9] Plato agrees wholeheartedly that conditioning must begin even before birth, echoing Lycurgus's belief that "children were not so much the property of their parents as of the whole commonwealth, ... [Lycurgus] ... would... have his citizens begot by the...best men that could be found...,"[9] choosing mating couples like breeders of prize dogs or horses. This applied to women as well, and both Plato and Lycurgus thought monogamy to be detrimental to their goals.

*Socrates: And this lawful use of them [powers of the philosopher-kings] seems likely to be often needed in the regulations of marriages and births.*
*Glaucon: How so?*
*Socrates: Why, I said, the principle has been already laid down that the best of either sex should be united with the best as often, and the inferior with the inferior, as seldom as possible; and that they should rear the offspring of the one sort of union, but not of the other, if the flock is to be maintained in first-rate condition.*[13]

Note that Plato states that the inferior sort of child should not be reared, even as Lycurgus taught that

> *"...The elders of the tribe to which the child belonged ... carefully ... view the infant, and, if they found it puny and ill-shaped, ordered it to be taken to ... a sort of chasm under Taygetus; as thinking it neither for the good of the child itself, nor for the public interest, that it should be brought up, if it did not, from the very outset, appear made to be healthy and vigorous."*[9]

Parallels emerge in the matter of preparing the men and women who would give birth to these perfect citizens, physically and mentally. Both Plato and Lycurgus wanted females to pursue exercise regimens in the same manner as men. Those who know the history of Greece know this meant exercising nude in public. Socrates and Glaucon banter about how people will think this odd but insist it must be carried through. Lycurgus demanded that the young women prepare themselves in this way, both for attracting mates and for producing superior offspring. Lycurgus was quite well aware of the traditional constraints of modesty upon women but meant to overcome them, as Plutarch reports, even giving a nod to the similarity of Plato's views on the subject.

> *[That] he might take away their ... fear of exposure to the air, and all acquired womanishness, he ordered that the young women should go naked in the processions, as well as the young men, and dance, too, in that condition, at certain solemn feasts, singing certain songs, whilst the young men stood around, seeing and hearing them.... These public processions of the maidens, and their appearing naked in their exercises and dancings, were incitements to marriage, operating upon the young with the rigour and certainty, as Plato says, of love, if not of mathematics.*[9]

According to Plutarch, Lycurgus carried on his radical reforms openly and the people accepted them, even to the point where "imperfect" men offered their "perfect" wives to other men and raised the offspring as their own just to be assured of continuing the "perfecting" of the race. "For example, an elderly man with a young wife, if he looked with favour and esteem on some fair and noble young man, might introduce him to her, and adopt her offspring by such a noble father as his own."[9] Plato did not believe people would be as accepting of his eugenics program, which included free interbreeding among the perfect specimens and none knowing which children they had sired.

"Then if any one at all is to have the privilege of lying, the rulers of the State should be the persons; and they ... may be allowed to lie for the public good. But nobody else should meddle with anything of the kind."[13] Plato feared an uprising among the ignorant and proposed that the general population be deceived into thinking traditional marriages were still taking place. "[Since] a lie is ...useful only as a medicine to men, then the use of such medicines should be restricted to physicians; private individuals have no business with them"[13] Here, too, is a parallel to Lycurgus, whom Plutarch describes by saying, "He must act as wise physicians do, in the case of one who labours under a complication of diseases, by force of medicines reduce and exhaust him, change his whole temperament, and then set him upon a totally new regimen of diet."[9]

*Socrates: Now these goings-on must be a secret which the rulers only know, or there will be a further danger of our herd, as the guardians may be termed, breaking out into rebellion.*
*Glaucon: Very true.*
*Socrates: Had we not better appoint certain festivals at which we will bring together the brides and bridegrooms, and sacrifices will be offered and suitable hymeneal songs composed by our poets: the number of weddings is a matter which must be left to the discretion of the rulers, whose aim will be to preserve the average of population?*[13]

Remember that marriage has nearly always been an important religious ceremony as well as a state-recognized institution. The legal and spiritual aspects are closely joined in the minds of most people. Plato suggests that pre-arranged sham marriages take place, complete with sham religious ceremonies. A form of lottery, rigged, of course, will convince the inferior types who do not "win" a superior partner that they just have bad luck. Everyone will think the process of selection is just. The marriages will "sanctify" Socrates' orgies of perfect partners and the production of children of unknown but superior parentage.

He wants to create the illusion that the society has not degenerated into "licentiousness," just as Lycurgus's followers insisted that adultery did not exist in Sparta. "Geradas, a Spartan of very ancient type,... asked by a stranger what the punishment for adulterers was ... answered ... 'But how could there be an adulterer in Sparta?'"[9]

*Socrates: True, I said; and this, Glaucon, like all the rest, must proceed after an orderly fashion; in a city of the blessed, licentiousness is an unholy thing which the rulers will forbid.*
*Glaucon: Yes, he said, and it ought not to be permitted.*
*Socrates: Then clearly the next thing will be to make matrimony sacred in the highest degree, and what is most beneficial will be deemed sacred?*[13]

Plato's State alone can make this matrimony sacred. Religion and government must go hand-in-hand to produce what man decides are the best people and the best place. Lycurgus and Plato both saw the need for public worship to support the state's aims, for ceremonies and songs and processions and feasts to glorify the perfecting of man and his government.

Having established the way to create perfect offspring, Lycurgus and Plato both went on to outline the education of their perfect citizens. "Every end and object of law and enactment it was his design education should effect ..."[9] Plutarch says of Lycurgus. Plato's educational system focused early on intellectual development.

"In the case of a young and tender [child] ...the character is being formed and the desired impression is more readily taken."[13] Socrates claims that he wants to take the youngest minds and shape their thoughts and beliefs by giving them fictional stories that teach important moral truths. This is why Bible "stories" are acceptable to Secular Humanists in preschool. They want them to be viewed just like fairy tales and animal fables – mainly fictitious while containing a few elements of truth. "Then the first thing will be to establish a censorship of the writers of fiction ...and we will desire mothers and nurses to tell their children the authorised ones only. Let them fashion the mind with such tales, even more fondly than they mould the body with their hands."[13]

The ancient Greeks taught as their religion a mythology based on false beliefs. These mythologies were just as false as the gods of the Sumerians, Egyptians and others. These gods may have been just statues, they may have been demons or human being given powers by Satan but their purpose was to replace the truth of God with a lie. For Socrates to say that stories of adultery, deception, selfishness and fickle punishments were not appropriate to teach young children seems like a good thing. But the point is that Socrates is rewriting the people's religion under complete government control. There is no better way to control people than to control what they believe. This is what an establishment of religion is.

Plato justifies "cleaning up" religious teachings, calling belief in these teachings "suicidal, ruinous, impious."[13] In the same manner secularists justify removing from the Bible God's "bullying" of man, especially any talk about punishing sin or about Hell. The same way Nimrod rewrote his people's religion, as described by Josephus at the beginning of the chapter, and the same way Plato rewrote Greek beliefs, the modern humanist censor rewrites the Bible.

Socrates uses flawed definitions of good and evil to rob God of most of His true nature and power. Socrates must establish a new state religion to secure his ends, and modern secularists have followed his example closely.

Lycurgus was less concerned with intellectual development than with physical and social training. He meant to build a certain type of character. Education included developing reasoning skills and the ability to make sound judgments according to the narrow and specific dictates of Spartan society. "The old men ... often raised quarrels and disputes among them [young boys], to have a good opportunity of finding out their different characters, and of seeing which would be valiant, which a coward... Reading and writing they gave them, just enough to serve their turn."[9]

Lycurgus was building a nation of acute observers of men and discerners of men's natures. "If they had not an answer ready to the question, who was a good or who an ill-reputed citizen, they were looked upon as of a dull and careless disposition, and to have little or no sense of virtue and honour."[9] As noted above, respected older citizens deliberately provoked and taunted boys to see if they showed "proper" spirit. The means of developing the desired character was harsh. "Besides this, they were to give a good reason for what they said, and in as few words and as comprehensive as might be; he that failed of this, or answered not to the purpose, had his thumb bit by the master."[9] They were spies-in-training, capable of informing on people who did not live up to the perfect standard and being a constant check on their freedom as well as the freedom of others. "They used them thus early to pass a right judgment upon persons and things, and to inform themselves of the abilities or defects of their countrymen."[9]

Both Lycurgus and Plato advised that the future leaders of their states be raised without any luxuries and apart from families and normal home life. It is important to remember that in both cases these people are completely state-controlled, prohibited from earning their own living, and from prospering freely.

"In the first place, none of them should have any property of his own beyond what is absolutely necessary; neither should they have a private house or store closed against any one who has a mind to enter; their provisions should be only such as are required by trained warriors, who are men of temperance and courage; they should agree to receive from the citizens a fixed rate of pay, enough to meet the expenses of the year and no more; and they will go and live together like soldiers in a camp."[13]

Lycurgus' plan for the upbringing of boys, beginning at age seven, was even more harsh and uncompromising. While it is good to train a soldier to "live off the land," forcing the population to commend success and punish failure at thievery breaks down morality on both sides.

> *They all lived under the same order and discipline... The whole course of their education was one of continued exercise of a ready and perfect obedience. ,,, their chief care was to make them good subjects, and to teach them to endure pain and conquer in battle. ... Heads were close-clipped, they were accustomed to go barefoot, and for the most part to play naked. ... After they were twelve years old, they were no longer allowed to wear any undergarments, they had one coat to serve them a year; ... but little acquaintance of baths and unguents... They lodged together in little bands upon beds made of the rushes ... which they were to break off with their hands without a knife; if it were winter, they mingled some thistle-down with their rushes, ... the weaker and less able [were sent] to gather salads and herbs, and these they must either go without or steal; ... if they were taken in the fact, they were whipped without mercy, for thieving so ill and awkwardly. They stole, too, all other meat they could lay their hands on... If they were caught, they were ... reduced to their ordinary allowance, which was but very slender.*[9]

Though there were differences, the similarities between Plato and Lycurgus' perfect states are many, and it is because their purposes were the same. They believed that the state should control people's lives in every aspect, because the state would be comprised of wise rulers who knew better than the people they governed what was best for them. They controlled marriages, births, upbringings, education, and especially religion. And the religion was to work hand in hand with the government to keep the controls tightly in place. Lycurgus' Spartans "neither would nor could live by themselves ...to make themselves one with the public good,"[9] Those who came up through Plato's Republic were to be "those who in their whole life show the greatest eagerness to do what is for the good of their country, and the greatest repugnance to do what is against her interests."[13] In other words, the state is more important than anything else, and in each of these "perfect" states, Lycurgus and Plato's, citizens were to be watched from the beginning to the end of their lives by the rulers and by each other. Any sign of "disloyalty" was to be dealt with immediately and harshly.

Sun Tzu, Chinese general and master strategist, wrote down the lessons he perfected earning his place in the king's army. His The Art of War is a timeless military manual as well as an influential philosophical treatise. Sun Tzu believed ardently in the possibility of perfect leaders and perfect soldiers.

> *5, 6. The Moral Law causes the people to be in complete accord with their ruler, so that they will follow him regardless of their lives, undismayed by any danger.*
> *9. The Commander stands for the virtues of wisdom, sincerity, benevolence, courage and strictness.*[11]
> *These five heads should be familiar to every general: he who knows them will be victorious; he who knows them not will fail.*[7]

Though he lived shortly after Lycurgus, Sun Tzu made no pretense of reliance upon the gods or even the "divine" emperor's authority. He believed superstition and reliance upon religious advice should be purged from the army. Following is biographical material included in the introduction to The Art of War.

> *Ho Lu, King of Wu, said to [Sun Tzu]: "I have carefully perused your 13 chapters. May I submit your theory of managing soldiers to a slight test?"*
>
> *Sun Tzu replied: "You may." Ho Lu asked: "May the test be applied to women?"*
>
> *... Sun Tzu divided [180 palace women] into two companies, and placed one of the King's favorite concubines at the head of each. ... "I presume you know the difference between front and back, right hand and left hand?"*
>
> *The girls replied: "Yes."*
>
> *Sun Tzu went on: "When I say "Eyes front," you must look straight ahead. When I say "Left turn," you must face towards your left hand. When I say "Right turn," you must face towards your right hand. When I say "About turn," you must face right round towards your back.*
>
> *Again the girls assented. ... Then, to the sound of drums, he gave the order "Right turn." But the girls only burst out laughing. Sun Tzu said: "If words of command are not clear and distinct, if orders are not thoroughly understood, then the general is to blame."*
>
> *So he ...gave the order "Left turn," ... the girls once more burst into fits of laughter. Sun Tzu said: "... if [the general's] orders ARE clear, and the soldiers nevertheless disobey, then it is the fault of their officers."*
>
> *So saying, he ordered the leaders of the two companies to be beheaded. Now the king of Wu ...was greatly alarmed ... "We are now quite*

*satisfied as to our general's ability to handle troops. ... It is our wish that [the two concubines] shall not be beheaded."*

*Sun Tzu replied: "Having once received His Majesty's commission to be the general of his forces, there are certain commands of His Majesty which, acting in that capacity, I am unable to accept."*

*Accordingly, he had the two leaders beheaded, and straightway installed the pair next in order as leaders in their place. When this had been done, the drum was sounded for the drill once more; and the girls went through all the evolutions, turning to the right or to the left, marching ahead or wheeling back, kneeling or standing, with perfect accuracy and precision, not venturing to utter a sound.*

*Then Sun Tzu sent a messenger to the King saying: "Your soldiers, Sire, are now properly drilled and disciplined, and ready for your majesty's inspection. They can be put to any use that their sovereign may desire; bid them go through fire and water, and they will not disobey."*

*But the King replied: "Let our general cease drilling and return to camp. As for us, we have no wish to come down and inspect the troops."*

*Thereupon Sun Tzu said: "The King is only fond of words, and cannot translate them into deeds."*

*After that, Ho Lu saw that Sun Tzu was one who knew how to handle an army, and finally appointed him general. In the west, he defeated the Ch`u State and forced his way into Ying, the capital; to the north he put fear into the*

> *States of Ch`i and Chin, and spread his fame abroad amongst the feudal princes.*[7]

This story is included to show that for the ruler to succeed, control is everything and must be maintained at any cost. The king set up the test conditions, and Sun Tzu followed through. Sun Tzu was not afraid to state that he had more strength than the king himself. Brutal, remorseless, but effective, Sun Tzu "shared in the might of the king."[7] From The Art of War itself come Sun Tzu's thoughts on seeking knowledge from a divine source.

> *4. Thus, what enables the wise sovereign and the good general to strike and conquer, and achieve things beyond the reach of ordinary men, is foreknowledge.*[5].
>
> *Now this foreknowledge cannot be elicited from spirits; it cannot be obtained inductively from experience, nor by any deductive calculation.*[6] *Knowledge of the enemy's dispositions can only be obtained from other men.*
>
> *26. Prohibit the taking of omens, and do away with superstitious doubts. Then, until death itself comes, no calamity need be feared.* [7]

---

1 Delivered Thursday, June 28, 1787, Philadelphia, PA.

2 Josephus, Flavius. *Antiquities of the Jews* I: iv: 2) William Whiston, Translator, 1737.

3 Dr. David P. Livingston,"Nimrod: Who Was He? Was He Godly or Evil?" *Associates for Biblical Research.* Originally published in ABR's BIBLE AND SPADE 14.3 (2001), pp. 67-72.

4*The LÎ KÎ* (The Book of Rites) Part I. Translated by James Legge (1885). *Sacred Books of the East*, vol. 27 "The Sacred Books of China," vol. 4.

5Marco Polo and Rustichello of Pisa, *The Travels of Marco Polo,* Volume 1, The Complete Yule-Cordier Edition, Including the unabridged third edition (1903) of Henry Yule's annotated translation, as revised by Henri Cordier; together with Cordier's later volume of notes and addenda. (1920) Chapter XVII).

6 Xenophon,"On Hunting," *Xenophon in Seven Volumes*, 7. E. C. Marchant, G. W. Bowersock, tr. Constitution of the Athenians. Harvard University Press, Cambridge, MA; William Heinemann, Ltd., London. 1925.

7Sun Tzu, *The Art of War*, 6th century BC, translated by Lionel Guiles, 1910.

8 Sayeed Abdul A'la Maududi, from an address given on April 13, 1939, translated on the site *IslamistWatch.org,* no translator credited.

9 Plutarch, from his *Life of Lycurgus,* translated by John Dryden and others, 1683.

10 Walt Whitman,"Song of Myself," from *Leaves of Grass*, first published 1855, revised and republished many times until the "deathbed" edition finished in 1892 and the "definitive version " published in 1900.

11 William Shakespeare, *Hamlet*, Act I Scene iii, Polonius to his son Laertes.

12 Adapted from, "Themis, Goddess of Justice," Prepared by Barbara Swatt, Reference Intern, Updated Oct. 31, 2007. *Marian Gould Gallagher Law Library, University of Washington School of Law.*

13 Plato, *The Republic* (c. 360 B.C.), translated by Benjamin Jowett over a period of 30 years until his death in 1893, completed posthumously by Lewis Campbell.

## 3. Where Did the Secular Humanists get Their Game Plan?

*"For legislators make the citizens good by forming habits in them, and this is the wish of every legislator, and those who do not effect it miss their mark, and it is in this that a good constitution differs from a bad one."*[1]

Aristotle

Today Secular Humanists claim they have grown past the need for gods, relying instead on belief in man and his reason and thereby creating god in their image. They rely heavily on ancient philosophy as the pinnacle of man's ability to solve his own problems and gain wisdom. From Homer through Diocletian, the Greeks and Romans that modern secularists rely on, however, found a belief in the gods useful. Their pantheons gained credibility through historians, poets, physicians and philosophers (the scientists of the period). They used religious ceremonies to unify people, to entertain and encourage socializing, and most important, to exercise control.

"... A lifeless lump, unfashion'd, and unfram'd,/Of jarring seeds; and justly Chaos nam'd."[2] Like the "big bang" of modern evolutionists, Ovid's "Creation" story begins with unknowable chaotic events in a distant past producing "seeds" or energy. He allows for gods in the far ancient times, creations and cataclysms in eons past. The later gods displayed characteristics embraced by modern secularists as vital to their society. Zeus/Jupiter produced heroes and rulers. Vulcan/Haephestus and Ceres/ Demeter demanded reverence for the earth,

Aphrodite/Venus and Dionysus/Bacchus encouraged personal gratification of every kind, Apollo/Helios/Horus/Marduk and Ares/Mars glorified man's personal accomplishments and earthly fame, and Artemis/Diana and Hera/Juno allowed women to be free of men or children, or choose lovers in scorn of marriage. The earliest Greek and Roman myths go from satyrs and centaurs living in fields and forests to complex societies with demigod heroes and statesmen, just as evolution demands primitive beginnings and complex advancements.

Though modern Secular Humanism says it has no gods, its beliefs are the same as the ancients. Modern Secular Humanists center on worship of the universe and the earth itself, substituting energy for divine power, vast distances and ages for activities of the gods in creation and tumultuous destruction which resulted in the formation of the present world. They update the attributes of the gods as unity or brotherhood of man, enjoying life and experiencing sexual freedom, loving and preserving the earth, encouraging men to live for society's recognition and "liberated" views of women and their place in society. Theologian Rousas John Rushdoony explained the real purpose behind the worship of mythological gods in ancient times.

> *The myth reveals a hatred of history . . . The purpose...is to end history, to make man the absolute governor ... where his myths acknowledge man's lot in history, man ascribes his sorry role, not to his depravity, but to the jealousy of the gods. The goal of the myth, progressively more clearly enunciated in time, has become the destruction of history and the enthronement of man as the new governor of the universe.*[3]

They rewrite history to insert evolutionary physical and social concepts. Modern literature desensitizes readers, promoting sexual freedom and emphasizing an inescapable randomness in life. Scientific discoveries must attach evolutionary significance and uniformitarian concepts in order to be published. Secularists attempt to divorce any other religion from every aspect of society. They demand the removal of references to the true God. But their preferred teachings simply scrape the explicit references to the mythological gods off of the same concepts they got from their "rational" philosophers and ancient writers chronicling the achievements of men who were treated as if they were gods among men. The attempt to ram the religion of secular humanism down our throats is as old as civilization.

"...Philosophers are to rule in the State,"[4] said Plato. Enlightened leaders guided by their feelings and emotions masquerading as reason, were to be the guides. "If you would build something solid, don't work with wind: always look for a fixed point, something you know that is stable ... yourself,"[5] advises an inscription at Karnak, Egypt. The same principles prevailed all around the ancient world. "This [Gilgamesh] was the man to whom all things were known; this was the king who knew the countries of the world. He was wise, he saw mysteries and knew secret things,"[6] The purpose of these wise rulers, according to Aristotle, was to teach men that through their reason they could learn that "to enjoy the things we ought and to hate the things we ought has the greatest bearing on virtue of character. For these things extend right through life."[1]

Visitors believed that some ancient kingdoms had already attained the perfect state. "... Cities are prosperous ... There are many guest houses for travelers. There are hospitals providing free medical service for the poor. ... People are free to choose their occupations. ... People are not addicted to drinks. They shun violence. The ... rulers [are] fair and just,"[7] wrote a fourth century A.D. Chinese traveler to India. This perfect state would result in stable economics and an end to conflict, poverty and overpopulation. “Poverty is the parent of revolution and crime,”[1] warned Aristotle, and the inscriptions at Karnack echo the need for enlightened rulers to bring order. “Organization is impossible unless those who know the laws of harmony lay the foundation.”[5] Socrates proposed that if everyone would fill his best place in society, guided by the enlightened rulers, all would prosper. If every person were to do the one task he excels at and no other, then “to every ... worker was assigned one work for which he was by nature fitted, ... he was not to let opportunities slip, and then he would become a good workman.”[8]

Socrates admonished that it was necessary to accept that there must be leaders, and that not just anyone could lead. “There will be discovered to be some natures who ought to study philosophy and to be leaders in the State; and others who are not born to be philosophers, and are meant to be followers rather than leaders.”[4] If everyone’s occupation was what he did best, true advancement would occur in the areas of communication, travel, arts, sciences and education. “... Libraries were built, monumental architecture was constructed, and a highly prestigious artistic ... class was cultivated. All of this created a “First World” aura of invincibility around the island-city of Tenochtitlan. ... All participants understand and accept common cultural “rules” in order to make the flow of imperial wealth as smooth as possible. The rules of empire in Mexico were old rules.”[9] By the time Columbus arrived in the New World, this Mexican alliance had been in existence for a century, operating on principles even more ancient.

In a “... government which depends [for] its sustenance upon the enlightenment of the populace, education is at once a social and political necessity.”[10] In first century BC India this lesson was already fixed. Compulsory education indoctrinated children because “virtue, like any art or facility, can only be acquired by education. Education must be regulated by the State. For as the end of the State as a whole is one, the education of all the citizens must be one and the same, and must therefore be an affair of the state. Every citizen should remember that he is not his own master but a part of the State."[1] Aristotle made the mandate of education clear, and left no doubt that it was the necessary catechism of the new society. "They all lived under the same order and discipline... The whole course of their education was one of continued exercise of a ready and perfect obedience. ... Their chief care was to make them good subjects."[11] Sparta sought to make perfect citizens of its children.

Karnack's walls declared the ancient message that the Secularist's version of Natural Law was the product of man's reason alone. "Knowledge is consciousness of reality. Reality is the sum of the laws that govern nature and of the causes from which they flow."[5] Children had to learn the perfectibility of man through reason, that what Epicurus said was true. "Chance seldom interferes with the wise man; his greatest and highest interests have been, are, and will be, directed by reason throughout his whole life,"[12] and that the evolution of the human race could only occur through man's improvements guided by the state. Aristotle did not believe man could rise to his best state without the guidance of the Enlightened Ruler. "Man, when perfected, is the best of animals, but when separated from law and justice, he is the worst of all."[1]

Egyptologist Isha Schwaller de Lubicz claimed that Karnack inscriptions using the word *neter*, usually translated "gods," meant "... a fundamental principle of nature, or a sort of causal agent." Therefore, "A man's heart is his own *Neter*."[5] Citizens of the perfect state had to learn that there was no supreme being, as Lucretius taught. "When once we know from nothing still/Nothing can create, we shall divine/More clearly what we seek: those elements/From which alone all things created are,/ And how accomplished by no tool of Gods."[13] They still had to have state-controlled ceremonies and festivals because "images are nearer reality than cold definitions."[5] Karnack's inscriptions spelled out the need for these visible symbols, which the people could be loyal to more than to mere spoken words.

Statues and temples like those at Karnack were fine, as long as it was understood that there were no actual gods, not even the concept of Intelligent Design. "All is within yourself. Know your most inward self and look for what corresponds with it in nature."[5] As was taught by the ancient Indian skeptics of Hinduism, only what man could reason out could exist. "Regard only that which is an object of perception, and cast behind your back whatever is beyond the reach of your senses."[14] They also had to be taught that there was no life after death. The teachings of Lucretius, according to Virgil, were designed to give man peace in this life. "Happy is he who has discovered the causes of things and has cast beneath his feet all fears, unavoidable fate, and the din of the devouring Underworld."[15]

The subjects of the perfect society needed to learn that service to mankind meant deciding what was best for others. At Karnack the message read, "Social good is what brings peace to family and society."[5] Seneca the Younger claimed that everyone had to conform to society's mold. "Therefore each one must accustom himself to his own condition and ... lay hold of whatever good is to be found near him."[16] This duty to determine the greatest good for others was a part of gratifying personal desires. "Stranger, here you will do well to tarry; here our highest good is pleasure,"[17] Epicurus assures us. "We conceive happiness as an end, something utterly and absolutely final and complete?" Aristotle asks. "If this is so, we shall pronounce those of the living who possess and are destined to go on possessing the good things we have specified to be supremely blessed."[1]

"And the higher the duties of the guardian ... the more time, and skill, and art, and application will be needed by him?"[8] Socrates asked, planning for the training of his state's law enforcement. "Have the wisdom to abandon the values of a time that has passed and pick out the constituents of the future."[5] Situation ethics was the order of the day according to the writings at Karnack. "An environment must be suited to the age and men to their environment."[5] Enlightened leaders guide the community to perfect its skills and also to choose its new values. "It is well said, then, that it is by doing just acts that the just man is produced, and by doing temperate acts the temperate man; without doing these no one would have even a prospect of becoming good,"[1] Aristotle said, firmly believing in the ability of a man to form his own habits of goodness through proper instruction.

"You will free yourself when you learn to be neutral and follow the instructions of your heart without letting things perturb you,"[5] Karnack's walls promised. "This is the way of *Maat*."[5] Worship of gods like Maat, the Egyptian goddess of Justice, was merely "code" for the following of a man-centered philosophy. The only restriction on personal freedom was what the leaders determined promoted the safety of all, as taught in the Hindu writings of the *Mahabharata*. "Let not any one do an act that injures another, nor any that he feels shame to do."[8] They remembered always to communicate that no consequences needed to be feared from non-existent future judgment. A first century BC Roman poet may have overcome the reluctance of his ladylove with such sentiments. "Let us live and love, my Lesbia .../Suns may set and rise again: for us, when our brief light has set,/there's the sleep of perpetual night."[19]

Personal possessions were to be considered evil because the state needed complete control of all property, sometimes masking this as equality. Like Lycurgus, the Egyptian King Sesostris was reported to have "... distributed an equal square portion to each man, and from this he made his revenue, ... if the river should take away anything ... ... the king [would] ... find out by measurement ... for the future the man might pay less."[20] Social contracts including marriage and acquiring material possessions must be regulated to avoid selfishness, greed and waste. "No itinerate fortune-teller, no harlot-monger, or gold or silversmith, engraver, or jeweler, set foot in a country which had no money; so that luxury, deprived little by little of that which fed and fomented it, wasted to nothing and died away of itself,"[11] reports Plutarch of Lycurgus's Sparta.

Rome's ancient law, the Twelve Tables, ordered that "an obviously deformed child must be put to death."[21] Society is responsible to prevent nonproductive, undesirable or inferior types, and Plato rose to the challenge in his Republic. "The best of either sex should be united with the best as often, and the inferior with the inferior, as seldom as possible; and that they should rear the offspring of the one sort of union, but not of the other."[4] This applied to all ages of life. "He did not want to lengthen out good-for-nothing lives," Socrates said of Asclepius, the renowned Greek physician, "or to have weak fathers begetting weaker sons--if a man was not able to live in the ordinary way he had no business to cure him; for such a cure would have been of no use either to himself, or to the State."[22]

The State could tolerate no other beliefs. Socrates advised telling "falsehood ... necessary for the good of their subjects... in the regulations of marriages ... appoint certain festivals at which we will bring together the brides and bridegrooms, ...sacrifices ... songs ..."[4] Plato admitted that Socrates invented ceremonies to legitimize his State functions, claiming these would make them "holy." The disobedient were profaning themselves in the state religion. "We shall say that he is raising up a bastard to the State, uncertified and unconsecrated."[4]

"[In pre-Columbian Peru] A definite ...worship of one god ... was not by the efforts of the priestly caste ... but rather by the will of the Inca Pachacutic, who seems to have been a monarch gifted with rare insight and ability... In Inca times the religion of the people was solely directed by the state, and regulated in such a manner that independent theological thought was permitted no outlet. ... the leaders ... had amalgamated the various faiths of the peoples whom they had conquered into one official belief."[23] When the ruler invented its tenets, it was clear that a religion was not real, merely a means of control. Ancient Indian skeptics accused organized religions of deception for personal gain. "The three authors of the Vedas were buffoons, knaves, and demons. ... all the various kinds of presents to the priests ... commanded by night-prowling demons."[14]

They also claimed that religion raised false hopes and restricted personal fulfillment. When Epicurus' books were burned, a first century A.D. Assyrian-Greek philosopher lamented the loss. "What blessings that book creates for its readers and what peace, tranquility, and freedom... liberating them as it does from terrors and apparitions and portents, from vain hopes and extravagant cravings, developing in them intelligence and truth, and truly purifying their understanding ... with straight thinking, truthfulness and frankness."[24] There was, after all, nothing non-material to believe in. "Alcmaeon also seems to have held a similar view about soul,"[1] Aristotle informs us while commenting on the writings of earlier philosophers. "He says that it is immortal because it resembles 'the immortals,' and that this immortality belongs to it in virtue of its ceaseless movement; for all the 'things divine,' moon, sun, the planets, and the whole heavens, are in perpetual movement."[1] The source of energy is natural, not supernatural. Natural Law means that matter and energy are without origin or ending. "Everything that depends on the action of nature is by nature as good as it can be, and similarly everything that depends on art or any rational cause,"[1] Aristotle says, claiming that nature itself is the origin of goodness.

Existence is a result of chance resulting from evolution, as a result of uniformitarianism. A surprising number of ancient beliefs did not mention a creator but seemed to be early versions of the belief that the living originated from the non-living. "Lakes, springs, rocks, mountains, precipices, and caves were all regarded by the various Peruvian tribes as *paccariscas*-places whence their ancestors had originally issued to the upper world. The *paccarisca* was usually saluted with the cry, "Thou art my birthplace, thou art my life-spring."[25] Secularists, who propose that life began in a "primordial soup," sometimes dismiss these all-too similar beliefs as nature-worship. Rather than credit a god with their creation, these people considered that their life had arisen from the water. Beliefs of many ancient American tribes included descent from animals. "A totem is an object or an animal, usually the latter, with which the people of a tribe believe themselves to be connected by ties of blood and from which they are descended. It later becomes the type or symbol of the tribe."[23] Are their stories so different from the teachings of Richard Dawkins, a popular modern science author? "We have proved that there exists a trajectory of stepwise change connecting beetle to deer and, by implication, a similar trajectory from any modern animal to any other modern animal."[26] (Note that Dawkins includes man among the "other modern animals.")

Disagreement or dissatisfaction with the perfect state was akin to rebellion against your own being, since you were part of a great whole. This was the form of worship of the Stoics, who insisted everything must be accepted and cooperation was the key to a peaceful and prosperous life. Marcus Aurelius believed we were all part of one interwoven tapestry of being.

> *Constantly regard the universe as one living being, having one substance and one soul; and observe how all things have reference to one perception, the perception of this one living being; and how all things act with one movement; and how all things are the cooperating causes of all things which exist; observe too the continuous spinning of the thread and the contexture of the web.*[27]

The stoics worshiped only gods who could do no wrong, and regarded public advisors to be just as infallible. Epictetus, a former slave who rose from "rags to riches." teaching a school of philosophy, insisted that, "every outcome is indifferent and nothing to you, and whatever it may be, it will be beautifully useful... So be confident in going to the gods as to counselors; and ... remember whom you ... disregard [when] disobeying ...do not divine if the danger should be incurred."[28]

Opposition must be suppressed, eradicated, and everyone forced into conformity. A prince of China's Han dynasty considered the people "royal resources." "Accordingly, in the country of an enlightened ruler ... they use the laws for instruction. ... They employ officials as their teachers. ... Everyone is sure to stay within the framework established by the laws, when they act everyone is certain to aim at real accomplishments. ...These are called 'royal resources.'"[29] Those who oppose the world community are fearful of change, divisive, bigoted, oppressive, or guilty of hatred. Plato caricatures this opponent to his new state in Thrasymachus' violent outburst toward poor, terrified Socrates. Note that Socrates, in spite of his "quivering" with fear, can still describe Thrasymachus as one of "you people who know everything," reflecting the common practice secularists have of using sarcasm rather than reason against opponents.

> *Thrasymachus ... came at us like a wild beast, seeking to devour us. ... He roared out, "...What folly. Socrates, has taken possession of you all? ... I must have...clearness and accuracy." I was panic-stricken ... and ...trembling. ... When I saw his fury rising. [Socrates said]... "You people who know all things should pity us and not be angry with us."*[30]

Modern secular humanists look to Plato for their master plan. In his Republic Plato has Socrates, the master twister of words and meanings, give modern secularists the means to successfully purge the true God from society. *The Republic* is the bridge between the humanism of paganism and modern secular humanism.

At the beginning of Plato's *Republic* Socrates is returning from a worship service in honor of "the goddess" [Athena]. In spite of this outward "devotion," the real religion he will go on to set up in his perfect state is secular humanism. It is clear that the form impresses Socrates more than any actual worship. Varying performances are praised as if the purpose of the ceremonies is just to be social gatherings and entertainments. He makes no mention of any spiritual purpose other than the vague "in honor of the gods." It is a secularized religion in which man's reason controls what is to be believed and taught.

As they are setting up their perfect state Socrates says to Adeimantus in Section II, that they must "Begin by telling children stories which...are in the main fictitious...when they are not of an age..."[8] He says that children learn both true and false stories at a very early age, beginning with false. "I do not understand your meaning,"[8] Adeimantus responds. Socrates explains the common educational method of using fiction to convey truth. He proposes supplying mothers with appropriate stories to read to their small children before the children enter the organized educational system, the *Gymnasium.*

"You know also that the beginning is the most important part of any work, especially in the case of a young and tender thing; for that is the time at which the character is being formed and the desired impression is more readily taken."[8] Socrates wants to form the youngest minds with works everyone knows are fiction but which convey important moral truths, which is a fine idea. Note, however, that this is why Bible stories are acceptable to Secular Humanists in preschool teaching situations. They want them to be viewed just like fairy tales and animal fables – mainly fictitious while containing a few elements of truth.

"And shall we just carelessly allow children to hear any casual tales ... and to receive into their minds ideas ... the very opposite of those which we should wish them to have when they are grown up?" Socrates asks. "We cannot," Adeimantus agrees. "Then the first thing will be to establish a censorship of the writers of fiction ...and we will desire mothers and nurses to tell their children the authorised ones only. Let them fashion the mind with such tales, even more fondly than they mould the body with their hands."[8]

Socrates picks and chooses what to tell children about the gods in the subjects under "music and literature education." "For a young person cannot judge what is allegorical and what is literal; anything that he receives into his mind at that age is likely to become indelible and unalterable; and therefore it is most important that the tales which the young first hear should be models of virtuous thoughts."[8] A child must not hear of bad behavior among the gods, which stories Socrates says are untrue in the first place, claiming that these fall into the "allegorical" category, and a bad example in the second place. In the same manner secularists justify the purging from the Bible of any "bad examples" (God's "bullying" acts of judgment on sin or any sins committed by respected persons). Thus the humanist censor gets to rewrite the Bible.

Recall that Socrates set up the Philosopher King as head of state and controller of all aspects of society. Here Socrates gives this ruler power to tell the poets what they may write. "The founders of a State ought to know the general forms in which poets should cast their tales, and the limits which must be observed by them, but to make the tales is not their business." "Very true," Adeimantus readily agrees. "But what are these forms of theology which you mean?"[8] By using the term theology, Adeimantus clearly indicates that the subject under discussion is education about the gods, not just teaching fiction as a vehicle of truth. Socrates originated the sanitizing of religious instruction; the picking and choosing of what children may learn about what is supposed to be their foundational beliefs about their gods. Socrates leads Adeimantus along in his usual style of presenting a one-dimensional argument that allows for no disagreement.

> *Something of this kind ... God is always to be represented as he truly is, whatever be the sort of poetry, epic, lyric or tragic, ... And is he not truly good? and must he not be represented as such?... And no good thing is hurtful?... And that which is not hurtful hurts not?... And that which hurts not does no evil?... And can that which does no evil be a cause of evil?... And the good is advantageous?... And therefore the cause of well-being?... It follows therefore that the good is not the cause of all things, but of the good only?*[8]

Whoa! Stop right there, Socrates. Where have you led us? Take a few steps back to where he says, "No good thing is hurtful?" He has just begun to redefine words for a cunning purpose. Good can in fact be hurtful, in the strict sense of causing pain. Training for sports and the military have always emphasized "no pain, no gain." Also, to punish those who do evil will probably result in pain but evil must be stopped, and stopping evil is good, not hurtful. Socrates wants you to believe good is one-dimensional. He creates a limitation on it, and he departs from the truth at that point. Wantonly causing pain is of course evil, but in this case, pain is a necessary byproduct of stopping evil.

Socrates has also inserted the concept that good might be thought of as the origin of evil, because God as creator is thought to be the origin of all things. But evil isn't a created thing as such, it's an activity of created things that arose later when they chose to rebel against God. It's a fallacy to believe that God created evil or to try to prove that He is limited because He can't have created evil if He's purely and exclusively good. Adeimantus agrees with Socrates like a good bobble-head but this is wrong, wrong, wrong. If you do not like the bobble-head analogy, you may think of Adeimantus as yes man instead.

> *Then God, if he be good, is not the author of all things, as the many assert, but he is the cause of a few things only, and not of most things that occur to men. For few are the goods of human life, and many are the evils, and the good is to be attributed to God alone; of the evils the causes are to be sought elsewhere, and not in him.... Let this then be one of our rules and principles concerning the gods, to which our poets and reciters will be expected to conform –that God is not the author of all things, but of good only.*[8]

Socrates lists stories and incidents where the gods have been recorded doing evil to men, planting guilt, causing pain and tragedy and sorrow by creating confusion or erroneous beliefs in their minds. Socrates says any story in which a good god does anything interpretable by him as evil is fiction. He discards a huge portion of his own state religion as lies. But his definitions of good and evil are flawed from the start, as shown above, and rob God of most of His true nature and power.

> *Then it is impossible that God should ever be willing to change; being, as is supposed, the fairest and best that is conceivable, every god remains absolutely and for ever in his own form. ... Then, I said, my dear friend, let none of the poets tell us that the gods, taking the disguise of strangers from other lands, walk up and down cities in all sorts of forms...*[8]

Socrates further denies gods the ability to change form by saying if they are only perfect and good in their true form they cannot become less than perfect by changing. He implies that the only reason a god would have for appearing like a man is to deceive. This is not even true in his own religion, where in the story of Baucis and Philomel gods took the form of men to test their moral character, to punish infidelity and to reward fidelity. Once again Socrates discounts his own national religion. This teaching also allows Secular Humanists to deny the possibility of *theophanies* (appearances of God and Jesus Christ in physical, manlike form such as to Abraham and Joshua). By extension the virgin birth of Christ is made impossible.

*The Republic* concludes with the story of the living man temporarily sent into the afterlife. This story includes a lengthy explanation of how men live a succession of lives. They go from heaven to earth, from the underworld to the earth, in an apparently endless cycle based upon choices made from available lives and the "genius" accompanying each life. Once a choice was made the three fates wound an irrevocable thread that completely determined the course of a person's next life. They drank of waters that made them forget, more or less completely, their past lives, depending on the degree of wisdom they had acquired, apparently. People could change sex, could become animals, and animals could become people. Virtuous people could become tyrants, world-famous heroes (Odysseus, for example) could become ordinary men without cares or responsibilities.

Socrates presents this story as authoritative and a necessary part of his perfect world system. The idea of reincarnation existed throughout the ancient world in opposition to the clear teachings of the Scriptures that a man lived once and made his choices to serve God or not to serve God while he lived. Socrates' tale, however, was essential to the "second-chance" humanism that believed man could just keep getting better and better if only he could tap into true wisdom, as slow as the process might be. He was responsible even in the afterlife for the way he turned out. Socrates believed this was the ultimate religion. He promised power over life and death through this teaching.

This is a typical "vision from the other side," man's adding to previous revelation, directly in contradiction to the finished revelation of the true Word of God. Socrates has gutted the ancient gods by focusing on stories of deception, lust and inconsistencies and dropped the ball of becoming virtuous and wise into man's lap. *Necessity* reigns supreme and fate only solidifies what you determine that your life will be. If you get it wrong, you'll have endless chances to correct. Those Secular Humanists who claim that this life is all are vindicated. All Socrates' talk about a thousand years of punishment or a thousand years of bliss is virtually irrelevant, simply temporary, a kick in the pants to make the next life better or prizes for the good life lived. There is no memory of them in the next cycle, only (possibly) a vague sense of ascending wisdom gained and a just and virtuous life to be lived here and now.

> *And thus, Glaucon, the tale has been saved and has not perished, and will save us if we are obedient to the word spoken; and we shall pass safely over the River of Forgetfulness and our*

> *soul will not be defiled. Wherefore my counsel is that we hold fast ever to the heavenly way and follow after justice and virtue always, considering that the soul is immortal and able to endure every sort of good and every sort of evil. Thus shall we live dear to one another and to the gods, both while remaining here and when, like conquerors in the games who go round to gather gifts, we receive our reward. And it shall be well with us both in this life and in the pilgrimage of a thousand years which we have been describing.*[4]

Behold, then, Socrates unmasked, the man who began the *Republic* by attending a worship service of his goddess and who before long has stripped his religion of most of its history and denied the truth of most of its accounts. Isn't it interesting that Socrates was executed on the charge of "corrupting the youth"? Could it have been at least in part because he destroyed their faith in the state-sanctioned religion (the established religion of Athens)? How could they help but question a religion gutted of most of its ages-old chronicles? (Not that they didn't need to be questioned, of course.) Why would they not regard worship as merely putting on the most impressive spectacles to draw the biggest crowds? What would be wrong with rewriting the stories to make them great moral tales, without regard to history or truth?

Aristotle, student of Plato, teacher at his school, and tutor to Alexander the Great, believed in the concept of "first principles," his ill-defined explanation for the origin of all things, Even the gods originated from these vague "first principles" rather than being creative agents. Aristotle naturalized the origins of soul and matter. He quoted such philosophers as Empedocles, who derived his four basic elements, Earth, Air, Fire, and Water, from attributes of gods and goddesses but seemed to be redefining the gods as natural forces rather than treating them as real beings. "The kindly Earth in its broad-bosomed moulds/Won of clear Water two parts out of eight,/And four of Fire; and so white bones were formed."[1] Aristotle says that earlier philosophers equated divinity and immortality with unceasing movement and on that basis claimed the soul was immortal. Though he finds contradictions and faults in these reasonings, clearly Aristotle seeks to find natural explanations for origins and especially in defining the soul only in terms of its action upon physical bodies and its ability to achieve virtue by the forming of man-defined habits, not by influence from any spiritual source.

Rome ordered its conquered people to practice religions that would make them moral people because moral people were easier to govern. Certainly it is most important that the people be united and controlled. As the secularists claim they hold diverse viewpoints and vary greatly in what they believe, yet demand unity and control, so the Incas gave them a blueprint for domination: Control the religion, control the people. Throughout the ancient world many prominent historical figures were guilty of the thinly–veiled practice of Secular Humanist principles.

Some "creation stories" speak of humans appearing and then being wiped out by natural catastrophes, with new races taking their place, in cycles over eons of time. (e.g., Greek, Meso-American.) In some cases, people arose out of the earth, caves or reeds in water, from "gods" who no longer live and are more like ancestors than divine creators. (This is distinct from such religions as Islam, Hinduism and even the truth of the Scriptures where man was physically formed out of dust or clay.) Notice the skepticism mixed with real confusion in the African speaker below. He does not find credible his elders' belief in this god *Umvelinqangi,* but he doesn't know what else to believe.

> *It was said at first ... if we asked, "By what were the stones made?"— "They were made by*

> *Umvelinqangi." It is said that we men came out of a bed of reeds, where we had our origin. ... For we used to ask when we were little, thinking that the old men knew all things which are on the earth; yet forsooth they do not know; but we do not contradict them, for neither do we know.*[31]

Gods and goddesses circulate freely in literature as ancient as that of Sumer but these are the same as the later versions, limited, unpredictable deities who cry helplessly over drums that fall into the netherworld (*Innana* of the Gilgamesh epic) or others that cannot be stopped from killing everyone except by getting them drunk with beer colored to resemble blood (*Sekhmet* of Egypt). They need at least partly mortal heroes like Gilgamesh, Hercules or Aeneas to fight their battles and defeat their fellow gods. Gods through the ages must sneak around behind each other's backs to help man or punish each other for variously helping or attacking him.

The focus is on man, his heroism, his longsuffering in the face of the gods' changeable behavior, his superiority to their petty lusts and irrational punishments. Lucretius understood the game when he said, "All religions are equally sublime to the ignorant, useful to the politician, and ridiculous to the philosopher."[13] These tales had a function, to exalt the ruler while building up national unity under him, as Ovid did in his tales of ancient Greeks. "It is expedient that gods should exist; since it is expedient, let us believe that they do."[2] Philosophers, the "true" thinkers of the day, had no delusions about the gods. Protagoras practically dismissed the subject as unimportant. "Concerning the gods, I have no means of knowing whether they exist or not or of what sort they may be. Many things prevent knowledge including the obscurity of the subject and the brevity of human life."[32] If they did deal with it, they sanitized the gods as Plato did, outright scoffed at them like Lucretius, or reasoned them away as a mere figment of the imagination. Since they had rejected "in the image of God created He [man]," and decided the "truth" must be the other way around, even before the time of Socrates, Xenophanes could confidently say,

> *The Ethiopians say that their gods are flat-nosed and black, while the Thracians say that theirs have blue eyes and red hair. Yet if cattle or horses or lions had hands and could draw, and could sculpt like men, then the horses would draw their gods like horses, and cattle like cattle; and each they would shape bodies of gods in the likeness, each kind, of their own.*[33]

Those who cherish the truths of the Scriptures and the traditions of the founding fathers sometimes struggle to "match wits" with these high and mighty thinkers of Secular Humanism. If they sometimes feel defeated by what seem to be more gifted speakers and more clever arguers, perhaps they would do well to remember Adeimantus, one of the players in Plato's *Republic* drama, and what he said in response to Socrates' carefully crafted argument for rule by philosophers. Adeimantus, named after a metal believed to be unbreakable by the ancient Greeks, brings up an argument that shows the indomitable spirit and the wise discernment of those who dare to tell the truth about the kind of leaders Socrates will end up with if he gets his way. (Emphasis added.)

> *Here Adeimantus interposed and said: "To these statements, Socrates, no one can offer a reply; but when you talk in this way,* ***a strange feeling passes over the minds of your hearers****: They fancy that they are* ***led astray a little at each step in the argument, owing to their own want of skill in asking and answering questions;*** *these littles accumulate, and at the end of the discussion they are found to have sustained a*

> *mighty overthrow and all their former notions appear to be turned upside down. And as unskillful players of draughts are at last shut up by their more skilful adversaries and have no piece to move, so they too find themselves shut up at last; for they have nothing to say in this new game of which words are the counters;* ***and yet all the time they are in the right.*** *The observation is suggested to me by what is now occurring. For any one of us might say, that although in words he is not able to meet you at each step of the argument,* ***he sees as a fact that*** *the votaries of* ***[those devoted to] philosophy****, when they carry on the study, not only in youth as a part of education, but as the pursuit of their maturer years, most of them* ***become strange monsters, not to say utter rogues, and that those who may be considered the best of them are made useless to the world by the very study which you extol.***[4]

Secular Humanists will dismiss all these examples as being irrelevant. They may claim that they do not see themselves and their beliefs in Lycurgus's rigid Spartan control or Plato's advice from the afterlife on how to "save" society. Clearly the ancient texts of Sumer, India and countries around the world relied on gods and the supernatural as the foundations of their societies. Or did they? Are these teachings so different from what secularists believe today? Do not many secularists even claim the *Republic* as their blueprint and Aristotle as their great teacher? Have they not already created their perfect state and established their religion as the law of the land in America?

---

1 *The Corpus Aristotelicum,* collected works preserved by medieval manuscript transmission. They are studies of philosophy made by Aristotle's school since many of his original works have been lost. Immanuel Bekker's nineteenth-century edition (1831-1836) is based on ancient classifications of these works.

2 Publius Ovidius Naso, the Roman poet known as Ovid, from his "Creation" story in the *Metamorphoses,* completed in AD 8, translated by Henry Thomas Riley, 1851.

3 Rousas Rushdoony, *The Mythology of Science.* Nutley, NJ: Craig Press, 1967.

4 Plato, *The Republic* (c. 360 B.C.), translated by Benjamin Jowett over a period of 30 years until his death in 1893, completed posthumously by Lewis Campbell, Book V.

5 Egyptian quotations from the temple areas of Karnak and Luxor, translated and interpreted by Isha Schwaller de Lubicz, taken from her two-part fictionalized Egyptian histories *Her-Bak: The Living Face of Ancient Egypt* and *Her-Bak: Egyptian Initiate.* Published 1978. Isha Schwaller de Lubicz lived for fifteen years among the temples and tombs of Luxor and Karnak, and studied under the direction of her husband and teacher, R. A. Schwaller de Lubicz.

6 *The Epic of Gilgamesh,* Cunningham, G., Fluckiger-Hawker, E, Robson, E., and Zólyomi, G. (Oriental Studies Faculty Members at Oxford), *The Electronic Text Corpus of Sumerian Literature,* Oxford, 1998.

7 Fa-Hien (or Fa-Xien), *A Record of Buddhistic Kingdoms, Being an Account by the Chinese Monk Fa-Hien of his Travels in India and Ceylon in Search of the Buddhist Books of Discipline,* written between A.D. 399 and 412. Translated by James Legge, 1886.

8 Plato, *The Republic,* Book II.

9 Bernal Diaz Del Castillo, *The Discovery And Conquest Of Mexico* 1517-1521, Edited by Genaro Garcia, Translated with an Introduction and Notes, A. P. Maudslay, first pub 1928. (This alliance was composed of the city-states of Tenochtitlan [founded in 1325], Texcoco, and Tlacopan.)

*10 Bhartruhari, Neeti Shatakan* (spelling varies; a work of Sanskrit philosophical verse). Former Raja who abdicated to become a scholar and poet. The empire in which he lived lasted from 185 B.C. to 135 A.D. Sahu Dharanidhar published An English Verse Translation of *Three Shatakas of Bhartruhari* in 2003.

11 Plutarch, from his *Life of Lycurgus*, translated by John Dryden and others, 1683.

12 Epicurus, from the *40 Sovran Maxims* (or "Sovereign Maxims"), in *Diogenes Laertus's Lives and Opinions of Eminent Philosophers,* 3rd Century AD, translated by Robert Drew Hicks, 1925.

13 Quotations from Titus Lucretius Carus (Lucretius), Roman poet and philosopher, (c 95-55 BC), unless otherwise noted, are from *Of The Nature of Things,* Translator: William Ellery Leonard, 1916.

14 from Charvaka teachings (ancient Indian skeptic philosophy) quoted in the *Ramayana,* approximately 600 BC. (Most original source material of the Charvaka beliefs was destroyed, and fragments are preserved in Hindu texts, where they are denounced as heresy.) Ravi Prakash Arya, (ed.*). Ramayana of Valmiki:* Sanskrit Text and English Translation. (English translation according to M. N. Dutt, introduction by Dr. Ramashraya Sharma, 4-volume set) Parimal Publications: Delhi, 1998.

15 Virgil, *Georgics,* Book Two, published c. 29 BC. Poetic translation by John Dryden, 1697.

16 Lucius Annaeus Seneca (Seneca the Younger) (c. 4 BC - 65 AD), Roman philosopher, statesman, dramatist, and humorist, in "A letter to Serenus," as translated in *Tranquillity of Mind and Providence* by William Bell Langsdorf, 1900.

17 Epicurus, 341 BC – 270 B.C., recorded by Seneca the Younger in his Epistle XX. From Lucius Annaeus Seneca. *Moral Essays.* Translated by John W. Basore. The Loeb Classical Library. London: W. Heinemann, 1928-1935. 3 vols.: Volume I. I.

18 *The Mahabharata, Santiparva,* cclx.20, 21, 23 and cxxiv.67, translated by Friedrich Max Müller and others in Sacred Books of the East (50 volumes), Oxford University Press, 1879-1910.

19 Gaius Valerius Catullus (c. 84 – c. 54 BC), Roman poet, in *Carmina.* Translated by Leonard C. Smithers, 1894.

20 Herodotus, *An Account of Egypt,* (484-425 ca BC) English translation: G. C. Macaulay, Macmillan, London and NY, 1890.

21 from *The Law of the Twelve Tables* (Duodecim Tabulae), the ancient foundation of Roman law. Frank Frost Abbott, Alan Chester Johnson, (authors, translators and editors), *Municipal Administration in the Roman Empire*, Princeton University Press, Princeton, NJ, 1926.

22 Plato, *The Republic*, Book III.

23 Lewis Spence, *The Myths of Mexico and Peru,* 1913.

24 Lucian of Samosata c. A.D. 125 – after A.D. 180. An Assyrian rhetorician, and satirist who wrote in the Greek language, translated by A. M. Harmon, 1936.

25 "El Inca" Garcilaso de la Vega (Gómez Suárez de Figueroa), *Comentarios Reales de los Incas*, Lisbon, 1609, trans. Harold V. Livermore. 1965.

26 Richard Dawkins, *The Extended Phenotype: The Long Reach of the Gene.* London: Oxford University Press, 1982, 1999.

27 Marcus Aurelius, *Meditations,* IV, 40, 167 AD, translated by George Long, 1862.

28 From the *Encheiridion of Epictetus* c. 135 BC, former slave, stoic philosopher, by Flavius Arrianus (his student and transcriber), Translated by Sanderson Beck, 1911.

29 Han Fei, c 200 BC., in his work *The Five Vermin,* W. K. Liao (translator and annotator), *The Complete Works of Han Fei Tzu.* London, 1939-59, 2 vols.

30 Plato, *The Republic,* Book I.

31Henry Callaway, *The Religious System of the Amazulu,* Springville, Natal, 1870, quoting native source Ufulatela Sitole.

32 Protagoras of Abdera (ca. 490-ca. 420 BC) Greek philosopher, agnostic, logician, believed to be from his lost work *On the Gods.* Included in the following work: *Aristophanes. Clouds.* Intro. and trans. by Carol Poster. In *Aristophanes 3,* ed. David Slavitt and Palmer Bovie. Philadelphia PA: University of Pennsylvania Press, 1999: 85-192.

33 Xenophanes, pre-Socratic philosopher, Diels, Hermann. *Die Fragmente der Vorsokratiker.* Rev. Walther Kranz. Berlin: Weidmann, 1972-1973.

## 4. How Was Secular Humanism Established? or Establishing America's Established Religion

*But, beyond all these matters, no purpose of action against religion can be imputed to any legislation, state or national, because this is a religious people. This is historically true. From the discovery of this continent to the present hour, there is a single voice making this affirmation.*[1]

Supreme Court Justice David Josiah Brewer

*It has long, however, been my opinion, and I have never shrunk from its expression... that the germ of dissolution of our federal government is in the constitution of the federal Judiciary; ... working like gravity by night and by day, gaining a little today and a little tomorrow, and advancing its noiseless step like a thief, over the field of jurisdiction, until all shall be usurped.*[2]

Thomas Jefferson

The case of *Church of the Holy Trinity v United States* in 1892 (see Appendix One, Court Cases, for more detail) involved a church that was fined in connection with a law prohibiting the importation of foreign workers to the United States. Holy Trinity hired a minister from England and so the court in the State of New York ruled the church had violated the law. The law was very detailed and specific and did include exceptions such as actors, artists, lecturers and domestic servants, but expressed no provision concerning ministers. Holy Trinity appealed when it lost the case to New York and the United States Supreme Court overruled the lower court decision.

The Act of February 26, 1880, "to prohibit the importation and migration of foreigners and aliens under contract or agreement to perform labor in the United States, its Territories, and the District of Columbia," 23 Stat. 332, c. 164, does not apply to a contract between an alien, residing out of the United States, and a religious society incorporated under the laws of a state, whereby he engages to remove to the United States and to enter into the service of the society as its rector or minister.[1]

As commendable as the attitude of Justice Brewster was in pointing out the religious character of the United States in the quote that begins the chapter, the decision of the court was made on the wrong basis. Supreme Court Justice Antonin Scalia believed that the Supreme Court should not have overturned the case. "Congress can enact foolish statutes as well as wise ones, and it is not for the courts to decide which is which and rewrite the former..." Scalia said the court was trying to interpret "unexpressed legislative intent" instead of just reading the law. "But to say that the legislature obviously misspoke is worlds away from saying that the legislature obviously overlegislated. *Church of the Holy Trinity* is cited to us whenever counsel wants us to ignore the narrow, deadening text of the statute and pay attention to the life-giving legislative intent, It is of course nothing but judicial law-making." In this sense, the Supreme Court opened the door to give Secular Humanists exactly what they wanted, and so, though secularists lost the battle, they found a way to win the war, through "judicial law-making."[3]

The constitutionality of the law was the real issue in *Holy Trinity*. The original statute did reveal the religious nature of the people, in the form of the creeping influence of Secular Humanism spreading its replacement religion through its favorite means, government. Legislation is a great way to undermine religious freedom, especially if it's not blatant. It apparently took them some time, ten years in fact, to get an application of the law to religion, but they found one in *Holy Trinity*. At that point secularists could exercise their greatest ally, the courts. The court in the State of New York went along gladly and tried to restrict the freedom of *Holy Trinity's* religious practice by limiting how it could choose its pastor.

As Scalia pointed out, the original law was indeed a case of overlegislation. The law was unconstitutional, seeking to restrict religious freedom. The First Amendment does not allow prohibiting free exercise of religion, and telling a church who it can and cannot have as pastor is prohibiting free exercise. Sadly, the Supreme Court didn't rule on that basis. Instead it established itself as having the right to judge "not only what the statute means abstractly, or even on the basis of legislative history, but also what it ought to mean in terms of the needs and goals of our present day society."[4] Along with the power to interpret original intent and modify laws for changing circumstances, judges before long would " . . . come to the point of exercising [the law revising authority he favors] through fictions, subterfuges, and indirection."[5] (Note that the words in brackets are Scalia's clarification, not those of the authors of this work.)

The Supreme Court's ruling made a fine statement of the country's religious nature. Brewster made noble an effort to protect the church in question. However, the court not only failed to come to the right decision, it set a precedent Scalia makes chillingly clear. "It is simply not compatible with democratic theory that laws mean whatever they ought to mean, and that unelected judges decide what that is."[3] Oliver Wendell Holmes, another Supreme Court Justice, warned against trying to guess what lawmakers might have had in mind, "We do not inquire what the legislature meant; we ask only what the statute means."[6] James Madison, in *Federalist* no. 47, quoted Montesquieu, French political theorist of the Enlightenment, as saying, "Were the power of judging joined with the legislative, the life and liberty of the subject would be exposed to arbitrary control, for the judge would then be the legislator."[7] Robert Rantoul, American judicial reform advocate, warned of this danger years before the *Holy Trinity* case.

> *Judge-made law is ex post facto law, and therefore unjust. An act is not forbidden by the statute law, but it becomes void by judicial construction. The legislature could not effect this, for the Constitution forbids it. The judiciary shall not usurp legislative power, says the Bill of Rights: yet it not only usurps, but runs riot beyond the confines of legislative power. Judge-made law is special legislation.*[7]

Did a breach occur in the judicial system with *Holy Trinity*? Certainly. More than one, in fact. Why? Scalia points out the mesmerizing effect of first-year law school on future judges, "How it changes their thinking and makes them to feel the power they have." He says this is just where the danger lies, that it "consists of playing king - devising, out of the brilliance of one's own mind, those laws that ought to govern mankind." Judges get used to feeling the power but abandon the strict guidelines of its use. "What a thrill! And no wonder so many lawyers, having tasted this heady brew, aspire to be judges!"[3] Common Law in England was practically created on a case-by case basis because it wasn't all written down and judges could reasonably write those laws. But judges in America have tried to make Statute law work the same way, and that is wrong. Statute law is written down and must be narrowly interpreted and followed.

Perhaps we have not yet left behind the need for the Founding Fathers to enlighten us on what we need to fear, even from their meticulous labors to craft a country and a government like no other. Thomas Jefferson wrote extensively on the judiciary. "They are irremovable but by their own body for any depravities of conduct, and even by their own body for the imbecilities of dotage."[9] Apparently Jefferson believed the system of appointing judges for life was flawed and that it left little means to remove them. This frequently resulted in their becoming incompetent at the least and arrogant and fearless at the worst.

> *...The judiciary bodies were supposed to be the most helpless and harmless members of the government. ... They were to become the most dangerous; that the insufficiency of the means provided for their removal gave them a freehold and irresponsibility in office; that their decisions...pass silent and unheeded by the public at large; that these decisions nevertheless become law by precedent, sapping by little and little the foundations of the Constitution and working its change by construction before any one has perceived that ... helpless worm has been busily employed in consuming its substance.*[10]

Jefferson said that the power usurped by the judiciary to make law resulted in " ... sapping and mining, slyly, and without alarm, the foundations of the Constitution" and said that it ".... can do what open force would not dare to attempt."[11] Jefferson conceded that there were times when deliberate wrongdoing was not the issue. "I do not charge the judges with willful and ill-intentioned error; but honest error must be arrested where its toleration leads to public ruin."[12] Jefferson did not flinch from declaring, however, that, intentional or not, the wrongs must be righted. "As for the safety of society, we commit honest maniacs to Bedlam; [a famous insane asylum] so judges should be withdrawn from their bench whose erroneous biases are leading us to dissolution."[12]

Jefferson may have even regretted soiling the reputation of a judge by removing him, but there were higher concerns than personal reputation, and especially more important than considerations of wealth and influence. "It may, indeed, injure them in fame or in fortune; but it saves the republic, which is the first and supreme law."[12] Jefferson bitterly denounced the practice of deliberate judicial legislating. "One single object... [will merit] the endless gratitude of society: that of restraining the judges from usurping legislation."[13] Jefferson considered them as potentially dangerous as a foreign power, accusing them of disloyalty when they stepped out of bounds. "And with no body of men is this restraint more wanting than with the judges of what is commonly called our General Government, but what I call our foreign department."[13] He did not even believe they had the power above any other branch to rule on constitutionality. "... Certainly there is not a word in the Constitution which has given that power to them more than to the Executive or Legislative branches."[14]

Jefferson had much more to say on the subject of ruling on constitutionality. "The Constitution... meant that its coordinate branches should be checks on each other."[15] Each branch was to inspect the work of the others, but the judicial had claimed the sole right of determining whether laws were constitutional. "But the opinion which gives to the judges the right to decide what laws are constitutional in their own sphere of action [as well as] the Legislature and Executive ... would make the Judiciary a despotic branch."[15] "Our judges are as honest as other men and not more so. They have with others the same passions for party, for power, and the privilege of their corps."[16] Even men who started out good could become corrupt, could arrive at the place where they sincerely believed that "[good justice is broad jurisdiction] (translation of a Latin judicial precept supplied by Jefferson's editor), and their power the more dangerous as they are in office for life and not responsible, as the other functionaries are, to the elective control."[16] Giving the judiciary exclusive power of this kind defeated the checks and balances and undermined the Constitution itself. "The Constitution on this hypothesis is a mere thing of wax in the hands of the judiciary, which they may twist and shape into any form they please."[17]

Jefferson expected the two other branches to combat this "by a strong protestation ... that such ... doctrines ... are contrary to the Constitution; and if ... they relapse into the same heresies, impeach and set the whole adrift. For what was the government divided into three branches, but that each should ... oppose their usurpations?"[18]

Again Jefferson charges these abusers with treasonous purpose and deadly power. "The original error [was in] establishing a judiciary independent of the nation, and which, from the citadel of the law, can turn its guns on those they were meant to defend, and control and fashion their proceedings to its own will."[19] He foresaw even our present predicament, that "The principal [leaders of the political opposition]" would "retreat ... into the judiciary as a stronghold..."[20] The subsequent attacks on basic Constitutional provisions have made Jefferson's fears all too real today.

Each of the freedoms guaranteed by the Bill of Rights was attacked during the ratification process, and has been continuously attacked ever since. Until the twentieth century, directly taking these rights away was never very effective in the United States. Since the Constitution was written there were many assaults through subversion. The greatest threat, however, came from a movement which called itself Liberalism. Liberalism was first and foremost a religious movement. The core of Liberalism is a man-centered approach. It emphasizes feelings, personal desires and situational ethics instead of eternal principles, self-denial and personal character. Liberals often used good causes, such as Henry Ward Beecher's opposition to slavery, to attack principles and principled men. Truth to a liberal depends on point of view. Liberalism used control of educational institutions to indoctrinate American children against religious freedom and to make Secular Humanism a federal American establishment of Religion.

Harvard University was named for John Harvard, a man who willed his library and financial resources to train men to preach the gospel of Jesus Christ. Less than a century after Harvard University was founded, men who did not believe in that purpose took positions on the faculty then gained control of Harvard. Then men who continued to believe in the gospel of Jesus Christ took their money and founded Yale. Yale, like Harvard, hired faculty who did not believe in the gospel of Jesus Christ and these men eventually controlled Yale. Men who understood the gospel of Jesus Christ left Yale, took their money and founded the College of New Jersey, which later changed its name to Princeton. One of Princeton's earliest presidents was Jonathan Edwards, the preacher of the Great Awakening (see the Great Awakening Appendix). Like Harvard and Yale, Princeton began hiring faculty members who did not believe in the gospel of Jesus Christ. The fall of Princeton through the replacement of godly faculty by liberals in the 1920's resulted in the Bible College Movement, the founding of hundreds of schools by those remaining faithful to the truth of Jesus Christ. These movements are explained in detail in Dr. David Beale's book *In Pursuit of Purity* and Dr. George Dollar's book *A History of Fundamentalism.*

Though religious freedom has been attacked since the creation of the world, the real turning point in the United States of America was the 1893 heresy trial of Charles Augustus Briggs. This important trial took place not in the US court system, but in the Presbyterian Church USA. In 1891 he was appointed to the position of

Chair of Biblical Theology at Union Theological Seminary. His inaugural sermon was entitled The Authority of Scripture. As professors at Harvard and Yale Theological seminaries had done before him, he took money given for the preaching of the Gospel and the defense of Christianity and used it to attack the absolute authority of Scriptures, what he called "bibliolatry." "In every department of Biblical study we come across error."[21] Briggs insisted. He also believed that "reason is a fountain of divine authority no less savingly enlightening than the Bible and the Church."[21]

> *There was a strong reaction throughout the PCUSA against Briggs' speech. ...In 1870 the General Assembly had been granted the power to veto the election of any professor in any seminary associated with the church. The GA of 1891 overwhelmingly voted (449-60) to veto Briggs' appointment to the chair of Biblical Theology at Union. The board and trustees of Union Seminary rallied behind Dr. Briggs and the Seminary after protesting left the PCUSA to avoid its control.*[22]

Union Theological Seminary withdrew from the Presbyterian Church USA one year before Charles Augustus Briggs was tried, found guilty and defrocked by the Presbyterian Church USA. Since Union Theological Seminary was no longer part of Presbyterian Church Union kept C. A. Briggs on as faculty and indoctrinated ministerial students into Higher Criticism (see Section Two Higher Criticism Appendix). The lesson for future liberals is: Tell a big enough lie and you get to keep the property and your job. These have been the tactics of Liberalism ever since. Liberals have found that they can control entire organizations if they firmly control the hiring and firing practices. Organizations with thousands on their payrolls, especially universities, can be controlled through less than a dozen key people. John Adams warned against allowing people who had no sense of their true duty to God and his Word to have free reign in our institutions. No government can protect against them. They should be stopped before they get into positions of power, or we are lost.

> *We have no government armed with power capable of contending with human passions unbridled by morality and religion. Avarice, ambition, revenge or gallantry [immoral behavior with women] would break the strongest cords of our Constitution as a whale goes through a net. Our Constitution is designed only for a moral and religious people. It is wholly inadequate for any other.*[23]

Beginning around 1900, the orthodox response to liberalism was the production of a series of twelve books called the Fundamentals. Leading conservative scholars of the time wrote these books. They were sent to as many pastors and Christian workers as could be found. These books popularized the term Fundamentalist for anyone who believed in the absolute authority of the Scriptures. However, Liberals went on a relentless crusade to fire any Fundamentalist and hire the most radical Liberals possible.

Samuel Adams knew that freedom had to be maintained with principle based on the Word of God or it would not survive. Secular Humanism's efforts to strip godliness from our country's foundations is deadly to all liberties. "Our contest is not only whether we ourselves shall be free, but whether there shall be left to mankind an asylum on earth for civil and religious liberty."[24]

With the beginning of the 21st century, traditional liberalism has been replaced by Secular Humanism as America's Established Religion. Faculty members lose their jobs by simply mentioning ID (Intelligent Design). Anyone who actually practices Christianity is portrayed as ignorant and backward. Americans are taxed to the point of slavery and then when they are without financial means to resist are further persecuted by courts. Modern persecution takes many forms.

> *A federal appeals court here declared today that the Pledge of Allegiance is unconstitutional because the phrase "one nation under God" violates the separation of church and state. In a decision that drew howls of protest across the political spectrum, a three-member panel of the United States Court of Appeals for the Ninth Circuit, ruled that the pledge could not be recited in schools because it violated the First Amendment's prohibition against a state endorsement of religion. In addition, the ruling, which will certainly be appealed, struck down a 1954 federal law in which Congress added the phrase "under God" to one of the most hallowed patriotic traditions in the nation.*[25]

This case involved, once again, the misinterpretation of the separation principle, but also included the false assumption that the government could remain religiously neutral. The words of Justice Arthur J. Goldberg clearly still apply:

> *The concept of neutrality can lead to a brooding and pervasive devotion to the secular and a passive, or even active, hostility to the religious. Such results are not only not compelled by the Constitution, but, it seems to me, are prohibited by it.*[26]

"He that spareth his rod hateth his son; but he that loveth him chasteneth him betimes."(Proverbs 13:24, KJV)

> *The highest state court in Massachusetts heard arguments today about whether spanking a child constituted abuse or was just good discipline. The case involved Donald Cobble, a*

*minister in Woburn, Mass., who in 1997 hit his son, Judah, then 9 years old, with the end of a leather belt after the boy came home with a bad report card. Judah told a teacher that his father had spanked him, and the teacher alerted the state's Department of Social Services. The agency, which considers spanking child abuse if it causes tissue swelling, filed abuse charges against Mr. Cobble. A lower court judge agreed with the agency, saying the spanking constituted abuse. But Mr. Cobble appealed, saying that "the Bible is absolutely clear that the rod is a necessary part to raising your child."*[27]

The Massachusetts Supreme court eventually ruled that there was not enough evidence of child abuse. These spankings left temporary red or pink marks on his buttocks that would fade after ten minutes or so.[27] Bills were later introduced in both California and Massachusetts to make spanking against the law, though neither bill had much support.

*In a rare victory for freedom of religion a German family was granted asylum in the United States after fleeing persecution because they homeschooled their children.*

*In a decision bound to send a shock wave through the European Union, a federal immigration judge today granted political asylum in the United States to a German family whose members feared persecution if returned to their home country because of their decision to homeschool.*

*"We can't expect every country to follow our Constitution," said federal Judge Lawrence O. Burman in Memphis, Tenn. "The world might be a better place if it did. However, the rights*

> *being violated here are basic human rights that no country has a right to violate," he said.*
>
> *"This decision finally recognizes that German homeschoolers are a specific social group that is being persecuted by a Western democracy," said Mike Donnelly, staff attorney and director of international relations for HSLDA. [Home School Legal Defense Association].*
>
> *"It is embarrassing for Germany since a Western nation should uphold basic human rights, which include allowing parents to raise and educate their own children. This judge understood the case perfectly and he called Germany out. We hope this decision will cause Germany to stop persecuting homeschoolers," he said.*[29]

Unfortunately U.S. courts are pressuring to be guided more and more by international law, and the following examples from Germany show clearly where that can lead. (Author's Note: The following paragraphs on German homeschooling are adapted from a *World Net Daily* article, abbreviated and reorganized, but still contain copyrighted material. See footnote below.)

Melissa Busckros, a fifteen-year-old German girl, was taken from her parents by 15 police officers and Youth Welfare Office representatives. A court order was issued because she was judged to have a "school phobia." It allowed them to take her "if necessary by force" to be committed to a Psychiatric Ward for evaluation because she was being homeschooled, which is illegal in Germany. Melissa was placed in a foster home. At midnight of the night she turned sixteen, she became subject to different laws and had more freedom. She left the foster home and returned to her parents at about 3 am.

"The minister of education does not share your attitudes toward so-called homeschooling," said a government letter concerning parents protesting when police arrived at their home to force their children into public school attendance. "... You complain about the forced school escort of primary school children by the responsible local police officers. ... In order to avoid this in future, the education authority is in conversation with the affected family in order to look for possibilities to bring the religious convictions of the family into line with the unalterable school attendance requirement."

Wolfgang Drautz, consul general for the Federal Republic of Germany, has explained that the German government "has a legitimate interest in countering the rise of parallel societies that are based on religion." Drautz said "school teaches not only knowledge but also social conduct, encourages dialogue among people of different beliefs and cultures, and helps students to become responsible citizens."

Lutz Gorgens, German consul general for the southeast U.S., has defended his nation's public education requirements. "For reasons deeply rooted in history and our belief that only schools properly can ensure the desired level of excellent education, we (Germany) go a little bit beyond that path which other countries have chosen." German homeschoolers have suffered thousands of dollars in fines, bank accounts frozen, and threats to sell their homes.[30]

People are ground down by taxes and regulations until their children are born dependent on the government for necessities like food and diapers. Both parents must work to pay taxes so the child goes into government-sponsored daycare. From infancy up through PhD the government provides babysitting services while indoctrinating each new generation to deny truth and fight it wherever they find it. They fight it with such concepts as "fairness," refusal to issue grades, rewarding mere attendance or participation rather than accomplishment, and drilling every child at every level to understand that beliefs are just opinions and everybody's entitled to one unless they defy the worship of man and his dogma of Secular Humanism. Thomas Jefferson warned of the dangers of allowing other forces to deprive Americans of the control of their money.

> *I believe that banking institutions are more dangerous to our liberties than standing armies. ... first by inflation, then by deflation, the banks and corporations that will grow ... will deprive the people of all property until their children wake-up homeless on the continent their fathers conquered.*[31]

America has an established religion. It is paid for by tax money and supported by law. Attendance is compelled. Belief is expected and required as a condition of employment. We are attempting to disestablish this religion. Those who fight against us are antidisestablishmentarians.

John Adams warned, "But a Constitution of Government once changed from Freedom, can never be restored. Liberty, once lost, is lost forever."[32] Attacks on liberty come hard and heavy through the Established Religion's education system. The persecution by Secular Humanists of those who try to hold onto the religious liberty forged into the founding documents is nowhere more evident than in the public schools. And this persecution is supported by the legal system.

The Court Cases Appendix includes more complete information on a number of court cases dealing with religion, public education, science instruction and evolution. Brief excerpts are included here. John Adams spoke prophetically when he said,

> *The management of the executive and judicial powers together always corrupts them, and*

> *throws the whole power into the hands of the most profligate and abandoned among themselves. The honest men are generally nearly equally divided in sentiment, and, therefore, the vicious and unprincipled, by joining one party, carry the majority; and the vicious and unprincipled always follow the most profligate leader, him who bribes the highest, and sets all decency and shame at defiance.*[33]

Both the law and the Congress have been virtually useless to protect our clear civil and religious liberties from the attacks of Secular Humanists. In fact, the courts have long given protected status to openly secularist people and organizations. The following three court cases directly relate to the legal status of Secular Humanism.

*Fellowship of Humanity v. County of Alameda, 1956*
The Fellowship of Humanity described itself as a non-theistic group but filed for tax-exempt status, which was granted on the basis that they held weekly Sunday meetings and met other criteria applied to religious groups. The Fellowship of Humanity case referred only to the term humanism. Justice Black apparently added the term secular when referring to the case in *Torcaso v Watkins* to distinguish the group from such beliefs as Christian Humanism.[34]

*Washington Ethical Society v. District of Columbia, 1957*
The Washington Ethical Society honors ethical living but does not require a supernatural origin for ethics. It considers itself nontheistic and was granted tax-exempt status as a religious organization on appeal. This case is considered to have established generic Secular Humanism as a religion.[35]

In the cases of both the Fellowship of Humanity and the Washington Ethical Society, the court decisions turned not so much on the particular beliefs of practitioners as on the function and form of the practice being similar to the function and form of the practices in other religious institutions. These organizations applied for and accepted tax-exempt status on this basis. "If it walks like a duck ..."

*TORCASO v. WATKINS, CLERK, 1961. APPEAL FROM THE COURT OF APPEALS OF MARYLAND. No. 373. Argued April 24, 1961. Decided June 19, 1961.* Justice Hugo Black commented in a footnote (emphasis added),"Among *religions in this country* which do not teach what would generally be considered a belief in the existence of God are Buddhism, Taoism, Ethical Culture, *Secular Humanism*, and others."[36]

Though humanism claims to have discarded its religious trappings, the behaviors documented by court cases and the very words of the Secular Humanists themselves say otherwise. Humanists like Carl Sagan are fond of referring to the past persecutions and repressions of State religions. They denounce the religion that enforces its will by stifling and obliterating all traces of beliefs that came before.

> *In the name of piety, in a mockery of their religion, the Spaniards utterly destroyed a society with an Art, Astronomy and Architecture the equal of anything in Europe. We revile the Conquistadors for their cruelty and shortsightedness, for choosing death.*[37]

They say they are not a religion. Yet they have beliefs about which they are certain, that if all people held them, mankind would be free and equal, the earth would be renewed and preserved, and peace and prosperity would reign supreme. Anyone who holds strong beliefs such as these would be a hypocrite if he did not also believe that all the world should hold his beliefs and he would be failing in an important duty if he did not seek to change the world to agree with his beliefs.

In a society such as that created by the founding fathers, such a believer is stuck with struggling to convince a few people to change and never achieving his objectives, while most people remain free to keep their own beliefs, misguided though they be. Anyone who truly accepted the American system of freedom of religion would let well enough alone. However, the Secular Humanist knows what is best for the rest of the world and cannot sit back and let mankind and the Earth be ruined by a little detail like that.

He knows the lesson religion learned centuries ago. The only way for a true believer to achieve his objectives and create believers where he is surrounded by pagans and heretics, the only way for a belief system to assert its control over others, for their salvation and the salvation of the Earth, is by becoming the state religion, to get the power of law behind it. Humanists repeat the mantra of "free inquiry" over and over and say democracy is essential to their ideals, yet they lobby and agitate and push for legislation that takes away freedom and democracy.

They got their foothold in the administration of Taft with the tool of income tax, funding an eventual government stranglehold and denying people power to use their own money. They solidified it under Woodrow Wilson. Today they are well on their way toward proselytizing the whole nation. With the funding in place and the "democratic" humanists in power they have infiltrated and taken over public education, teaching their Science, their History, their Literature, and most of all, their religion. They are just picking off the last few pockets of resistance. Only a few are left who are foolish enough to believe America will remain free while we let the government take control of educating our children from birth (Can you say "Headstart"?) because, like educator John Dunphy, secularists cry that we cannot progress without their help.

> *I am convinced that the battle for humankind's future must be waged and won in the public school classroom by teachers that correctly perceive their role as proselytizers of a new faith: a religion of humanity that recognizes and respects the spark of what theologians call divinity in every human being... The classroom must and will become an arena of conflict between the old and new -- the rotting corpse of Christianity, together with all its adjacent evils and misery, and the new faith of humanism, resplendent with the promise of a world in which the never-realized Christian ideal of 'love thy neighbor' will finally be achieved.*[38]

Following are court cases directly related to the public education system and the attempts by Secular Humanism to oust biblical truth from education.

*State v. Scopes, Scopes v. State, 152 Tenn. 424, 278 S.W. 57 (Tenn. 1926), Scopes vs. The State of Tennessee*

In 1925 Tennessee passed a statute known as the Butler Act.

(Tenn. HB 185, 1925) "...It shall be unlawful for any teacher ... supported in whole or in part by the public school funds of the State, to teach any theory that denies the Story of the Divine Creation of man as taught in the Bible, and to teach instead that man has descended from a lower order of animals."

The ACLU (American Civil Liberties Union) placed ads offering to defend any teacher accused of violating the law. John Scopes was an athletic coach with no science background who had substitute-taught a few classes reviewing for a Science unit test. He participated in a publicity ploy for the potential benefit of the town, the ACLU and the cause of Secular Humanism. "If you can prove that I've taught evolution and that I can qualify as a defendant, then I'll be willing to stand trial," Scopes told the "town committee" that approached him, since he didn't even recall whether he'd taught human evolution or not. Students were subsequently found who were persuaded to testify against Scopes, with his encouragement.

The simple facts of the case were that the statute was clear and the prosecution presented satisfactory evidence that Scopes had violated it. Scopes was found guilty and fined $100 by the judge.

The involvement of Clarence Darrow and William Jennings Bryan in the case obscured the original, simple point, but that was the point, for the Secular Humanists. It was a sham and a true "monkey trial" in the sense that Darrow managed to monkey with the facts concerning the Bible and Christianity and none of that was relevant to the case. The judge rightly narrowed the scope of evidence that could be presented. He threatened Darrow with a contempt charge for his arrogant, insulting attitude toward the court (forcing a stammering apology from the great orator). He threw out the "testimony" of Bryan being asked endless irrelevant and largely unanswerable questions by Darrow. Only a few statements out of the whole trial bear repeating.

Bryan brought up the fact that the previous year Darrow had defended Leopold and Loeb, two university students, charged with murdering a young acquaintance, an infamous "thrill-killing" case. Bryan reminded the jury that Darrow's defense hinged upon what they had been taught. "This terrible crime was inherent in his organism, and it came from some ancestor ... Is any blame attached because somebody took Nietzsche's philosophy seriously and fashioned his life upon it? ... It is hardly fair to hang a 19–year–old boy for the philosophy that was taught him at the university." The reason the statute was enacted was to protect the students of Tennessee from teaching believed to be dangerous. Nietzsche's philosophy was an outgrowth of Darwin's philosophy.

Darrow's attack on the constitutionality of the statute ran as follows:

> *"Ignorance and fanaticism is ever busy and needs feeding. ... It is the setting of man against man and creed against creed until ... we are marching backward to ... when bigots lighted fagots to burn the men who dared to bring any intelligence and enlightenment and culture to the human mind."*

He didn't address the constitutionality. He ranted about the dangers of ignorance and fanaticism. Darrow also protested the fact that each day the judge opened with prayer. "Your honor... I object to prayer ... it is claimed by the state that there is a conflict between science and religion, ... [there should be] no attempt by means of prayer ... to influence the deliberation and consideration of the jury of the facts in this case." The judge wisely replied:

> *"This court has no purpose except to find the truth and do justice to all the issues involved in this case. ... I have instructed the ministers ... to make no reference to the issues involved in this case. I see nothing that might influence the court or jury as to the issues. I ... constantly invoke divine guidance ... on the bench and off the bench; I see no reason why I should not continue to do this."*

Defense team member Dudley Field Malone presented a case for academic freedom, an impassioned plea that got a standing ovation.

> *"... The least that this generation can do...is to give the next generation all the facts, ... all the theories, all the information ... give it to the children in the hope of heaven that they will*

> *make a better world ...We have just had a war with twenty million dead.... Civilization need not be so proud of what the grown-ups have done. For God's sake let the children have their minds kept open... shut no door from them. Make the distinction between theology and science. ... Let them both be taught. Let them both live ...We feel we stand with progress. We feel we stand with science. We feel we stand with intelligence. We feel we stand with fundamental freedom in America. We are not afraid. Where is the fear? We meet it! Where is the fear? We defy it!"*

What he did, while pretending to champion freedom and equality, was reiterate the secularist demand that "theology" be separated from science. He got a standing ovation for saying that the Bible has nothing to do with science, that its study has nothing to do with progress, intelligence or freedom except as his secularist beliefs allow it limited freedom to exist as far away from "real" education as possible.

The conviction was upheld on appeal, though subsequently overturned by the state Supreme Court only on the technicality that the jury, not the judge, should have done the fining because judges weren't permitted to levy fines over $50.[39]

*Epperson vs. Arkansas,* 1968, United States Supreme Court dealt with an Arkansas statute that was interpreted to prohibit the teaching of evolution in the schools. The statute was written forty years earlier and never enforced. A teacher brought action against the state, claiming she feared reprisals if she taught evolution. Justice Black gave a concurring opinion striking down the statute as unconstitutional but raising serious doubts about the wisdom of bringing such a case before a federal court. He stated that the Federal court seemed to be intruding on state sovereignty in the area of "subjects and schoolbooks." He admitted that the Arkansas Supreme Court did not support the same interpretation of the law that the U.S. Supreme Court came up with. In order to arrive at the ruling that the highest court reached, it was necessary to interfere with a state's governing powers, which the federal government was never supposed to do.

> *"Notwithstanding my own doubts as to whether the case presents a justiciable controversy, the Court brushes aside these doubts and leaps headlong into the middle of the very broad problems involved in federal intrusion into state powers to decide what subjects and schoolbooks it may wish to use in teaching state pupils. ... But, agreeing to consider this as a genuine case or controversy, I cannot agree to thrust the Federal Government's long arm the least bit further into state school curriculums than decision of this particular case requires. And the Court, in order to invalidate the Arkansas law as a violation of the First Amendment, has been compelled to give the State's law a broader meaning than the State Supreme Court was willing to give it. This Court, however, treats the Arkansas Act as though it made it a misdemeanor to teach or to use a book that teaches that evolution is true. But it is not for this Court to arrogate to itself the power to determine the scope of Arkansas statutes. Since the highest court of Arkansas has deliberately refused to give its statute that meaning, we should not presume to do so."*[40]

*Segraves vs. State of California,* 1981, took up the case of a man who sued because he said his children's free exercise rights were being violated by the teaching of evolution in the schools. California had a provision of accommodation that included the following:

> *The anti-dogmatism policy provided that class discussions of origins should emphasize that scientific explanations focus on "how," not "ultimate cause," and that any speculative statements concerning origins, both in texts and in classes, should be presented conditionally, not dogmatically.*[41]

Superior Court Judge Irving Perluss promised the father that he would make sure the school board made sure everybody understood and practiced that policy. Yet the judge himself negated what might have been accomplished with the following statement.

> *Now, when you begin to think of textbooks that talk about belief, now to me belief is not a scientific word. One knows, one accumulates data, one has a comprehension of, one understands, one does a lot of things, but to me belief always, in my situation, has been something I associate with my theology. I would not like to see my theology and my science get mixed. I have never dealt with a scientific process where somebody says, 'I believe.' I have dealt with theological processes where one believes. In short, I think at that point you begin to mix epistemologies, and that's confusing.*[41]

The judge seems to have forgotten his historic jurisprudence, because belief is a legal term. It's like a jury examining evidence on a case and reaching a verdict. It's not even primarily a religious term, and it applies to Science as well as law when properly defined. There's no question that Evolution is a belief by the judge's definition, dealing in more presuppositions and theories than facts. And it certainly can become confusing when it gets mixed up with Science.

*McLean v. Arkansas Board of Education,* 1982, was the case that redefined the role of the government in education. Or, rather, it made clear what had actually been true for a long time. Government is the only proper educator of children. Government defines all the terms, makes all the rules, and clearly has the power to wipe religious freedom out of the schools. The judge makes it sound like he's protected people from something evil, chasing Creation Science out of the schools and deciding that it can't be a Science at all but must be solely a religion, therefore having no place in the schools because religion has no place in the schools.

The Court closes this opinion with a thought expressed eloquently by the great Justice Frankfurter:

"We renew our conviction that 'we have at stake the very existence of our country on the faith that complete separation between the state and religion is best for the state and best for religion.' *Everson v. Board of Education*, 330 U.S. at 59. 'If nowhere else, in the relation between Church and State, 'good fences make good neighbors.'" *[McCollum v. Board of Education,* 333 U.S. 203, 232 (1948)][42]

The Court Cases Appendix deals with the quote taken out of context from Robert Frost's "Mending Wall," but it is sufficient to say that the judge wants his wall high and strong and religion cut off from, not protected by, the state.

*Edwards v. Aguillard, U.S. Supreme Court,* 1987 is essentially the same case as the previous one, only this one went to the Supreme Court. Read carefully the dissenting opinion of Justice Antonin Scalia in the Court Cases Appendix. Chief Justice Rehnquist agreed with him as well but the rest of the court continued the downhill rush to keep Secular Humanism reigning supreme as the protected established religion and true belief suppressed. One sentence of Scalia's opinion makes a point not to be missed.

*One could argue, I suppose, that any time Congress acts with the intent of advancing religion, it has enacted a "law respecting an establishment of religion;" but far from being an unavoidable reading, it is quite an unnatural one."*[43]

This is the exact premise used to prevent religion from being protected. Unnatural it may be, constitutionally prohibited it may be, but Secular Humanism has no interest in what is natural or constitutional. If twisting even the Constitution's meaning gets the desired end accomplished, Secular Humanists will do it without hesitation.

*Webster v. New Lenox School District,* 1990, the Seventh Circuit Court of Appeals. A Social Studies teacher, not a Science teacher, objected to a statement in his classroom textbook asserting that the earth was over four billion years old. He explained that the statement was presented by the textbook as a fact, not a theory, as it should have been. He also talked about Creation in class as an alternative theory to Evolution. For this he was censured. The School board was cleared of charges it violated his right to freedom of speech because it had told him he could teach historic Church-State relationships. Part of the ruling includes this:

*Epperson, 393 U.S at 106* (school may not adopt programs that aid or oppose any religion). As the district court noted, the superintendent's letter is directed to this concern. "Educators do not offend the First Amendment so long as their actions are reasonably related to legitimate pedagogical concerns."[44]

The quote says,"aid or oppose" any religion. The teacher believed his religion was being opposed and it seems he was correct if he was not permitted to speak about it. Remember that Thomas Jefferson said,"... all men shall be free to profess, and by argument to maintain, their opinions in matters of religion, and that the same shall in no wise diminish, enlarge, or affect their civil capacities."[45]

*Peloza v. Capistrano School District,* 1994

This case resulted in nothing less than a gag order on a teacher. The School board was permitted to order him to refrain from any discussion of religion with students, even ones initiated by a student. One judge dissented, and his statement is well worth reading. Though his interpretation of the "Establishment Clause" is also very flawed, since he says he would agree with the majority on much of the decision, he makes the point that the decision is based on an assumption that it is possible to know in advance what kind of religious discussion the teacher would have, and that it would automatically be a violation. One paragraph is included here to show the point he tries to make.

> *Religion has been used to justify the suppression of speech for centuries. See Everson V. Board of Ed, 330 U.S. 1, 8-10, 67 S.Ct. 504, 5074)9, 91 L.Ed. 711 (1947). With the development of a vigorous First Amendment jurisprudence, we have quelled some of the worst abuses. But points of tension remain. We must thus remain vigilant to ensure that in our rush to preserve certain fundamental rights, we do not trample others. Caution is of the essence; only through a methodical and fact-specific jurisprudence can we hope to achieve a proper accommodation.*[46]

In a case beginning in 2005 U.S. district Judge James Otero ruled that the University of California could deny science credit for students from Christian high schools. The following is a paragraph from the article.

*Among the books used in rejected courses were Christianity's Influence on America and Biology for Christian Schools, both of which instruct that the Bible is the inerrant starting point for knowledge. "[If scientific] conclusions contradict the Word of God, the conclusions are wrong," Otero cited from the latter book as a reason for its rejection.*[47]

Evolution stated as a fact has been permitted for decades in textbooks, but a student can be denied admission to college because his textbook states that the words of the Bible are facts. The rejected books present evolutionary theory, but since they state a reliance on the authority of Scripture they are of no value.

Secular Humanism became America's established religion in large part through judicial action. Courts speculated on legislative intent and engaged in judicial lawmaking. In *Holy Trinity* judges ignored the obvious unconstitutionality of restricting religious freedom of a church to choose its own pastor. Distinctions between Common Law and Statute Law have consistently been violated.

Thomas Jefferson warned against judicial power, especially its unelected and virtually unremovable status and the danger of judges being corrupted by partisanship. He demanded that the system of checks and balances be strictly maintained, especially in the area of determining constitutionality, seeing even in his own time that the judiciary was trying to usurp this power entirely from the other two branches and become the sole decider.

The Briggs heresy trial marked the fall of ministerial schools to liberalism and secularism. The rise of Fundamentalism preserved doctrinal purity. Public sector "religious neutrality" masked secularist hostility. Support for the secularist educational system came through taxation, which reduces people to poverty (no ability to support or fight for their free exercise rights) and two-income dependence (forcing children into the secularist public babysitting system). Government sponsored indoctrination begins in infancy at daycares and preschools and continues throughout education system. Legal persecution of parents for biblical discipline and homeschooling causes further wearing away of government protection and financial stability.

Early twentieth-century court cases established Secular Humanism as a religion by granting it tax exemption based on its practices and beliefs. Secularists used this power to cause states to strike down statutes supportive of free religious expression and practice and promote secularism in its place. An artificial separation of church and state was created to shut out God from education.

Education-related court cases follow a pattern of separating the Scripture and science, creating an imagined distinction between "religious truth" and "scientific truth." Also included are the redefining of legal terms, intrusion of the federal government into state issues and the redefining of the "separation principle." These led to censuring those who protested teaching theories as facts and to prohibit expression of scriptural viewpoints, disallowing college admission because coursework was not Secular Humanist.

It is possible that some may still doubt Secular Humanists are responsible for this Establishment of Religion in America, this destruction of freedom of religion and the reduction of every aspect of education to government indoctrination in anti-god dogma. So come along and hear from the mouths, the pens, the typewriters, and the word processors of the true believers themselves. Let them dispute these claims and say these allegations are lies. Listen to the words they claim as their own, and judge for yourself.

---

1 *Church of the Holy Trinity v. United States, 143 U.S. 457* (1892)

2 Thomas Jefferson, "A letter to Charles Hammond," August 18th, 1821.

3 Antonin Scalia, *Common-Law Courts in a Civil-Law System: The Role of United States Federal Courts in Interpreting the Constitution and Laws,* THE TANNER LECTURES ON HUMAN VALUES, Princeton University, March 8 and 9, 1995.

4 Quoted by Scalia, from William Eskridge, Jr., *Dynamic Statutory Interpretation,* copyright by the President and Fellows of Harvard College, 1994.

5 Quoted by Scalia, from Guido Calabresi, *A Common Law for the Age of Statutes,* copyright by the President and Fellows of Harvard College, 1982.

6 Quoted by Scalia from Oliver Wendell Holmes, "The Theory of Legal Interpretation," 12 *Harvard Law Review,* 417, 419 (1899).

7 Quoted by Scalia from James Madison, in *Federalist* No. 47, quoting Montesquieu (Charles de Secondat, Baron de Montesquieu, 1689-1755), *The Spirit of the Laws*, vol. 1, trans. Thomas Nugent (London: J. Nourse, 1777).

8 Quoted by Scalia from a Robert Rantoul Fourth-of-July address in Scituate, Massachusetts, in 1836.

9 From the University of Virginia Library *Collection of the letters and papers of Thomas Jefferson.* Thomas Jefferson to Samuel Kercheval, 1816. ME 15:34.

10 -------Thomas Jefferson to A. Coray, 1823. ME 15:486.

11 -------Thomas Jefferson to Edward Livingston, 1825. ME 16:114.

12 -------Thomas Jefferson: Autobiography, 1821. ME 1:122.

13 -------Thomas Jefferson to Edward Livingston, 1825. ME 16:113.

14 -------Thomas Jefferson to W. H. Torrance, 1815. ME 14:303.

15 -------Thomas Jefferson to Abigail Adams, 1804. ME 11:51.

16 -------Thomas Jefferson to William C. Jarvis, 1820. ME 15:277.

17 -------Thomas Jefferson to Spencer Roane, 1819. ME 15:212.

18 -------Thomas Jefferson to Nathaniel Macon, 1821. FE 10:192.

19 -------Thomas Jefferson to John Wayles Eppes, 1807. FE 9:68.

20 -------Thomas Jefferson to Joel Barlow, 1801. ME 10:223.

21 Sydney F. Ahlstrom. *A Religious History of the American People*. New Haven: Yale University Press, 1972 and from Randall Balmer and John R. Fitzmier. The Presbyterians. Westport, CT: Praeger, 1994.

22 from the Presbyterian Church history section of the website *americanpresbyterianchurch.org*

23 John Adams, President, to the 1st Brigade of the 3rd Division of the Militia of Massachusetts. OCTOBER 11, 1798.

24 Samuel Adams, Speech, State House of Pennsylvania, Philadelphia, 1 August 1776.

25 *The New York Times,* September 14, 1999.

26 Justice Arthur J. Goldberg, quoted in *The Supreme Court of the United States No. 02-1574 UNITED STATES OF AMERICA, PETITIONER v. MICHAEL A. NEWDOW, ET AL. ON PETITION FOR A WRIT OF CERTIORARI TO THE UNITED STATES COURT OF APPEALS FOR THE NINTH CIRCUIT REPLY BRIEF FOR THE UNITED STATES* July 2003.

27 November 19, 1999, Massachusetts Supreme Court decision.

28 *World Net Daily* Posted: December 16, 2007 1:00 am EST.

29 *World Net Daily* Posted: January 26, 2010 11:02 pm Eastern By Bob Unruh 2010.

30 Adapted from an article in *World Net Daily*, Posted: April 23, 2007 12:33 pm Eastern By Bob Unruh.

31 Thomas Jefferson Letter to the Secretary of the Treasury Albert Gallatin (1802).

32 John Adams, letter to Abigail Adams, July 7, 1775.

33 John Adams, *The Works of John Adams*, vol. 6 (*Defence of the Constitutions* Vol. III cont'd, Davila, Essays on the Constitution) [1851] *The Works of John Adams, Second President of the United States: with a Life of the Author, Notes and Illustrations, by his Grandson Charles Francis Adams* (Boston: Little, Brown and Co., 1856). 10 volumes. Vol. 6.

34 *Fellowship of Humanity v. County of Alameda*, 1956.

35 *Washington Ethical Society v. District of Columbia,* 249 F.2d 127 (D.C. Cir. 1957).

36 *TORCASO v. WATKINS, CLERK,* 1961. APPEAL FROM THE COURT OF APPEALS OF MARYLAND. No. 373. Argued April 24, 1961. Decided June 19, 1961.

37 Carl Sagan, From *Cosmos: A Personal Voyage* (Updated), 1989.

38 John J. Dunphy, Quoted in *Humanist* Magazine, January-February 1983.

39 Scopes Trial background information and quotations adapted from "State v. John Scopes" ("The Monkey Trial") by Douglas O. Linder *http://www.law.umkc.edu/faculty/projects/ftrials/scopes/ evolut.htm*

40 *Epperson v. Arkansas* (1968) 393 U.S. 97, 37 U.S. Law Week 4017, 89S. Ct. 266, 21 L. Ed 228) excerpts

from the Supreme Court transcript of this trial, taken from the website *www.bc.edu/bc_org/avp/cas/comm /free_speech/epperson.*

41 *Segraves v. California* (1981) Sacramento Superior Court #278978) excerpts from the personal website built by Frank Fire.

42 *McLean v. Arkansas Board of Education* (1982) 529 F. Supp. 1255, 50 U.S. Law Week 2412.

43 *Edwards v. Aguillard, U.S. Supreme Court,* 1987.

44 *Webster v. New Lenox School District #122, 917 F. 2d* 1004.

45 Thomas Jefferson, "Draft for a Bill for Establishing Religious Freedom." Proposed to the Virginia Assembly, 1779.

46 *John E. Peloza v. Capistrano Unified School District,* (1994) 917 F. 2d 1004.

47 *Answers in Genesis News to Note*, Aug 16, 2008, *San Francisco Chronicle*: "Judge Says UC Can Deny Religious Course Credit."

## 5. How Can You Say That?

*The Cosmos is all that is or ever was or ever will be. Our feeblest contemplations of the Cosmos stir us — there is a tingling in the spine, a catch in the voice, a faint sensation of a distant memory, as if we were falling from a great height. We know we are approaching the greatest of mysteries.*[1]

Carl Sagan

Modern Secular Humanists seem like positive people. "We are part of something greater than ourselves,"[2] Edward Osborne Wilson, Pulitzer prize-winning biologist, insists. Politician Robert Ingersoll wants "to ... render all the service possible in the holy cause of human progress."[3] They have groups that meet for fellowship on Sundays, listening to motivational speakers with messages like that of Stephen Covey. "Our ultimate freedom is the right and power to decide how anybody or anything outside ourselves will affect us."[4]

Secularists exchange inspiration and learning at these meetings. "Our species is young and curious and brave and shows much promise." They hold fundraisers where they sell donated books and videos. "In the last few millennia we have made the most astonishing and unexpected discoveries about the Cosmos."[1] Popular writers and TV personalities like Carl Sagan churn out ample material for their fundraisers. They even enjoy potlucks and occasionally make jokes about themselves.

> *Don't forget to bring food and/or drink along, too. ... "Atheists will bring only food whose ingredients they can see. Agnostics are not sure*

> *what they will bring or whether there really is food, skeptics will argue whether we really should have a potluck supper at all, pagans will bring wine, anarchists may bring whatever they ... please, and humanists optimistically believe they will help to complement the meal and make it a wonderful experience for all."*[5]

"Unity and secularism will be the motto of the government," promised Manmohan Singh, the first Sikh prime minister of India. "We can't afford divisive polity."[6] They believe in a democratic society. "I am the most intensely religious man I know," American General and later President Dwight Eisenhower stated. " . . . That does not mean I adhere to any sect. ... I believe in Democracy."[7] They encourage free inquiry. "The things we live by," visionary American animator Walt Disney believed,"... are preserved or diminished by how freely we exchange ideas and feelings."[8] They seek to broaden knowledge, like UNESCO's first director and World Wildlife founder Julian Huxley. "Man can now see himself as the sole agent of further evolutionary advance on this planet, and one of the few possible instruments of progress in the universe at large."[9]

Secularists are "wide open" to all knowledge. "Sit down before fact as a little child," urges British scientist and Darwin contemporary Thomas Henry Huxley. "... Follow humbly wherever and to whatever abysses nature leads, or you shall learn nothing. I have only begun to learn contentment and peace of mind since I have resolved at all risks to do this."[10] French mathematician Henri Poincaré echoes the sentiment of Huxley. "The scientist does not study nature because it is useful to do so. ...He takes pleasure in it because it is beautiful. ... That more intimate beauty which comes from the harmonious order of its parts, and which a pure intelligence can grasp."[11]

Roy Wood Sellars and Raymond Bragg, authors of the original Humanist Manifesto I draft, made a call for unity that seemed to be far-reaching, even including theists. "Religions have always been means for realizing the highest values of life." Their claim that "today man's larger understanding of the universe, his scientific achievements," must be taken into consideration even seems reasonable, and they say modern secularists have a "deeper appreciation of brotherhood."[12] Surely, then, theists are part of that brotherhood, aren't they?

Things became a bit confusing when onetime NAACP vice president Algernon David Black said, "Why not let people differ about their answers to the great mysteries of the Universe?" This sounds like a positive goal, but "mysteries" is the key term. "Let each seek one's own way to the highest, to one's own sense of supreme loyalty in life, one's ideal of life." The highest what? Supreme loyalty to what? What does "an ideal of life" mean? "Let each philosophy, each world-view bring forth its truth and beauty to a larger perspective." How can it be that everybody gets to have his/her own truth? How can "people ... grow in vision, stature and dedication"[13] when religion can only have mysteries and relativism that fit in with a "larger perspective?"

Terry Sanderson, president of the National Secular Society of the UK, suddenly loses his positive outlook on the subject of "...conservative religious beliefs that sometimes shock and repel the majority." Immigrants bringing their theism into the UK are divisive. "...Full of hatred and intolerance and crazy, senseless rules." They oppose democracy. "When religion ... bids for temporal power ...it isn't long before demands for privilege ensue and eventually the brutality begins."[14] Theists restrict learning and discovery. "History is full of people who out of fear, or ignorance or lust for power," said American popular science writer Carl Sagan, "have destroyed knowledge of immeasurable value which truly belongs to us all. We must not let it happen again."[1]

Emily Dickinson chided the narrow view of using "holy writings" as the only authority. "The Bible is an antique Volume/Written by faded men ...Boys that 'believe' are very lonesome/Other Boys are 'lost'/Had but the Tale a warbling Teller/All the Boys would come/Orpheus' Sermon captivated/It did not condemn."[15] Some Secularists put on a brave front and claim to be tolerant of theists, like American author James Baldwin. "If the concept of God has any validity or any use, it can only be to make us larger, freer, and more loving." But if God fails to conform to secularist ideals, "if God cannot do this, then it is time we got rid of Him."[16]

"The church of this country is not only indifferent to the wrongs of the slave, it actually takes sides with the oppressors." The truth is, theists disgust and horrify the secularist like Fredrick Douglass. ".... For my part, I would say, welcome infidelity! Welcome atheism!" He lumps all manner of worshipers together and convinces himself they all believe the same as those who admittedly wronged him. "Welcome anything! in preference to the gospel, as preached by these Divines! They convert the very name of religion into an engine of tyranny and barbarous cruelty."[17]

George Bernard Shaw mocked the very idea that theists might be better off than secularists. "The fact that a believer is happier than a skeptic is no more to the point than the fact that a drunken man is happier than a sober one." He deeply distrusted the possibility of true belief. "The happiness of credulity is a cheap and dangerous quality."[18] Secularists claim to expect censorship, personal attacks, venomous hatred, possibly to be burned at the stake, as Clarence Darrow warned at the Scopes trial. "... Bigots lighted fagots to burn the men who dared to bring any intelligence and enlightenment and culture to the human mind."[19]

Science Fiction writer Robert A. Heinlein said,"One man's religion is another man's belly laugh."[20] Some secularists claim, like Heinlein and American educator and poet Lizette Reese, not to be frightened by theists. "The old faiths light their candles all about, but burly truth comes by and blows them out."[21] Secularists still will not listen to any point of view involving theism, saying, like Sigmund Freud, "religion is comparable to a childhood neurosis,"[22] and ridiculing them all. "So oft in theologic wars,/The disputants, I ween,/Rail on in utter ignorance/Of what each other mean,/And prate about an Elephant/Not one of them has seen!"[23] John Godfrey Saxe, 19th century poet, echoing the writings of the Buddhist *Udana* and many eastern folktales, dismissed the possibility of real knowledge of God.

They do not want anyone else to listen to theist viewpoints, either. "An Inuit hunter asked the local missionary priest: 'If I did not know about God and sin, would I go to hell?' 'No,' said the priest, 'not if you did not know.'" While individual missionaries might teach this, it is not a scriptural teaching or the official doctrinal position of any Christian religion. Man is obligated to follow as much light as he has, and God has obligated Himself to provide more light to him. Still, it is clear from the rest of the story that Pulitzer prize-winning author Annie Dillard has judged all missionary and evangelistic efforts to be reprehensible. "'Then why,' asked the Inuit earnestly, 'did you tell me?'"[24]

Those who follow and proclaim the Scriptures are enemies of secularist progress. "Fundamental, Bible believing people do not have the right to indoctrinate their children in their religious beliefs," warned Peter Hoagland, American lawyer and congressman. "We, the state, are preparing them for the year 2000, when America will be part of a one-world global society and their children will not fit in."[25] Apparently not every "world view" is permitted. "There is not sufficient love and goodness in the world to permit us to give some of it away to imaginary beings,"[26] warned Friedrich

Nietzsche. Religious belief cannot be allowed if it conflicts with the secularist agenda.

> *"On religion ...the time [has]... come," said John Stuart Mill, "when ... all who, being qualified in point of knowledge, have ... satisfied themselves that the current opinions are not only false, but hurtful, to make their dissent known. ... Over himself, over his own body and mind, the individual is sovereign."*[27]

Secularists believe the world would be better off with theistic teaching out of the schools, out of public meetings, out of government buildings. "The abolition of religion as the illusory happiness of the people is the demand for their real happiness,"[28] Karl Marx insisted. Religious teaching should be purged out of anyplace where it might ever be heard. "It is not hardness of heart or evil passions that drive certain individuals to atheism," said TV personality and prolific author Steve Allen, "but rather a scrupulous intellectual honesty."[29] Karl Marx judged religious expression to be a fruitless attempt to avoid despairing over physical problems. "To call on them to give up their illusions about their condition is to call on them to give up a condition that requires illusions."[28]

Secularists absolutely do not think theists have a right to be afraid of them, because they are positive people. "When religion sanctifies hatred, it lends to that hatred a special ferocity," warned Johannes Cardinal Willebrands, Dutch Roman Catholic ecumenist. "Normal moral inhibitors are erased."[30] The fact that they feel free to say these things about every person who practices a religion should not terrify us.

A "Christian Manifesto" recently signed by cross-denominational leaders taking a stand against same-sex marriage, abortion and euthanasia drew a warning from Peter Montgomery of *AlterNet.org*. "But it also reflects a potentially more troubling hardening of right-wing resistance to legal abortion." The claim is that the majority favors these "freedoms" and therefore Christians stand opposed to " ... a nation increasingly supportive of equality for LGBT people." Montgomery claims these leaders are just trying to get attention for themselves. "In a diverse and increasingly pluralistic nation, these conservative Christian leaders are inflaming false fears of religious persecution in order to justify their own intransigence and unwillingness to abide by legal, political and cultural changes they don't like."[31] The fears of persecution are not false.

The Nazis put those who opposed them in concentration camps. The U.S. House of Representatives in 1971 referred to this event in a Committee on the Judiciary report. "It is extremely easy for us to say that the German people, for instance, even under the threat of physical violence, shouldn't have allowed their government to do what it did."[32] Stalin and Soviet Communism put them in the gulag. "Prisoners were engaged in a variety of economic activities, but their work was typically unskilled, manual, and economically inefficient. The combination of endemic violence, extreme climate, hard labor, meager food rations and unsanitary conditions led to extremely high death rates in the camps."[33] North Korea, Vietnam and China put them in "reeducation camps." "The new Vietnamese government decides to "re-educate" thousands of former American allies, government workers, intellectuals and merchants by transforming them into agricultural workers. They are forced from the cities to Vietnam's 'new economic zones.'"[34] More people died in these reeducation camps than all who were put to death by Hitler and Stalin combined. Ho Chi Min of Vietnam and the Khmer Rouge under Pol Pot in Cambodia simply murdered millions of those who opposed them, stacking their dead bodies without burial. "Cambodia probably lost slightly less than 4,000,000 people ...The vast majority, almost 3,300,000 men, women, and children (including 35,000 foreigners), were murdered within the years 1970 to 1980 ... Most of these, a likely near 2,400,000, were murdered by the communist Khmer Rouge."[35] All of these mass murderers were Secular Humanists.

America has already built or refurbished detention camps, such as those used in the forced relocation of Japanese-Americans during WWII, The same 1971 Judiciary Committee report mentioned above also informs us of a chilling reality. "We can only feel repugnance and fear at the fact that today we have locations available for another round-up [1970's and again in 1999] and that we live under a law which would permit another mass detention of people without any proof that they had committed any illegal actions."[32] and for the Korean war-era Detention Act of 1950 to deal with "subversives." "Congress's anxiety over the existence of communist groups located in the United States also grew. In 1952, Congress appropriated $775,000 for the activation and rehabilitation of six camps. "[36]

Some of these facilities have been converted to ordinary prisons or memorial sites. Others stand empty, but they have rail service like the Soviet gulag. "It is estimated that there are between 160 – 190 detention (internment) facilities in the United States, each capable of housing between 10,000 to 300,000 civilians. Most of these camps are located on active military bases, or closed military bases which have been converted to detention facilities."[36] Some reports say these camps can hold as many as 400, 000 people. Various executive orders have permitted the president to order containment or relocation and confinement of people within the United States. FEMA has control of these facilities in some cases and legislation is being proposed that claims to allow for the creation of emergency evacuation centers in case of disasters, terrorism or other threats to public safety.

> *Photos do exist of detention camps at Camp Grayling in Grayling, Michigan; Fort Dix, New Jersey; and the Federal Transfer Center-Temporary Facility at Will Rogers Airport in Oklahoma City, Oklahoma. Miscellaneous pictures have been taken of other sites showing empty fields with ten foot fences topped with razor wire creating holding pens. These sites also have stadium lighting and guard towers surrounding the sites. The question that should be asked is who are these holding pens for, because cattle do not climb fences, and they don't need guard towers?*[36]

The wording of some of these executive orders and legislative proposals is vague, though. "Should this country experience a national emergency, whether real or fabricated, that grows into a perceived crisis situation, the President, through *Executive Order 12919* [President Bill Clinton, June 3, 1994 37] may declare Martial Law, and federal resources will be committed with or without local or state requests."[36] Across the ideological spectrum people question the power and control being used to conduct preparedness drills for possible invasions. "The Army and National Guard are posting for 'Internment/Resettlement Specialists' for 'confinement,' 'control,' 'custody,' 'supervision' and 'counseling individual prisoners in rehabilitative programs.'"[38] They question the allocation of funds to erect chain-link fences with barbed wire around empty facilities. The stated purpose may be to deal with terrorism, disease outbreaks or natural disasters, but almost any pretext could be used to relocate or confine American citizens.[36]

President Jimmy Carter established FEMA and began paving the way for these camps. More work was done during the Cold War era and in 1999 during the Clinton administration. The trend continued during the Bush and Obama administrations. Much of the actual physical evidence is only in proposals, drills such as Rex 84 and contingency plans. Little hard evidence can be presented. When questioned about these camps, US officials say that they are in case of an invasion of illegal aliens.[36]

What the camps might really be for is to segregate a violent segment of the population. Secularists constantly use of the terms “brutality,” “cruelty,” “fanatics,” “oppression,” “tyranny,” and the like when referring to theists. Fundamentalism has been linked to radical Islam and made synonymous with terrorism. Christian behavior during such times as the Crusades has been irretrievably distorted. Hence the government or the public might feel justified in opposing all religion because it will encourage violent behavior. They may even consider theists a threat to public safety, people who need to be locked up for the good of all.

Aaron Cline, *About.com's* Agnosticism/atheism expert, confidently affirms that “People ... seem to act even more brutally when they believe that they have religious or even divine sanction for that cause.” Secularists demand respect and toleration. They deny it to theists, however, because theists are brutal and God makes them so, meaning they will never be able to change until they give up God. “God becomes an ‘amplifier’ ... even more respect, deference, and reverence is expected for religious beliefs...”[39] The only way theists can earn respect is to stop being theists. Secularists have apparently already earned respect and toleration, though Cline does not explain how.

Walter Savage Landor, English poet, demanded freedom to attack with impunity belief in any god. “Even the weakest disputant is made so conceited by what he calls religion, as to think himself wiser than the wisest who thinks differently from him.”[40] The positive message has largely disappeared from secularist thinking by this time, replaced by a plan of attack. “Religion: a daughter of Hope and Fear, explaining to Ignorance the nature of the

Unknowable,"[41] *Devil's Dictionary* author Ambrose Bierce sneered.

"They'll take food out of the mouths of children in order to give tax cuts to the wealthiest."[42] Speaker of the House Nancy Pelosi meant Republicans, but secularists equate conservativism with "extremist" religion and use the same attacks against them. The attack on biblically based moral principles is essential to secular humanism. "I say quite deliberately that the Christian religion, as organized in its churches," said mathematician Bertrand Russell, "has been and still is the principal enemy of moral progress in the world."[43] Morality originates from human reason, according to *Atlas Shrugged* author Ayn Rand. "Achievement of your happiness is the only moral purpose of your life, and that happiness ... is the proof of your moral integrity," not obedience to God's teaching, "since it is the proof and the result of your loyalty to the achievement of your values."[44]

They also believe that morality must be free from dogmatic, outdated writings like the Scriptures. "The only possible basis for a sound morality is mutual tolerance and respect," said British philosopher A .J. Ayer. "Tolerance of one another's customs and opinions; respect for one another's rights and feelings; awareness of one another's needs."[45] This respect did not apply to any institutions that promoted morality based on the Scriptures or that reference God as the source of morality. Peter Ustinov, British actor, diplomat, and prolific author, said,

> *"People ... I don't think they should be judged at all ... feel towards people according to their behavior and not according to their beliefs. ... An Atheist who would help an old lady across the street is probably doing a more... Christian act than a highly religious person who's so wrapped up in his own thoughts that he didn't*

> *notice that the old lady was trying to get across."*[46]

Speaker of the House Nancy Pelosi exclaimed,"The Republicans did not have an election about jobs, health care, education, environment, national security, they had an election about wedge issues in our country." "Wedge issues" is code meaning someone was being divisive again. "They exploited the loveliness of the American people, the devoutness of people of faith for a political end." This time Republicans bamboozled a bunch of ignorant Bible-thumpers into going along with their schemes for domination. "Democrats are going to ban the Bible if they are elected. Imagine the ridiculousness of that, if it won votes for them."[47] Imagine secularists banning the Bible. Oh, wait. They don't need to, because they pretty much already have.

"God wants unbelievers to suffer, and what could be more noble than to help him a little?" According to philosopher Simon Blackburn, "When religion rules, toleration disappears, for you cannot cherish the verdict of death to the infidels, yet also tolerate those who disagree - for those are the very same infidels..."[48] It is common among secularists to ascribe to all theists the beliefs which some hold and which they despise, and to attack all equally. "With or without it (Religion) you would have good people doing good things and evil people doing evil things." Steve Weinberg, physicist and author, believes. "But for good people to do evil things, that takes religion."[49] It is popular to make God the author of all that is wrong with religion. But, since He is supposed to be perfectly good, that is too much of a contradiction. Therefore the existence of God can be dismissed as impossible. "God is a hypothesis, and, as such, stands in need of proof; the onus probandi [burden of proof] rests on the theist,"[50] Percy Bysshe Shelley challenged.

"I don't believe in the 'sky bully' (referring to God)," said Joseph Hill "Joss" Whedon, creator of SciFi/Occult series including *Buffy the Vampire Slayer* and *Serenity*. Whedon answered an interview question asking, "Is there a God?" with one word: "No." The interviewer followed up with: "That's it, end of story, 'no?'" Whedon answered: "Absolutely not. That's a very important and necessary thing to learn."[51] To make certain everyone learns that lesson, Secularists seek to discredit belief in God. "All religions, with their gods, demigods, prophets, messiahs and saints, are the product of the fancy and credulity of men who have not yet reached the full development and complete possession of their intellectual powers,"[52] said Mikhail Bakunin, theorist of collectivist anarchism, dismissing religion as childish.

"The Universe is an entirely natural process," claims David Nicholls of the Atheist Foundation of Australia. "Religion is of such a serious concern to planet Earth, that its guessings are no longer good enough." Some people are not content to dismiss theism as something we'll grow out of, though. Note again that certain knowledge where religion is concerned is an absurd idea for secularists. "Reaching a full potential of life before death is only afforded to those who reject the notion of life after death."[53] Life after death must be refuted because there can be no fear of judgment or consequences of sin. "I anticipate death will be a totally unconscious void in which you float through eternity with no particular consciousness of anything."[54] Rod Serling, producer and writer of the *Twilight Zone*, said in his last interview. "I don't believe in an afterlife, so I don't have to spend my whole life fearing hell, or fearing heaven even more. For whatever the tortures of hell, I think the boredom of heaven would be even worse,"[55] Isaac Asimov said.

Secularists have redefined freedom to suit their goals. "...The illegality of cannabis is outrageous, ... a drug which helps produce the serenity and insight, sensitivity and fellowship so desperately needed in this increasingly mad and dangerous world."[56] Carl Sagan's argument uses strongly emotional terms, in spite of the secularist claim to be guided by reason. "No woman can call herself free," was Margaret Sanger's passionate cry as the founder of Planned Parenthood, "until she can choose consciously whether she will or will not be a mother. ... Regardless of what man's attitude may be... She goes through the vale of death alone."[57] Tenzin Gyatzo, 14th Dalai Lama, equates happiness with freedom and speaks of it as a right. "All beings are equal in both their desire for happiness and their right to obtain it, ... there is no logical basis to discriminate ... or to alter your concern for them if they behave negatively."[58] Some secularists, like Aldous Huxley, openly proclaim that their real goal in seeking universal freedom is "liberation from a certain system of morality. We objected to the morality because it interfered with our sexual freedom."[59]

Issues of morality are excellent examples of the practical application of secularist principles. "We're going to take things away from you on behalf of the common good."[60] Hillary Clinton, former first lady, senator and Secretary of State, was talking about tax cuts, but the principle applies to freedom to practice morality as well when secularists are around. When the courts ruled that the Boy Scouts of America did not have to accept homosexuals as members or leaders, Florida news commentator Bill Maxwell grudgingly admitted that private organizations had rights and freedoms. "But officials should bear in mind that they, like the Christian Right and the Anglican bishops, are disserving the nation's boys -- mere children -- when teaching them to hate fellow humans."[61] It should have been clear that this issue had nothing to do with hatred of fellow humans. It especially had nothing to do with freedom or equality, in spite of what Coretta Scott King, wife of Martin Luther King, civil rights leader, proclaimed. "Homophobia is like racism and anti-Semitism and other forms of bigotry in that it seeks to dehumanize a large group of people, to deny their humanity, their dignity and personhood."[62]

The word "homophobia" means fear of homosexuals. It, along with the terms "gay-bashers" or "anti-gay," presupposes that the only reason anyone can possibly oppose homosexuality is because of fear or hatred of the people who practice it. "In fact, it is a farce to call any being virtuous whose virtues do not result from the exercise of its own reason,"[63] *Frankenstein* author Mary Shelley said, scoffing at the idea that biblical obedience can produce any morals worth having. Some people may be actual homophobes. But by including everyone who does not accept homosexual behavior as haters of homosexuals, there is left no room for the possibility of opposing the homosexual act as sin, yet having compassion for the souls of the people who are trapped by it.

"Sex and race, because they are easy and visible differences, have been the primary ways of organizing human beings into superior and inferior groups." Gloria Steinem championed feminism, but the logical extension of this kind of equality applies to Homosexuality as well, as secularists themselves will tell you. "We are talking about a society in which there will be no roles other than those chosen or those earned. We are really talking about humanism."[64] By ascribing the role of the hater or the oppressor to people who follow the Scriptures, secularists create an enemy that does not exist.

Though the Boy Scouts is not technically a biblical or even Christian organization, it has been strongly connected to and heavily supported by religious or formerly religious organizations like the YMCA, the United Methodist denomination, and the Latter Day Saints. "The greatest tragedy in mankind's entire history may be the hijacking of morality by religion."[65] Arthur C. Clarke lamented, outraged that everyone has not long ago abandoned connections to churches as support for moral character. Many churches have used the Boy Scouts as a youth outreach program. The attack on the organization by homosexuals only intensified after the Supreme Court ruling. "Shouldn't we consider ... a fundamental restructuring of economic political social and religious institutions?" Carl Sagan's topic was the terrors of nuclear holocaust, but secularists want us to believe that all "divisive" issues are going to destroy us and must be snuffed out. "We've reached a point where there can be no more special interests or special cases."[1]

Activist-harassed local governments and the United Way tried to bully the Scouts into "non-discrimination" by suddenly charging rent for formerly free meeting places and denying funding that was previously shared among old established charities. "We do not need any more preaching about right and wrong," insisted Dr. Sidney Simon, speaking of classroom education, but certainly wanting his principles applied across society. "The old 'thou shalt nots' simply are not relevant." Homosexuals claimed that the Boy Scouts suffered declining membership and financial losses after the Supreme Court decision, with most major newspapers reporting these exaggerations and lies as facts. "Values clarification is a method for teachers to change the values of children without getting caught."[66] Dr. Simon would have been proud of how his lessons live on in the lives of public-school educated moral relativists. The truth is that the Boy Scouts experienced an upturn in membership and support, though they continue to face persecution.

Former scout John Faulkner, who is homosexual but apparently never disclosed the fact while he was a scout, said, "I was angry with the Boy Scouts of America," when the policy officially won protection. "... Their policy ... denies the truth that many men who happen to be gay have made significant, wholesome contributions to the growth and development of young boys in scouting..."[67] Yet parents, church groups and community leaders who insist they do not discriminate against or hate homosexuals as individuals have all said they cannot comfortably endorse homosexual leadership in the Scouts.

Faulkner does not care about the comfort of the people who have loved and supported the standards of the Boy Scouts for generations. "Youth who are questioning their sexual identity will be shamed into feeling inferior to their peers," he warns. Many people have indeed been turned from wrong behavior by the positive example of their peers, whether it seems like "shaming" at the time or not. Shaping good character and preventing bad is exactly what the Boy Scouts were formed to do. But Faulkner claims future potential homosexuals will be forced "into a critically wounded sense of self-worth."[67]

Such a "discriminatory" purpose must be combated, however, if the homosexual movement is to survive. "The youth of today is ever the people of tomorrow," said Adolph Hitler, ever mindful of the need for unity. "For this reason we have set before ourselves the task of inoculating our youth with the spirit of this community,"[68] Considering the difficulties of perpetuating their "species," homosexuals can't lose potential converts to people who insist boys have to be "morally straight." Gays could have started their own organizations and governed members and leaders according to their own set of bylaws. (There is an all-gay group within the Canadian Boy Scout organization.) That would have resulted in freedom and equality.

But homosexuals didn't want what the Boy Scouts offered when they sought to "come out" within or volunteer for leadership in the existing Boy Scouts. They didn't even want their own segregated group. They understood the need Adolph Hitler expressed, echoing Plato, to shape "people at a very early age, ... still unperverted and therefore unspoiled," as Hitler went on to say. "This Reich stands, and it is building itself up for the future, upon its youth. And this new Reich will give its youth to no one." Instead, they wanted to try to change the Boy Scouts. And they still claim they "will... take youth and give to youth [their] own education and [their] own upbringing."[68] They wanted the Boy Scouts to become a different organization, to no longer exist as "morally straight."

"Every child in America entering school at the age of five is mentally ill because he comes to school with certain allegiances ..." psychiatrist Chester M. Pierce warned future teachers, "toward his parents, toward a belief in a supernatural being, ... It's up to you as teachers to make all these sick children well--by creating the international child of the future."[69] Behold in these activists the child of the future realized.

Homosexuals took more direct action against Mount Hope Church in Lansing, Michigan, which had spoken out publicly against their behavior as sin. An organization calling itself "Bash Back," which posed for a website photo in pink headscarves, brandishing club like sticks, mimicking terrorists, invaded a service at the church in 2008. Here is the organization's own report on the incident. (Note that the use of the term "queer" is the spokesperson's choice, not the authors'. This is an "official report" from the group claiming responsibility.)

"The Mount Hope Church is a deplorable, anti-queer mega-church. ... *Bash Back*! ain't down with that. And so on Sunday November 9th, about thirty radical queers from Lansing, Chicago, Memphis and Milwaukee disrupted the church's most well-attended sermon.

> *[We] began demonstrating outside the church. The group was extremely loud and wildly offensive. Another group threw over a thousand fliers to the entirety of the congregation. The fire alarm was pulled. Queers began making out in front of the pastor. And within a matter of minutes, everyone had evaded the guards and made*

> *their escapes. Let it be known: So long as bigots kill us in the streets, this pack of wolves will continue to BASH BACK!*[70]

These people came in as visitors to the service and distributed themselves throughout the auditorium. In addition to what they describe above, the group threw condoms into the air, hung a poster proclaiming that "Jesus Was Gay" from the balcony, and pushed through crowds of worshippers, trying to provoke a violent reaction. (No church member "bashed back.")[70] Because certain people commit acts of violence against homosexuals, homosexuals proclaim that everyone who calls homosexuality a sin is out to kill them. Or so they say, since, truthfully, it's doubtful they would have risked their safety or their lives by going into a church full of people they believed hated them and wanted to kill them. Nothing, absolutely nothing, proves that their blanket attacks against Bible-believers are based on false claims like this incident.

Secularists also heavily back "reproductive freedom" as a "right." Margaret Sanger promised that "a mutual and satisfied sexual act is of great benefit to the average woman, the magnetism of it is health giving."[71] Mostly she means the freedom *not* to reproduce, though vigorous sexual activity is absolutely encouraged. "*The Satanic Verses* (A novel condemned by Islamist extremists which earned death threats for its author and publishers) celebrates hybridity, impurity, intermingling, the transformation that comes of new and unexpected combinations of human beings, cultures, ideas, politics, movies, songs."[72] Salman Rushdie, Indian writer of historical fantasies on east-west relations, may not have been advocating free sex but his ideals involve breaking down traditional barriers to secularist freedoms and, indiscriminately applied, will result in moral breakdown.

"There is a great deal of political pressure to only talk about abstinence, and to deny support for condoms and education on using them." Former first lady, U.S. senator and Secretary of State Hillary Clinton informs us that abortion and contraception are essential to this "freedom" because they are supposed to keep people from dying from this exercise of their "rights." "This [abstinence] policy will lead to the unnecessary deaths of many people."[73] Clinton can call us practical murderers simply because we believe that there are negative consequences, in spite of Margaret Sanger assuring us there are none, to having"... unlimited sexual gratification without the burden of unwanted children ... to live ... to love ..." When Sanger declared that "the marriage bed is the most degenerative influence in the social order ..."[57] secularists no doubt cheered.

The delusion of contraception as health care is deeply entrenched. "War, famine, poverty and oppression of the workers will continue while woman makes life cheap." Sanger claimed that mere control of baby making could end all manner of societal ills. "They will cease only when she limits her reproductivity and human life is no longer a thing to be wasted."[57] "Protection" is a myth, because people don't need to be protected from babies and they can't be protected from STDs unless they practice true "safe sex" and abstain from casual "hook-ups," multiple partner sex and other extreme risk situations. The failure rate of condoms is roughly the same as playing Russian roulette with a 7-chambered revolver.

Yet these are not the people Sanger describes as "irresponsible and reckless ones having little regard for the consequences of their acts, or whose religious scruples prevent their exercising control over their numbers." Here she manages to expand the definition of protection to include "protecting" society from both the poor and the religious, relegating them to the category of defectives. "Many of this group are diseased, feeble-minded, and are of the pauper element dependent upon the normal and fit members of society for their support."[57]

Sanger despises charity, as does the French novelist and feminist Amantine Aurore Lucile Dupin, better known as George Sand, who ridicules "...those who threw themselves into the flood to save some debris of humanity. The debris is not worth the effort..."[74] Charity is the weak draining the resources of the strong, bad policy according to social Darwinism. "There is no doubt in the minds of all thinking people that the procreation of this group should be stopped."[57] Sanger asserts. Social engineering appeals so strongly to secularists they can even forgive those in their past like W.E.B. Du Bois, founder of the NAACP and close associate of Margaret Sanger. "The mass of ignorant Negroes still breed carelessly and disastrously." Du Bois engaged in blatant racism for the good of society. "The increase among Negroes, even more than the increase among whites, is from that portion of the population least intelligent and fit, and least able to rear their children properly."[75]

Sanger considered social and physical eugenics critical to societal progress. She attributed the fact that humanity wasn't perfect yet to "our foolhardy and extravagant sentimentalism..." Again she attacks charity for holding up the progress of Darwinism. "[Philanthropists] encourage the healthier and more normal sections of the world to shoulder the burden of unthinking and indiscriminate fecundity of others." Imagine the strong caring for the weak instead of being socially responsible enough to see them snuffed out, since they are "a deadweight of human waste. ... We are paying for, and even submitting to, the dictates of an ever-increasing, unceasingly spawning class of human beings who never should have been born at all."[71] What a positive message of inclusiveness. Sanger is almost as adept as the man who inspired all this social Darwinian sentiment in the first place, Reverend Thomas Robert Malthus.

> *"All children born, beyond what would be required to keep up the population to a desired level, must necessarily perish, unless room is made for them by the deaths of grown persons. We should facilitate, instead of foolishly and vainly endeavoring to impede, the operations of nature in producing this mortality."*[76]

Don't forget that secularists want us all to come together and agree, as long as we agree with them. "Technology tools help us to gather and disseminate information, but we also need qualities like tolerance and compassion to achieve greater understanding between peoples and nations." Arthur C. Clarke, British science fiction author urged. "... So I hope we've learnt something from the most barbaric century in history — the 20th." Clarke probably judged the twentieth century this way because of the world wars, since peace at any price is a secularist dogma. "I would like to see us overcome our tribal divisions and begin to think and act as if we were one family. That would be real globalisation..."[77]

Carl Sagan assured us that "National boundaries are not evident when we view the Earth from space." Sagan's pet device is to imagine all of us coming together for the grand uniting cause of flinging ourselves out among the stars. "Fanatical ethnic or religious or national identifications are a little difficult to support when we see our Earth as a fragile blue crescent fading to become an inconspicuous point of light against the bastion and the citadel of the stars."[1] At the very least he hopes to find that space aliens have been observing our world and failing to understand, because they are so advanced, what it is that still divides us.

Roger Nash Baldwin was the first president of the ACLU. Its agenda hasn't changed much. "I have continued directing the unpopular fight for the rights of agitation..." Baldwin was a little radical even for his time, stating the obvious goals which secularists today are trying harder to obscure but are just as determined to achieve. "I am for socialism, disarmament and ultimately for abolishing the state itself as an instrument of violence and compulsion." Things have changed a little, actually, since secularists realize they need the government to help them get their beliefs made into policy. "I seek the social ownership of property, the abolition of the propertied class and sole control by those who produce wealth."[78]

John Lennon, British singer, songwriter and social activist, claimed the message of one of his most famous songs, *Imagine,* was obscured and "sugar-coated" to conceal its real purpose. "Imagine no possessions/I wonder if you can/No need for greed or hunger/A brotherhood of man..." Seems pretty clear, actually. Another verse states that we must also imagine there's "no religion" or heaven or hell and says "it's easy if you try."[79] (Note: after Lennon's death Yoko Ono sued to keep people from using this song if she disagreed with them, in spite of its apparently "inclusive" message.) Lawsuits are an indispensable part of the secularist dogma, of course.

Secularists need their established religion to elevate its own writings to sacred and infallible status in place of those outdated Scriptures. "Human beings must have an epic, a sublime account of how the world was created and how humanity became part of it ..." Edward Osborne Wilson declared. They understand that certain components must be a part of the mix of the new holy writ. "The way to achieve our epic that unites human spirituality, instead of cleav[ing] it, is to compose it from the best empirical knowledge that science and history can provide." Note that former religious epics have divided men in their beliefs. "The true evolutionary epic retold as poetry, is as intrinsically ennobling as any religious epic."[80] This one won't be divisive because secularists have already been established as the only ones who can present true science and history instead of mysteries and myths.

What is the central tenet of the established religion, the foremost article of secularist faith? “Evolution is a fact, and [my] book will demonstrate it. No reputable scientist disputes it, and no unbiased reader will close the book doubting it,”[81] Richard Dawkins promised in *The Greatest Show on Earth.* Dawkins is simply the latest high priest. More than one hundred years ago, Ernst Haeckel, originator of the fascinating illustrations of how every embryo carries the imprint of how its form evolved (a theory now discredited because those drawings were completely falsified), still had one premise secularists embrace. “In consequence of Darwin’s reformed Theory of Descent, we are now in a position to establish scientifically the groundwork of a non-miraculous history of the development of the human race...”[82]

Even if it’s not that easy to show how evolution took place, it’s essential to use it to discredit theism. “Those afraid of the universe as it really is,” Carl Sagan sneers, “those who pretend to nonexistent knowledge,” that is, the theists who can’t already have true knowledge in the form of scriptural revelation, “and envision a Cosmos centered on human beings will prefer the fleeting comforts of superstition.” The accusation of fear is that all-purpose dismissal used by every kind of secularist who despises theists. They won’t believe we already have certain knowledge and don’t need to look for ways to make up a tale of beginnings. “They avoid rather than confront the world. But those with the courage to explore the weave and structure of the Cosmos, even where it differs profoundly from their wishes and prejudices, will penetrate its deepest mysteries.”[1] Knowledge comes to the evolutionist alone, because he rejects the Scriptures and jumps off into a search for “real truth.”

“When it comes to the Origin of Life there are only two possibilities: creation or spontaneous generation,” stated evolutionist George Wald, Harvard University biochemist and Nobel Laureate. "There is no third way. Spontaneous generation was disproved one hundred years ago, but that leads us to only one other conclusion, that of supernatural creation." So, an evolutionist admitted in an article written in 1954 in Scientific American that evolution can't be true, and that creationism is the only way left to consider. Unfortunately, Wald goes on to make the religiously dogmatic statement, "We cannot accept that on philosophical grounds; therefore, we choose to believe the impossible: that life arose spontaneously by chance!"[83]

So, onward to proving what was disproved a hundred years before 1954. Richard Dawkins tells us he already did prove evolution, in that book he wrote. Or those many books he wrote, all adopting the same insulting, sarcastic tone, that creationists are stupid and evolutionists are smart, nyaah, nyaah, nyaah, so evolution must be true. He never wavers from the pattern of insults, assumptions of facts not in evidence, and "irrelevant, incompetent, and immaterial" arguments, to quote Perry Mason author Earle Stanley Gardner.

Dr. Antony Flew, former atheist, embraced deism and came out in support of intelligent design in his eighties. His work, *There is a God: How the World's Most Notorious Atheist Changed his Mind,* written with the assistance of Christian author Roy Varghese. Dawkins claimed that Flew was used by Varghese and didn't know what his own book contained. That and Flew's review of Richard Dawkins' *The God Delusion* gave Dawkins an opportunity to express himself in his most tolerant and inclusive manner.

> *"Antony Flew, having lost the ability to write a book, was persuaded by a Christian ghost writer, Roy Varghese, to let him write it*

> *instead. It is one thing for a footballer or a supermodel to use a ghost writer, but there is something absurd about a philosopher using a ghost writer. Flew has now apparently lost the ability to read a book, too, for his 'review' of The God Delusion turns out to be a review of its index and nothing but its index. He only needed to read Chapter 1, in order to see the absurdity of his claims about my treatment of Einstein."*[84]

That's the secularist spirit of brotherhood at its finest. The flap that Flew brought up about The God Delusion concerns whether or not Einstein was an atheist. Simple answer: no one knows. Einstein wrote and spoke prolifically over a lifetime and he made some highly confusing and contradictory statements. On one occasion Einstein wrote, "I'm not an atheist and I don't think I can call myself a pantheist."[78] Many other Einstein quotes sound like Einstein was an atheist, however. Difficulty in pinning down exactly what a prolific writer believes is not all that unusual. John Calvin believed in and taught about God and the Scriptures at least from the time he was fifteen, when he began his lifelong work on the *Institutes of the Christian Religion*. Still, he managed to write down some rather confusing and contradictory interpretations over so many years writing so many works. Yet Dawkins believes that he has locked down that Einstein was an atheist and no one should doubt it. To prove it, he browbeats an eighty-four year-old man about how he's too feeble to be listened to anymore. That's solid evidence, all right.

However, Anthony Flew isn't the man to be browbeaten. "The idea that someone manipulated me because I'm old is exactly wrong. I may be old but it is hard to manipulate me. That is my book and it represents my thinking."[84] His review of Dawkin's book is as incisive as anyone could wish in spite of the fact that it comes from what Dawkins probably wished he could dismiss as a doddering old fool. Check out a sample of the "old fool's" ability to see through dogma substituting for evidence.

> *"The whole enterprise of The God Delusion was not, as it at least pretended to be, an attempt to discover and spread knowledge of the existence or non-existence of God but rather an attempt - an extremely successful one - to spread the author's own convictions in this area.*
>
> *"But an academic attacking some ideological position which s/he believes to be mistaken must of course attack that position in its strongest form. This Dawkins does not do in the case of Einstein and his failure is the crucial index of his insincerity of academic purpose and therefore warrants me in charging him with having become, what he has probably believed to be an impossibility, a secularist bigot."*[84]

Evolution is woven into the fabric of today's writings across disciplines. No one who wishes to be published can neglect it. "How man evolved with such an incredible reservoir of talent and such fantastic diversity isn't completely understood... he knows so little and has nothing to measure himself against,"[85] exclaimed Edward T. Hall, Anthropologist. "No single discovery from any of these fields denotes proof of evolution, but together they reveal that life evolved in a certain sequence by a particular process,"[86] Michael Shermer, science writer, confidently affirms in his works debunking the supernatural. "We observe closely related species in sympatry [living near each other but not interbreeding] and infer how they evolved from a common ancestor,"[87] explains Peter R. Grant, evolutionary biologist working with Darwin's finches. Darwin arrived at his ports of call, made observations, and wrote down what he thought it all meant, inferring, not scientifically testing or proving. In the same way these folks carry on, generation after generation of inferences substituting for facts.

Charles Darwin wasn't the founder of evolutionary theory, of course. Even ignoring the atomists and naturalists of ancient times, we still find that even Darwin's grandfather had his piece to say on the subject, and many others wrote of natural origins in the century before Darwin and around the same time. But it's interesting to note that Darwin had far more training in theology than he did in natural science when he joined the crew of the Beagle. Either that made him a bad father to give birth to a naturalistic theory of origins, or it made him the perfect man to bring together and commit to writing the new holy writ. Sometimes, however, the theologian got the better of the "truth-seeker" and resulted in some interesting footnotes to the sacred texts of Origin of Species and Descent of Man.

"I am quite conscious that my speculations run quite beyond the bounds of true science."[88]

"By nature, I mean the laws ordained by God to govern the Universe."[89]

> *"I had no intention to write atheistically....I can see no reason, why a man, or other animal, may not have been aboriginally produced by other laws; & that all these laws may have been expressly designed by an omniscient Creator, who foresaw every future event & consequence. But the more I think the more bewildered I become."*[90]

Darwin wasn't so sure God didn't fit in somewhere. The heresy of theistic evolution resulted from some of this uncertainty on the part of Darwin and others who weren't ready for the radical abandonment of God later secularists insist on. Darwin's writings have been pretty much supplanted by the hardliners like Dawkins who know God is a bit of madness absurd folk cling to.

Dawkins and others spend less time seeking evidence for evolution than they do fighting creationism.

If creationism is preposterous and laughable, why write book after book after book to refute it, Richard? If there is no God, why bother to tell people he's a delusion? Won't an error that's ignored die on its own? Why keep bringing it up? Is there something nagging at the back of your mind that won't be quiet, something that nagged Darwin, has nagged others for centuries, and still nags them today?

François-Marie Arouet, better known as Voltaire, was an undisputed rationalist. So why does he say something positively disloyal to the cause of secularism like this? "We are intelligent beings: intelligent beings cannot have been formed by a crude, blind, insensible being: there is certainly some difference between the ideas of Newton and the dung of a mule. Newton's intelligence, therefore, came from another intelligence."[91]

A few of secularism's most well-known adherents will still not go as far as their established religion demands. Just to cite one example, do they know what one of their most popular scientists and authors, Stephen Hawking, has said about this same cherished fundamental that there can be no creator, not even a waffling on the possibility of "divine inspiration"?"The whole history of science has been the gradual realization that events do not happen in an arbitrary manner, but that they reflect a certain underlying order, which may or may not be divinely inspired."[92]

Secularists can afford a few uncertain voices in their past as long as they can find strong enough voices to drown them out. After all, an established religion needs a priesthood, perhaps even a high priest. The message is simple: there is no god but man, no temple but the billions of years of time and the infinite cosmos, no rites and rituals but sexual license and the extermination of the undesirable, no holy scriptures but the infallible word of "a scientific study says."

Richard Dawkins seems like a good candidate for the current high priesthood, but he's a little strident, a little crude at times. Secularists had a high priest capable of gentler mockery, a more eloquent tongue to lay out the enemy's supposed weaknesses,"pseudo-science," "unreason," "prejudices," "fanaticism," and to restate secular strengths. He reassured secularists that they could fight back with the weapons of "self-esteem" and "nerve." Theists lacked courage and resolve because they "agonized about their place in the cosmos," since they couldn't have truth or certainty. Secularists must have mourned the passing of Carl Sagan, the snuffing out of his candle. It is interesting that he chooses to describe reliance on the Scriptures ("habits of thought from ages past") as "darkness," and likens acknowledgment of the reality of God as "The Demon-Haunted World."

> *"I worry that, especially as the Millennium edges nearer, pseudo-science and superstition will seem year by year more tempting, the siren song of unreason more sonorous and attractive. Where have we heard it before? Whenever our ethnic or national prejudices are aroused, in times of scarcity, during challenges to national self-esteem or nerve, when we agonize about our diminished cosmic place and purpose, or when fanaticism is bubbling up around us-then, habits of thought familiar from ages past reach for the controls. The candle flame gutters. Its little pool of light trembles. Darkness gathers. The demons begin to stir."*[93]

---

1 Carl Sagan, *Cosmos*, Random House, New York, NY, 1980.

2 Edward Osborne Wilson, American biologist, researcher and author. Two-time winner of the Pulitzer Prize for General Non-Fiction. Environmental advocate. From *On Human Nature*, Harvard University Press, Cambridge, MA, 1979.

3 Robert Ingersoll, politician and defender of agnosticism, from *Ingersoll the Magnificent*, by Joseph Lewis, dedicated at a memorial address in 1954, printed by American Atheist Press, 1983.

4 Stephen Covey, Latter-Day Saints motivational speaker and writer, in *Principle-Centered Leadership,* Chapter 4, Fireside, Simon and Schuster, Rockefeller Center, New York, NY, 1992.

5 *The Separationist*, Newsletter of the "Secular Humanists of the Lowcountry," advertising a meeting and potluck, May 2002.

6 Manmohan Singh, Sikh prime minister of India, at his first press conference, reported by George Iype in *Rediff, India Abroad,* May 20, 2004.

7 General Dwight David Eisenhower, in a speech when he was installed as president of Columbia University in 1948.

8 Walt Disney, cited on *justDisney.com*, an official Disney quote compilation site.

9 Commentary with quotations citing and explaining the beliefs of evolutionists Julian Huxley and Alfred Russell Wallace in "The conflict between Science and Faith," by Rama Coomaraswamy, M.D., surgeon, Ecclesiastical History Professor, Traditionalist Catholic essayist, from his online archives.

10 Thomas Henry Huxley, letter to Charles Kingsley, 23 September 1860.

11 Henri Poincaré (1854 - 1912) in "Science et méthode" ("Science and Method"), 1908, English translation in *The*

*Foundations of Science: Science and Hypothesis, The Value of Science, Science and Method,* The Science Press, translated by George Bruce Halstead, 1913.

12 Roy Wood Sellars and Raymond Bragg, authors of the original *Humanist Manifesto I* draft, 1933.

13 Algernon David Black, vice president for the NAACP from 1950 to 1966, from an essay, "Are We Religious?" collected in *Understanding Ethical Religion,* Chapter 1, "Why an Ethical Religion," by Howard B. Radest, produced for the American Ethical Union Library, 1975.

14 Terry Sanderson, president of the *National Secular Society of the UK*, from an address on Dec 17, 2009.

15 Emily Dickinson, from "The Bible Is an Antique Volume," poem # 1545, Johnson, Thomas H., ed. *Complete Poems*. Boston: Little, Brown, 1960.

16 James Baldwin, from The Fire Next Time, Copyright 1962, 1963 by James Baldwin originally published by the Dial Press, 1963.

17 Frederick Douglass, from an address entitled "What, to the Slave, is the Fourth of July?" given to a women's anti-slavery society in Rochester, New York, 1852.

18 George Bernard Shaw, from the play "Androcles and the Lion," 1913.

19 *State v. Scopes, Scopes v. State, 152 Tenn. 424, 278 S.W. 57* (Tenn. 1926), *Scopes vs. The State of Tennessee.*

20 Robert A Heinlein, *The Notebooks of Lazarus Long,* 1978, Pomegranate Publications, Inc., 1999.

21 Lizette Reese 1856-1935, from the poem "Truth," *American Women Poets of the Nineteenth Century, an Anthology,* edited by Cheryl Walker, 1992 Rutgers University, New Jersey.

22 Sigmund Freud, *The Future of an Illusion,* German version 1927, translated by W.D Robson-Scott, English

translation published by Horace Liveright and the Institute of Psychoanalysis, 1928.

23 John Godfrey Saxe, (1816 - 1887), from his poem, "The Blind Men and the Elephant," *The Poems of John Godfrey Saxe* (Highgate Edition), Boston. MA, Houghton, Mifflin and Company, 1881.

24 Annie Dillard, from *Pilgrim at Tinker Creek,* Harper's Magazine Press, New York, NY, 1974.

25 Peter Hoagland, American lawyer and congressman (US House of Representatives, Democrat, Nebraska), in a radio speech with Pastor Everett Silevan, 1983, documented in *Bill Clinton: Friend or Foe?* by Ann Wilson, J. W. Publishing Company, 1993, page 170.

26 Friedrich Nietzsche, Philosopher known for existentialism, anti-Christian writings and for associations with Nazism, from *Human, All-Too-Human, A Book for Free Spirits,* German version 1878. Translated by Marion Faber and Stephen Lehmann. English version published by Lincoln: University of Nebraska Press, 1984.

27 John Stuart Mill, philosopher, utilitarianist, from his *Autobiography,* 1873.

28 Karl Marx, from a *Contribution to the Critique of Hegel's Philosophy of Right,* 1843-44, Translated by Joseph O'Malley, English edition published by Oxford University Press, 1970.

29 Steve Allen, American television personality, musician, actor, commedian, prolific author, quoted in *2000 Years of Disbelief: Famous People with the Courage to Doubt*, by James A. Haught, Prometheus Books, Amherst, NY, 1998.

30 Johannes Cardinal Willebrands, in a speech responding to the Boy Scouts of America official position on the admission of homosexual members and leaders, 2000.

31 Peter Montgomery of *AlterNet.org*. (Feb. 10, 2010).

32 Committee on the Judiciary House of Representatives, Prohibiting Detention Camps, March 18, 1971, Pg. 93.

33 *gulaghistory.org*

34 *cbc.ca digital archives*, "Boat People, a Refugee Crisis."

35 *STATISTICS OF DEMOCIDE* "Chapter 4 Statistics of Cambodian Democide Estimates, Calculations, And Sources," By R.J. Rummel from *Hawaii.edu*.

36 Adapted from "civilian detention camps," from the website *D.program.net* posted October 1, 2008, from an article by Carl Jensen, Source: *http://web.archive.org/web/20050831053419/www.pbnnews*.

37 *disastercenter.com* contains the full text of the executive order.

38 "Forced Vaccines: Ready For Yours?" Janet Porter, *Faith2action*, posted: August 18, 2009 1:00 am Eastern © 2010 *World Net Daily. wnd.com.*

39 Aaron Cline, *About.com,* Agnosticism/atheism columnist for 10 years.

40 Walter Savage Landor, "Melanchthon and Calvin," *Imaginary Conversations* (1824-29).

41 Ambrose Bierce, author, from *The Enlarged Devil's Dictionary,* 1906.

42 Nancy Pelosi, Speaker of the House, concerning Republicans, quoted in *National Review Online* by John Tamny, "Where Are the Supply-Side Democrats?" November 18, 2005.

43 Bertrand Russell, Mathematician, logician, nuclear disarmament proponent, from a lecture, "Why I am Not

a Christian," delivered to the *National Secular Society*, March 6, 1927.

44 Ayn Rand, author, originator of objectivism, from *Atlas Shrugged,* 1957 first Signet printing, New American Library, Penguin, 1996.

45 A. J. Ayer, *The Humanist Outlook,* Rationalist Press Association, Ltd, 1968.

46 Peter Ustinov, British actor, diplomat, Goodwill Ambassador for UNICEF, prolific author, columnist, president of the *World Federalist Movement,* in an interview with Mike Wallace, March 29, 1958.

47 Nancy Pelosi, Minority Leader, later Speaker of the House, commenting on the 2004 elections.

48 Simon Blackburn, member of the Humanist Philosophers' Group, Independent on Sunday, from the *National Secular Society Newsline,* 12 May 2002.

49 Steve Weinberg, physicist, author, strong supporter of Israeli Nationalism, from "A Designer Universe?" A version of the original quote from address at the *Conference on Cosmic Design, American Association for the Advancement of Science,* Washington, D.C. in April 1999.

50 Percy Bysshe Shelley, poet, from the pamphlet, *The Necessity of Atheism* (1811), to serve as a note to the line in Queen Mab, "There is no God", 1813.

51 Joseph Hill "Joss" Whedon, Television and movie writer and producer, creator of SciFi/Fantasy series including *Buffy the Vampire Slayer* and *Serenity,* from the commentary on *Buffy the Vampire Slayer* DVD series, episode 5.16 ( "The Body") (Season 5, released December 9, 2003), and an interview by Tasha Robinson for *The Onion,* (an online satirical magazine) September 5, 2001.

52 Mikhail Bakunin Russian revolutionary and theorist of collectivist anarchism, *God and the State* February-March, written 1871, First published 1882 (Discovered posthumously by Carlo Cafiero and Elisée Reclus), Translated by Benjamin R. Tucker, Published by Mother Earth Publishing Association, New York, 1916.

53 David Nicholls, Atheist Foundation of Australia, in an undated article on the Foundation's website.

54 Rod Serling, producer and writer of the *Twilight Zone* and *Night Gallery* TV series, in his last interview before his death in 1975.

55 Isaac Asimov, Biochemist, Author in many fields including Science Fiction and Religion, quoted in *Philosophy on the Go* (2007) by Joey Green and Alan Corcoran, Running Press, Philadelphia, PA, 2007, p. 222.

56 Carl Sagan, popular science teacher and TV host, published in Dr. Lester Grinspoon's *Marihuana Reconsidered,* Harvard University Press, Cambridge, MA, 1971.

57 Margaret Sanger, founder of Planned Parenthood, in *The Woman Rebel,* Volume I, Number 1. Reprinted in *Woman and the New Race.* New York: Brentanos Publishers, 1922.

58 Tenzin Gyatzo, 14th Dalai Lama, leader of Tibetan Buddhism, from the *Dalai Lama website*, "Compassion and the Individual: thc Purpose of Life."

59 Aldous Huxley, author of social commentary novels such as *Brave New World.* "Confessions of a Professed Atheist," *Report: Perspective on the News*, Vol. 3, June 1966, p. 19.

60 Hillary Clinton, First Lady, US Senator, Secretary of State, in a speech in San Francisco, CA, June 28th, 2004.

61 Bill Maxwell,"Intolerance as policy," *St. Petersburg Times,* August 9, 1998.

62 Coretta Scott King, wife of Martin Luther King, civil rights leader, in a speech at the Palmer House Hilton in Chicago, April 1, 1998.

63 Mary Wollstonecraft Shelley, author of *Frankenstein,* feminist, in *A Vindication of the Rights of Woman With Strictures on Political and Moral Subjects,* 1792.

64 Gloria Steinem, author, publisher, feminist, from an "Address to the Women of America," at the founding of the National Women's Political Caucus in 1971.

65 Arthur C. Clarke, British science fiction author, inventor and television host, in "Credo" (1991); also in *Greetings, Carbon-Based Bipeds! : Collected Essays,* 1934-1998 (1999), p. 360.

66 Sidney Simon, Lecturer and Educator, *Values Clarification,* originally published 1972, Warner Books revised edition by Grand Central Publishing September 1, 1995.

67 Allen H. Johnson, "James Dale, the Supreme Court and fond memories of Troop 148," *News and Record I,* 7-30-00. *Gay Straight Advocates for Education Website (gsafe.org).*

68 Adolph Hitler, German Nazi party leader, in a speech given May 1, 1937.

69 Chester M. Pierce, Psychiatrist and Harvard University Professor, in his address to teachers at the 1973 Childhood International Education Seminar.

70 Adapted from a posting by contributor Nick De Leeuw, Monday, Nov. 10, 2008 on the *Right Michigan.com* website, from an email he received from a friend who attends Mount Hope Church in Lansing, Michigan and who witnessed the actions of *Bash Back,* and from the public statement released by the group.

71 Margaret Sanger, social activist, founder of Planned Parenthood , in *The Pivot of Civilization,* 1932.

72 Salman Rushdie, Indian writer of historical fantasies on east-west relations, signer of a declaration against religious totalitarianism and in favor of secularism (directed at radical Islam), in a 1996 speech.

73 Hillary Clinton, First Lady, US Senator, presidential candidate, Secretary of State, in a speech given Wednesday, Sept. 28, 2005, at the *Global Business Coalition on HIV/AIDS Annual Awards for Business Excellence Gala* at the Kennedy Center in Washington, D.C.

74 Amantine Aurore Lucile Dupin (George Sand), 1804-1876 Letter to Gustave Flaubert, 14 September, 1871, translated by A.L. MacKenzie, 1921.

75 W.E.B. DuBois, founder of the NAACP, in a 1932 essay on birth control in Margaret Sanger's *Birth Control Review.*

76 Reverend Thomas Robert Malthus, 18th/19th century clergyman, professor, and proponent of population control, in a 1798 tract called *An Essay on the Principle of Population.*

77 Arthur C. Clarke, British science fiction author, inventor and television host, in his *90th Birthday Reflections,* 2007.

78 Roger Nash Baldwin, President of ACLU and its predecessor, American Union Against Militarism. From the *Harvard Class Book of 1935,* entitled "Thirty Years Later", spotlighting Baldwin's class of 1905 on its thirtieth anniversary, as quoted in a *1997 Insight on the News* article.

79 John Lennon, British singer, songwriter, social activist, in the title song from the *Imagine* album released 1971. In the book *Lennon in America* (2000), by Geoffrey Giuliano, Lennon is quoted as saying that

*Imagine* was an "anti-religious, anti-nationalistic, anti-conventional, anti-capitalistic [song], but because it's sugar-coated, it's accepted."

80 Edward Osborne Wilson, American biologist, researcher and author. Two-time winner of the Pulitzer Prize for General Non-Fiction. Environmental advocate. From *On Human Nature*, Harvard University Press, Cambridge, MA, 1979.

81 Richard Dawkins, from *The Greatest Show on Earth, The Evidence for Evolution,* Ch. 1, Free Press, Simon and Schuster, New York, NY, 2009.

82 Ernst Haeckel, artist, originator of the discredited theory that the evolution of an organism can be seen in its development from an embryo, from *The History of Creation* (1876), Vol. 1, 6-9. Translated by Joseph McCabe, Watts & Company, London, 1912.

83 George Wald, Evolutionist, Harvard University biochemist and Nobel Laureate, from an article, "The Origin of Life," *Scientific American,* 191:48, May 1954.

84 Martin Beckford, Antony Flew, Richard Dawkins, excerpted from an article published: at *www.telegraph.co.uk/ science/science-news,* 9:30PM BST 02 Aug 2008, by Martin Beckford, Religious Affairs Correspondent. "Flew Speaks Out: Professor Antony Flew reviews The God Delusion." (Flew's review is copyrighted as follows) Antony Flew, 2008, *bethinking.org.*

85 Edward T. Hall, Anthropologist, cross-cultural researcher, author of *Beyond Culture,* Anchor Books, Random House, New York, NY, 1976.

86 Michael Shermer, "The Fossil Fallacy: Creationists' demand for fossils that represent 'missing links' reveals a deep misunderstanding of science," *Scientific American,* 21 February 2005.

87 Peter R. Grant and B. Rosemary Grant, evolutionary biologists, working with Darwin's finches, in *The National Academy of Sciences of the USA Colloquium Paper,* "Genetics and the origin of bird species," 1997.

88 Charles Darwin, in a letter to Asa Gray, Harvard Professor of Biology.

89 Darwin to Asa Gray, 22 May 1860, in *The Correspondence of Charles Darwin.* Vol. 8 (Cambridge University Press), 224

90 Charles *Darwin's Natural Selection, Being the Second Part of his Big Species Book* Written from 1856 to 1858, ed. R.C. Stauffer (Cambridge 1975), 224.

91 Voltaire (François-Marie Arouet), *Atheism I,* Section I,"Of Modern Atheists, Reasons of the Worshipers of God," c 1764, Selected and Translated by H.I. Woolf, Knopf, New York, NY, 1924.

92 Stephen Hawking, *The Illustrated A Brief History of Time.* New York, NY: Bantam Dell, a division of Random House, 1996.

93 Carl Sagan, popular Science teacher and TV Host, in *The Demon-Haunted World: Science as a Candle in the Dark,* Ballantine Book, Random House, 1996.

# Appendixes

## Appendix One: Court Cases

*Church of the Holy Trinity v. United States 1892* U.S. Supreme Court Church of the Holy Trinity v. United States, 143 U.S. 457 (1892) No. 143

Argued and submitted January 7, 1892 Decided February 29, 1892 143 U.S. 457

ERROR TO THE CIRCUIT COURT OF THE UNITED

STATES FOR THE SOUTHERN DISTRICT OF NEW YORK

Syllabus

The Act of February 26, 1880, "to prohibit the importation and migration of foreigners and aliens under contract or agreement to perform labor in the United States, its Territories, and the District of Columbia," 23 Stat. 332, c. 164, does not apply to a contract between an alien, residing out of the United States, and a religious society incorporated under the laws of a state, whereby he engages to remove to the United States and to enter into the service of the society as its rector or minister.

THE case is stated in the opinion.

MR. JUSTICE BREWER delivered the opinion of the Court.

Plaintiff in error is a corporation duly organized and incorporated as a religious society under the laws of the State of New York. E. Walpole Warren was, prior to September, 1887, an alien residing in England. In that month the plaintiff in error made a contract with him by which he was to remove to the City of New York and enter into its service as rector and pastor, and in pursuance of such contract, Warren did so remove and enter upon such service. It is claimed by the United States that this contract on the part of the plaintiff in error was forbidden by 23 Stat. 332, c. 164, and an action was commenced to recover the penalty prescribed by that act. The circuit court held that the contract was within the prohibition of the statute, and rendered judgment accordingly, 36 F.3d 3, and the single question presented for our determination is whether it erred in that conclusion.

The first section describes the act forbidden, and is in these words:

"Be it enacted by the Senate and House of Representatives of the United States of America in Congress assembled, that from and after the passage of this act it shall be unlawful for any person, company, partnership, or corporation, in any manner whatsoever, to prepay the transportation, or in any way assist or encourage the importation or migration, of any alien or aliens, any foreigner or foreigners, into the United States, its territories, or the District of Columbia under contract or agreement, parol or special, express or implied, made previous to the importation or migration of such alien or aliens, foreigner or foreigners, to perform labor or service of any kind in the United States, its territories, or the District of Columbia."

We find, therefore, that the title of the act, the evil which was intended to be remedied, the circumstances surrounding the appeal to Congress, the reports of the committee of each house, all concur in affirming that the intent of Congress was simply to stay the influx of this cheap unskilled labor.

But, beyond all these matters, no purpose of action against religion can be imputed to any legislation, state or national, because this is a religious people. This is historically true. From the discovery of this continent to the present hour, there is a single voice making this affirmation.

The commission to Christopher Columbus, prior to his sail westward, is from "Ferdinand and Isabella, by the grace of God, King and Queen of Castile," etc., and recites that "it is hoped that by God's assistance some of the continents and islands in the ocean will be discovered," etc. The first colonial grant, that made to Sir Walter Raleigh in 1584, was from "Elizabeth, by the grace of God, of England, Fraunce and Ireland, Queene, defender of the faith," etc., and the grant authorizing him to enact statutes of the government of the proposed colony provided that "they be not against the true Christian faith nowe professed in the Church of England." The first charter of Virginia, granted by King James I in 1606, after reciting the application of certain parties for a charter, commenced the grant in these words:

"We, greatly commending, and graciously accepting of, their Desires for the Furtherance of so noble a Work, which may, by the Providence of Almighty God, hereafter tend to the Glory of his Divine Majesty, in propagating of Christian Religion to such People, as yet live in Darkness and miserable Ignorance of the true Knowledge and Worship of God, and may in time bring the Infidels and Savages, living in those parts, to human Civility, and to a settled and quiet government; DO, by these our Letters-Patents, graciously accept of, and agree to, their humble and well intended Desires."

Language of similar import may be found in the subsequent charters of that colony, from the same king, in 1609 and 1611, and the same is true of the various charters granted to the other colonies. In language more or less emphatic is the establishment of the Christian religion declared to be one of the purposes of the grant.

The celebrated compact made by the pilgrims in the *Mayflower*, 1620, recites:

"Having undertaken for the Glory of God, and Advancement of the Christian Faith, and the Honour of our King and Country, a Voyage to plant the first Colony in the northern Parts of Virginia; Do by these Presents, solemnly and mutually, in the Presence of God and one another, covenant and combine ourselves together into a civil Body Politick, for our better Ordering and Preservation, and Furtherance of the Ends aforesaid."

The fundamental orders of Connecticut, under which a provisional government was instituted in 1638-39, commence with this declaration:

"Forasmuch as it hath pleased the Allmighty God by the wise disposition of his diuyne pruidence so to Order and dispose of things that we the Inhabitants and Residents of Windsor, Hartford, and Wethersfield are now cohabiting and dwelling in and vppon the River of Conectecotte and the Lands thereunto adioyneing; And well knowing where a people are gathered togather the word of God requires that to mayntayne the peace and vnion of such a people there should be an orderly and decent Gouerment established according to God, to order and dispose of the affayres of the people at all seasons as occation shall require; doe therefore assotiate and conioyne our selues to be as one Publike state or Comonwelth, and doe, for our selues and our Successors and such as shall be adioyned to vs att any tyme hereafter, enter into Combination and Confederation togather, to mayntayne and presearue the liberty and purity of the gospell of our Lord Jesus weh we now prfesse, as also the disciplyne of the Churches, weh according to the truth of the said gospell is now practiced amongst vs."

In the charter of privileges granted by William Penn to the province of Pennsylvania, in 1701, it is recited:

"Because no People can be truly happy, though under the greatest Enjoyment of Civil Liberties, if abridged of the Freedom of their Consciences, as to their Religious Profession and Worship; And Almighty God being the only Lord of Conscience, Father of Lights and Spirits, and the Author as well as Object of all divine Knowledge, Faith, and Worship, who only doth enlighten the Minds, and persuade and convince the Understandings of People, I do hereby grant and declare," etc.

Coming nearer to the present time, the declaration of independence recognizes the presence of the Divine in human affairs in these words:

"We hold these truths to be self-evident, that all men are created equal, that they are endowed by their Creator with certain unalienable Rights, that among these are Life, Liberty, and the pursuit of Happiness. . . . We therefore the Representatives of the United States of America, in General Congress, Assembled, appealing to the Supreme Judge of the world for the rectitude of our intentions, do, in the Name and by Authority of the good these Colonies, solemnly publish and declare," etc.; "And for the support of this Declaration, with a firm reliance on the Protection of Divine Providence, we mutually pledge to each other our Lives, our Fortunes, and our sacred Honor."

If we examine the constitutions of the various states, we find in them a constant recognition of religious obligations. Every Constitution of every one of the forty-four states contains language which, either directly or by clear implication, recognizes a profound reverence for religion, and an assumption that its influence in all human affairs is essential to the wellbeing of the community. This recognition may be in the preamble, such as is found in the Constitution of Illinois, 1870: "We, the people of the State of Illinois, grateful to Almighty God for the civil, political, and religious liberty which He hath so long permitted us to enjoy, and looking to Him for a blessing upon our endeavors to secure and transmit the same unimpaired to succeeding generations," etc.

It may be only in the familiar requisition that all officers shall take an oath closing with the declaration, "so help me God." It may be in clauses like that of the Constitution of Indiana, 1816, Art. XI, section 4: "The manner of administering an oath or affirmation shall be such as is most consistent with the conscience of the deponent, and shall be esteemed the most solemn appeal to God." Or in provisions such as are found in Articles 36 and 37 of the declaration of rights of the Constitution of Maryland, 1867: "That, as it is the duty of every man to worship God in such manner as he thinks most acceptable to Him, all persons are equally entitled to protection in their religious liberty, wherefore no person ought, by any law, to be molested in his person or estate on account of his religious persuasion or profession, or for his religious practice, unless, under the color of religion, he shall disturb the good order, peace, or safety of the state, or shall infringe the laws of morality, or injure others in their natural, civil, or religious rights; nor ought any person to be compelled to frequent or maintain or contribute, unless on contract, to maintain any place of worship or any ministry; nor shall any person, otherwise competent, be deemed incompetent as a witness or juror on account of his religious belief, provided he believes in the existence of God, and that, under his dispensation, such person will be held morally accountable for his acts, and be rewarded or punished therefore, either in this world or the world to come. That no religious test ought ever to be required as a qualification for any office of profit or trust in this state, other than a declaration of belief in the existence of God; nor shall the legislature prescribe any other oath of office than the oath prescribed by this constitution."

Or like that in Articles 2 and 3 of part 1st of the Constitution of Massachusetts, 1780: "It is the right as well as the duty of all men in society publicly, and at stated seasons, to worship the Supreme Being, the great Creator and Preserver of the universe. . . . As the happiness of a people and the good order and preservation of civil government essentially depend upon piety, religion, and morality, and as these cannot be generally diffused through a community but by the institution of the public worship of God and of public instructions in piety, religion, and morality, therefore, to promote their happiness, and to secure the good order and preservation of their government, the people of this commonwealth have a right to invest their legislature with power to authorize and require, and the legislature shall, from time to time, authorize and require, the several towns, parishes, precincts, and other bodies politic or religious societies to make suitable provision at their own expense, for the institution of the public worship of God and for the support and maintenance of public Protestant teachers of piety, religion, and morality, in all cases where such provision shall not be made voluntarily."

Or, as in sections 5 and 14 of Article 7 of the Constitution of Mississippi, 1832: "No person who denies the being of a God, or a future state of rewards and punishments, shall hold any office in the civil department of this state. . . . Religion morality, and knowledge being necessary to good government, the preservation of liberty, and the happiness of mankind, schools, and the means of education, shall forever be encouraged in this state."

Or by Article 22 of the Constitution of Delaware, (1776), which required all officers, besides an oath of allegiance, to make and subscribe the following declaration: "I, A. B., do profess faith in God the Father, and in Jesus Christ His only Son, and in the Holy Ghost, one God, blessed for evermore, and I do acknowledge the Holy Scriptures of the Old and New Testament to be given by divine inspiration."

Even the Constitution of the United States, which is supposed to have little touch upon the private life of the individual, contains in the First Amendment a declaration common to the constitutions of all the states, as follows: "Congress shall make no law respecting an establishment of religion, or prohibiting the free exercise thereof," etc., and also provides in Article I, Section 7, a provision common to many constitutions, that the executive shall have ten days (Sundays excepted) within which to determine whether he will approve or veto a bill.

There is no dissonance in these declarations. There is a universal language pervading them all, having one meaning. They affirm and reaffirm that this is a religious nation. These are not individual sayings, declarations of private persons. They are organic utterances. They speak the voice of the entire people. While, because of a general recognition of this truth, the question has seldom been presented to the courts, yet we find that in Updegraph v. Commonwealth, 11 S. & R. 394, 400, it was decided that "Christianity, general Christianity, is, and always has been, a part of the common law of Pennsylvania; . . . not Christianity with an established church and tithes and spiritual courts, but Christianity with liberty of conscience to all men."

And in People v. Ruggles, 8 Johns. 290, 294-295, Chancellor Kent, the great commentator on American law, speaking as Chief Justice of the Supreme Court of New York, said: "The people of this state, in common with the people of this country, profess the general doctrines of Christianity as the rule of their faith and practice, and to scandalize the author of these doctrines is not only, in a religious point of view, extremely impious, but, even in respect to the obligations due to society, is a gross violation of decency and good order. . . . The free, equal, and undisturbed enjoyment of religious opinion, whatever it may be, and free and decent discussions on any religious subject, is granted and secured; but to revile, with malicious and blasphemous contempt, the religion professed by almost the whole community is an abuse of that right. Nor are we bound by any expressions in the Constitution, as some have strangely supposed, either not to punish at all, or to punish indiscriminately the like attacks upon the religion of Mahomet or of the Grand Lama, and for this plain reason, that the case assumes that we are a Christian people, and the morality of the country is deeply engrafted upon Christianity, and not upon the doctrines or worship of those impostors."

And in the famous case of Vidal v. Girard's Ex'rs, 2 How. 127, 198, this Court, while sustaining the will of Mr. Girard, with its provision for the creation of a college into which no minister should be permitted to enter, observed: "It is also said, and truly, that the Christian religion is a part of the common law of Pennsylvania."

If we pass beyond these matters to a view of American life, as expressed by its laws, its business, its customs, and its society, we find everywhere a clear recognition of the same truth. Among other matters, note the following: the form of oath universally prevailing, concluding with an appeal to the Almighty; the custom of opening sessions of all deliberative bodies and most conventions with prayer; the prefatory words of all wills,"In the name of God, amen;" the laws respecting the observance of the Sabbath, with the general cessation of all secular business, and the closing of courts, legislatures, and other similar public assemblies on that day; the churches and church organizations which abound in every city, town, and hamlet; the multitude of charitable organizations existing every where under Christian auspices; the gigantic missionary associations, with general support, and aiming to establish Christian missions in every quarter of the globe. These, and many other matters which might be noticed, add a volume of unofficial declarations to the mass of organic utterances that this is a Christian nation. In the face of all these, shall it be believed that a Congress of the United States intended to make it a misdemeanor for a church of this country to contract for the services of a Christian minister residing in another nation?

Suppose, in the Congress that passed this act, some member had offered a bill which in terms declared that if any Roman Catholic church in this country should contract with Cardinal Manning to come to this country and enter into its service as pastor and priest, or any Episcopal church should enter into a like contract with Canon Farrar, or any Baptist church should make similar arrangements with Rev. Mr. Spurgeon, or any Jewish synagogue with some eminent rabbi, such contract should be adjudged unlawful and void, and the church making it be subject to prosecution and punishment. Can it be believed that it would have received a minute of approving thought or a single vote? Yet it is contended that such was, in effect, the meaning of this statute. The construction invoked cannot be accepted as correct. It is a case where there was presented a definite evil, in view of which the legislature used general terms with the purpose of reaching all phases of that evil, and thereafter, unexpectedly, it is developed that the general language thus employed is broad enough to reach cases and acts which the whole history and life of the country affirm could not have been intentionally legislated against. It is the duty of the courts under those circumstances to say that, however broad the language of the statute may be, the act, although within the letter, is not within the intention of the legislature, and therefore cannot be within the statute.

The judgment will be reversed, and the case remanded for further proceedings in accordance with this opinion.

*Epperson vs. Arkansas, 1968, United States Supreme Court*

(Author's Note: Italicized material represents direct quotations. Material in regular type represents the author's comments.)

(The following paragraph is not part of a trial transcript, but is quoted from the website *Voices For Evolution.*)

In 1968, in Epperson v. Arkansas, the United States Supreme Court invalidated an Arkansas statute that prohibited the teaching of evolution. The Court held the statute unconstitutional on grounds that the First Amendment to the U.S. Constitution does not permit a state to require that teaching and learning must be tailored to the principles or prohibitions of any particular religious sect or doctrine.

(Epperson v. Arkansas (1968) 393 U.S. 97, 37 U.S. Law Week 4017, 89S. Ct. 266, 21 L. Ed 228)

Following are excerpts from the Supreme Court transcript of this trial, taken from the website www.bc.edu/ bc_org/avp/cas/comm/ free_speech/epperson. Background material in the transcript explains that a teacher hired in 1964 to teach High School Biology completed her first year without incident. Her second year, however, a new textbook was obtained for her class which included a chapter on Darwin's theory. The teacher was apparently aware of the state's constitutional issue and decided to protect herself from disciplinary action before any was taken by suing the state to have the statue voided. The excerpt begins by stating the position of the attorney representing the State of Arkansas explaining how the state would interpret the statute.

On the other hand, counsel for the State, in oral argument in this Court, candidly stated that, despite the State Supreme Court's equivocation, Arkansas would interpret the statute "to mean that to make a student aware of the theory . . . just to teach that there was [103] such a theory" would be grounds for dismissal and for prosecution under the statute; and he said "that the Supreme Court of Arkansas' opinion should be interpreted in that manner." He said: "If Mrs. Epperson would tell her students that 'Here is Darwin's theory, that man ascended or descended from a lower form of being,' then I think she would be under this statute liable for prosecution."

In any event, we do not rest our decision upon the asserted vagueness of the statute. On either interpretation of its language, Arkansas' statute cannot stand. It is of no moment whether the law is deemed to prohibit mention of Darwin's theory, or to forbid any or all of the infinite varieties of communication embraced within the term "teaching." Under either interpretation, the law must be stricken because of its conflict with the constitutional prohibition of state laws respecting an establishment of religion or prohibiting the free exercise thereof. The overriding fact is that Arkansas' law selects from the body of knowledge a particular segment which it proscribes for the sole reason that it is deemed to conflict with a particular religious doctrine; that is, with a particular interpretation of the Book of Genesis by a particular religious group.

The following excerpt includes the specific opinion of Justice Black on this matter.

MR. JUSTICE BLACK, concurring.

I am by no means sure that this case presents a genuinely justiciable case or controversy. Although Arkansas Initiated Act No. 1, the statute alleged to be unconstitutional, was passed by the voters of Arkansas in 1928, we are informed that there has never been even a single attempt by the State to enforce it. And the pallid, unenthusiastic, even apologetic defense of the Act presented by the State in this Court indicates that the State would make no attempt to enforce the law should it remain on the books for the next century. Now, nearly 40 years after the law has slumbered on the books as though dead, a teacher alleging fear that the State might arouse from its lethargy and try to punish her has asked for a declaratory judgment holding the law unconstitutional. She was subsequently joined by a parent who alleged his interest in seeing that his two then school-age sons "be informed of all scientific theories and hypotheses ..."

Notwithstanding my own doubts as to whether the case presents a justiciable controversy, the Court brushes aside these doubts and leaps headlong into the middle of the very broad problems involved in federal intrusion into state powers to decide what subjects and schoolbooks it may wish to use in teaching state pupils. ... But, agreeing to consider this as a genuine case or controversy, I cannot agree to thrust the Federal Government's long arm the least bit further into state school curriculums than decision of this particular case requires. And the Court, in order to invalidate the Arkansas law as a violation of the First Amendment, has been compelled to give the State's law a broader meaning than the State Supreme Court was willing to give it. The Arkansas Supreme Court's opinion, in its entirety, stated that:

"Upon the principal issue, that of constitutionality, the court holds that Initiated Measure No. 1 of 1928, Ark. Stat. Ann. § 80-1627 and § 80-1628 (Repl. 1960), is a valid exercise of the state's power to specify the curriculum in its public schools. The court expresses no opinion on the question whether the Act prohibits any explanation of the theory of evolution or merely prohibits teaching that the theory is true; the answer not being necessary to a decision in the case, and the issue not having been raised."

It is plain that a state law prohibiting all teaching of human development or biology is constitutionally quite different from a law that compels a teacher to teach as true only one theory of a given doctrine. It would be difficult to make a First Amendment case out of a state law eliminating the subject of higher mathematics, or astronomy, or biology from its curriculum. And, for all the Supreme Court of Arkansas has said, this particular Act may prohibit that and nothing else. This Court, however, treats the Arkansas Act as though it made it a misdemeanor to teach or to use a book that teaches that evolution is true. But it is not for this Court to arrogate to itself the power to determine the scope of Arkansas statutes. Since the highest court of Arkansas has deliberately refused to give its statute that meaning, we should not presume to do so.

The Supreme Court struck down this Arkansas statue partly because it believed the state was violating the first and fourteenth amendments and partly because it believed the law to be too vaguely worded. The significant fact is in Black's statement that Arkansas had a chance to deal with the issue without federal interference and failed to do so. Black did not like even the idea that a Federal hand might be reaching into a state issue. Education specifics were supposed to be up to the states in those days. Arkansas gave away its state's right, and the rights of states in the future, by allowing the Supreme Court to establish this precedent.

The important issue of this case is just what Black said. The federal government made a ruling in a state issue and that shouldn't have happened. Time after time cases like this one have whittled away autonomy and replaced it with precedent. The power of the federal courts took away, little by little, the control of states over education and transferred it to the federal government. The Supreme Court has been a powerful tool in taking away our protection, our freedom, our rights and our property.

*Segraves vs. State of California,* 1981

(Author's Note: Italicized material represents direct quotations. Material in regular type represents the author's comments.)

(The following paragraph is not part of a trial transcript, but is quoted from the website Voices For Evolution)

In 1981, in Segraves v. State of California the Court found that the California State Board of Education's Science Framework, as written and as qualified by its anti-dogmatism policy, gave sufficient accommodation to the views of Segraves, contrary to his contention that class discussion of evolution prohibited his and his children's free exercise of religion. The anti-dogmatism policy provided that class discussions of origins should emphasize that scientific explanations focus on "how", not "ultimate cause," and that any speculative statements concerning origins, both in texts and in classes, should be presented conditionally, not dogmatically. The court's ruling also directed the Board of Education to widely disseminate the policy, which in 1989 was expanded to cover all areas of science, not just those concerning issues of origins. (Segraves v. California (1981) Sacramento Superior Court #278978)

Following are excerpts from the oral presentation of the case. Superior Court Judge Irving Perluss adopted a very friendly and informal tone, insisting on the oral format, making light of the need for huge amounts of documentation, and so it's a bit difficult to find a clean copy of this transcript to draw from. Most of the sections are the opinion of the judge, but there is an instance where a witness, Dr. Meyer, is called upon to speak.

These excerpts come from a personal website built by Frank Fire, who says he is "a firefighter/ paramedic. (with a name like that, what else would I be?) I also built it to promote critical thinking and to promote the defense of the First Amendment." The text contained a number of typos and formatting errors which have been corrected for ease of reading, but the basic format is that of the original transcript.

The judge's tone seemed to imply that the case was not important enough to be recorded and everyone should just get together as friends and settle things. It established an important precedent, however, and Frank Fire performed an important service by posting a copy of the transcript.

And isn't it truly wonderful that in our country we can seek to invoke the awesome authority of the courts to assuage the feelings of a single child, a child. And in the final analysis, I believe that is what this case is all about. The play between establishment on the one hand, in terms of accommodation, and free exercise on the other. Now, fortunately -- I say "fortunately" because I'm the fellow that has to make the decision -- the issues have been narrowed here to the point where we are not faced with such a dilemma, and thus there is on contention here that evolution should not be taught in the public schools. I think you've heard me say on several occasions that if there were, it would be rejected as an impermissible accommodation, for that battle was fought and resolved by the Supreme Court of the United States, in Epperson versus Arkansas. Now, moreover, the Plaintiffs have disclaimed any interest in an accommodation which would require the teaching of special creation in the public schools. And I might say, in -- and of course, this is what they call, "dicta," this is not part of the decision in this case, but this is my -- my view -- that is was appropriate that they do so, for I have no doubt, whatever, that such an accommodation would be held to be violated with the establishment clause, and forbidden. I think this is so, as a matter of law. It was basically held to be such in the -- in the opinion of the California Attorney General in 58 Attorney General Opinions, 262. And of course, it was held in the decision of Daniels versus Waters in the Sixth Circuit, which was referred to during the course of our trial.

Now, the issue, simply stated, accordingly, is whether or not the free exercise of religion by Mr. Segraves and his children was thwarted by the instruction in science that children had received in school, and if so, has there been sufficient accommodation for their views?

The Court, in addition, is prepared to find and does find that the science framework, as written, and if qualified by the policy of the Board exemplified by Exhibit N, does provide sufficient accommodation for the views of the Plaintiff. This is so, in my judgment, even if, as was alluded to by Mr. Turner, there is some problem about whether that was ever officially adopted as a policy by the Board because the fact is now that by virtue of the statement of the representative of the Board, more than one, not only the Attorney General but the representatives of the Board, that is current Board policy and shall remain as current Board policy until a Board changes it. I think all teachers -- I hope all teachers endeavor to follow the Code of Ethics and the administrative regulation that we have read 80130 of Title Five. But nevertheless, all of us conclude, and I conclude myself, sometimes are needed -- we need to be reminded of our responsibilities. It seems to me that what has happened here has developed from a lack of communication from the Board to the school to the classroom teacher. I think it is the emphasis on tolerance and understanding that should be communicated as a fundamental policy of the State Board of Education. This is true not only in science, but it's true throughout the entire public school system. I must add that it seems to the Court, also, that persons seeking tolerance and understanding must practice it, also. Only in this way can all of us enjoy the religious liberty which is our fundamental right.

Mr. Turner has already quoted from the concurring opinion of Justice Stewart, and Sherbert versus Vernor. I think it's worth repeating because those are resounding and beautiful words where he said, "I am convinced that no liberty is more essential to the continued vitality of the free society which our constitution guarantees than is the religious liberty protected by the free exercise clause explicit in the First Amendment and embedded in the Fourteenth." I think Justice Stewart has spoken well.

In the final analysis, ladies and gentlemen, counsel, all that Plaintiffs seek, in the Court's view, presently is contained in Board policy. It appears, however, that this Board policy may not have been communicated to all who should know of it, and who should be guided by that policy. As this is a Court of equity, it seems to the Court that an appropriate remedy may be fashioned.

It will be the order of the Court that there shall be disseminated to all the publishers, institutions, school districts, schools, and persons regularly receiving the science framework a copy of the Board policy set forth in Exhibit N. By this, the Court means, insofar as possible, the policies shall -- the policy shall be sent to those who have received the framework in the past. It shall be included in the framework disseminated in the future. It follows that if there are violations of this policy when disseminated it becomes a matter of concern for students and parents to adjust with their local teachers, their local schools, and their local school boards.

"Now, when you begin to think of textbooks that talk about belief, now to me belief is not a scientific word. One knows, one accumulates data, one has a comprehension of, one understands, one does a lot of things, but to me belief always, in my situation, has been something I associate with my theology. I would not like to see my theology and my science get mixed. I have never dealt with a scientific process where somebody says, 'I believe.' I have dealt with theological processes where one believes. In short, I think at that point you begin to mix epistemologies, and that's confusing."

And then I said to him,

"But I see, as I comprehend this case, we are talking about the very kind of disclaimer that you have just told us about, that you have just told us about, that at the beginning of a science textbook should there not be a statement --because not everyone is a scientist and knows all the background of scientists -- but shouldn't there be a statement saying, 'this does not deal with theology?'"

Dr. Mayer,

"Absolutely. I would -- I would say there should be a clear explanation that perhaps should run through the entire textbook within the student's mind what it is he's dealing with. He's dealing with science. We are not making a pretense to teach him music, art, poetry, theology, or any other discipline. Science does these things, and outside of that realm, science is not only moot, but might even be harmful."

Court,

"And, moreover, science is not dogmatic in that it is open ended and there is an absence of preset conclusions?"

The witness,

"Yes sir."

Now, there is one additional statement from Justice Stewart -- forgive me if I quote from him often, but our son clerked for him as a clerk, and so I -- I think he's a great man.

Justice Stewart also said in the concurring opinion, and in the Sherbert case, and these are the words that I felt were most pertinent to our case where he said, "And I think that the guarantee of religious liberty embodied in the free exercise clause affirmatively requires government to create an atmosphere of hospitality and accommodation to individual belief or disbelief. In short, I think our constitution commands the positive protection by government of religious freedom, not only for a minority, however small, not only for the majority, however large, but for each of us." I don't think any of us could really quarrel with that.

As I view this case, accordingly, counsel, I really don't believe that either side has lost. I truly believe that both sides have won. I think that we have all won because hopefully what we have achieved in this case is understanding.

California had a policy to make sure teachers didn't make evolution a dogma. The judge made a very kind and inclusive statement that everybody won but the man and his children lost the case.

The anti-dogmatism policy provided that class discussions of origins should emphasize that scientific explanations focus on "how," not "ultimate cause," and that any speculative statements concerning origins, both in texts and in classes, should be presented conditionally, not dogmatically.

This California statute may or may not have been sufficient to protect the religious beliefs of students. The intended result seems to have been that each side is free to believe what it will about origins. A consequence that may have been unintended is that by accepting and operating under this standard, by attempting to place both sides on an equal footing, Evolutionists reveal that they really do regard Evolution as a set of beliefs, in spite of the judge's contention that Science doesn't deal with beliefs.

*McLean v. Arkansas Board of Education, 1982*

(Author's Note: Italicized material represents direct quotations. Material in regular type represents the author's comments.)

(The following paragraph is not part of a trial transcript, but is quoted from the website Voices For Evolution.)

In 1982, in McLean v. Arkansas Board of Education, a federal court held that a "balanced treatment" statute violated the Establishment Clause of the U.S. Constitution. The Arkansas statute required public schools to give balanced treatment to "creation-science" and "evolution-science". In a decision that gave a detailed definition of the term "science," the court declared that "creation science" is not in fact a science. The court also found that the statute did not have a secular purpose, noting that the statute used language peculiar to creationist literature in emphasizing origins of life as an aspect of the theory of evolution. While the subject of life's origins is within the province of biology, the scientific community does not consider the subject as part of evolutionary theory, which assumes the existence of life and is directed to an explanation of how life evolved after it originated. The theory of evolution does not presuppose either the absence or the presence of a creator. (McLean v. Arkansas Board of Education (1982) 529 F. Supp. 1255, 50 U.S. Law Week 2412)

Following are excerpts from the trial transcript. The source is *www.talkorigins.org/faqs/mclean-v-arkansas*.

Special attention should be paid to the notation in the preceding paragraph, however, the one that says While the subject of life's origins is within the province of biology, the scientific community does not consider the subject as part of evolutionary theory, which assumes the existence of life and is directed to an explanation of how life evolved after it originated. The theory of evolution does not presuppose either the absence or the presence of a creator. Keep this idea in mind for later consideration.

On March 19, 1981, the Governor of Arkansas signed into law Act 590 of 1981, entitled "Balanced Treatment for Creation-Science and Evolution-Science Act." The Act is codified as Ark. Stat. Ann. &80-1663, et seq., (1981 Supp.). Its essential mandate is stated in its first sentence: "Public schools within this State shall give balanced treatment to creation-science and to evolution-science." On May 27, 1981, this suit was filed challenging the constitutional validity of Act 590 on three distinct grounds.

First, it is contended that Act 590 constitutes an establishment of religion prohibited by the First Amendment to the Constitution, which is made applicable to the states by the Fourteenth Amendment. Second, the plaintiffs argue the Act violates a right to academic freedom which they say is guaranteed to students and teachers by the Free Speech Clause of the First Amendment. Third, plaintiffs allege the Act is impermissibly vague and thereby violates the Due Process Clause of the Fourteenth Amendment.

The following excerpt is significant because it tells you that the courts have taken upon themselves the right to sole and indisputable power to tell us what the Constitution says and what it means. The courts can tell you how to think about this because people let them tell you how to think about it before. Now you're stuck.

There is no controversy over the legal standards under which the Establishment Clause portion of this case must be judged. The Supreme Court has on a number of occasions expounded on the meaning of the clause, and the pronouncements are clear. Often the issue has arisen in the context of public education, as it has here. In Everson v. Board of Education, 330 U.S. 1, 15-16 (1947), Justice Black stated:

The "establishment of religion" clause of the First Amendment means at least this: Neither a state nor the Federal Government can set up a church. Neither can pass laws which aid one religion, aid all religions, or prefer one religion over another. Neither can force nor influence a person to go to or to remain away from church against his will or force him to profess a belief or disbelief in any religion. No person can be punished for entertaining or professing religious beliefs or disbeliefs, for church-attendance or non-attendance. No tax, large or small, can be levied to support any religious activities or institutions, whatever they may be called, or what ever form they may adopt to teach or practice religion. Neither a state nor the Federal Government can, openly or secretly, participate in the affairs of any religious organizations or groups and vice versa. In the words of Jefferson, the clause ... was intended to erect "a wall of separation between church and State."

The Establishment Clause thus enshrines two central values: voluntarism and pluralism. And it is in the area of the public schools that these values must be guarded most vigilantly.

Designed to serve as perhaps the most powerful agency for promoting cohesion among a heterogeneous democratic people, the public school must keep scrupulously free from entanglement in the strife of sects. The preservation of the community from divisive conflicts, of Government from irreconcilable pressures by religious groups, or religion from censorship and coercion however subtly exercised, requires strict confinement of the State to instruction other than religious, leaving to the individual's church and home, indoctrination in the faith of his choice. [McCollum v. Board of Education, 333 U.S. 203, 216-217 (1948), (Opinion of Frankfurter, J., joined by Jackson, Burton, and Rutledge, J.J.)]

What Black said was proper and correct, up to the point where he inserted Jefferson's explanation about the "wall of separation." People have gotten to think that that's actually in the Constitution because of mentions like this, but it isn't. And it's been used to promote the idea that all mention of any religion must be excised from education because education must be a state function. What Thomas Jefferson actually meant is just the opposite of what Justice Black says. Thomas Jefferson, the extreme leftist of his day, meant that the state must not interfere in the affairs of the Church; the wall was to protect the Church from the state. Thomas Jefferson meant what all of the founding fathers meant. No aspect of the federal government, including the courts, had any power, any authority to do anything at all with any aspect an establishment of religion. An Establishment of Religion is welfare, education and worship. Yet Justice Black in this case doesn't even stop there. He goes on to quote Frankfurter, and Frankfurter goes too far. He presupposes that the government must be the teacher or the people can't be cohesive.

Education wasn't originally a state function. It was usurped by the state from religious leaders and parents. In every society from ancient times to the present, where the government took over teaching the children, the seeds of that government's destruction were sown. The teaching of religion doesn't automatically mean that there will be strife or coercion or even indoctrination. Who puts up a fuss about religious instruction? People who don't want to be reminded that they are responsible to God. Look for them, and you'll see where the strife and coercion is coming from.

In the second place, no one even pretends that all religion has been excised from the public school. Yoga classes are taught in Physical Education. Teaching the Crusades in History class can't be done without bringing up religious issues, wrong ones and right ones. Teachers interweave culture and religion with Foreign Language study, and even studying Science brings up medical treatments at the Temple of Aesclipius and Egyptian pharmaceutical papyri ceremonially buried with priests.

The term "scientific creationism" first gained currency around 1965 following publication of *The Genesis Flood* in 1961 by Whitcomb and Morris. There is undoubtedly some connection between the appearance of the BSCS texts emphasizing evolutionary thought and efforts of Fundamentalist to attach the theory. (Mayer)

In the 1960's and early 1970's, several Fundamentalist organizations were formed to promote the idea that the

Book of Genesis was supported by scientific data. The terms "creation science" and "scientific creationism" have been adopted by these Fundamentalists as descriptive of their study of creation and the origins of man. Perhaps the leading creationist organization is the Institute for Creation Research (ICR), which is affiliated with the Christian heritage College and supported by the Scott Memorial Baptist Church in San Diego, California. The ICR, through the Creation-Life Publishing Company, is the leading publisher of creation science material. other creation science organizations include the Creation Science Research Center (CSRC) of San Diego and the Bible Science Association of Minneapolis, Minnesota. In 1963, the Creation Research Society (CRS) was formed from a schism in the American Scientific Affiliation (ASA). It is an organization of literal Fundamentalists who have the equivalent of a master's degree in some recognized area of science. A purpose of the organization is "to reach all people with the vital message of the scientific and historical truth about creation." Nelkin, The Science Textbook Controversies and the Politics of Equal Time, 66.

The preceding quote sets up the case being presented, the argument, not about whether teachers should have the freedom to teach what they believe is important and right, but whether a particular teaching must be attacked, discredited and beaten out of the schools. The court has already made itself the authority on what the state is and what religion is and how they can't be in the same room together. That includes the concept that the school is the state. A lengthy summary of the history of Fundamentalism is included in the transcript, because it's necessary for an inextricable bond to be formed between Creation Science and religious extremists. The transcript contends that proponents of this bill were on a religious crusade and that they attempted to conceal the fact to allow their bill to pass.

Senator James L. Holsted [was chosen to] introduce the act. Holsted, a self-described "born again" Christian Fundamentalist, introduced the act in the Arkansas Senate. He did not consult the State Department of Education, scientists, science educators or the Arkansas Attorney General. The Act was not referred to any Senate committee for hearing and was passed after only a few minutes' discussion on the Senate floor. In the House of Representatives, the bill was referred to the Education Committee which conducted a perfunctory fifteen minute hearing. No scientist testified at the hearing, nor was any representative from the State Department of Education called to testify.

The State failed to produce any evidence which would warrant an inference or conclusion that at any point in the process anyone considered the legitimate educational value of the Act. It was simply and purely an effort to introduce the Biblical version of creation into the public school curricula. The only inference which can be drawn from these circumstances is that the Act was passed with the specific purpose by the General Assembly of advancing religion. The Act therefore fails the first prong of the three-pronged test, that of secular legislative purpose, as articulated in Lemon v. Kurtzman, supra, and Stone v. Graham, supra.

An immediate attack is made on the bill's credentials. There were no scientists, no Department of Education input, no senate committee ruled on it, so it can't be valid. More about the issue of scientists later, but at least the last two entities can be identified as instruments of government control. The state must retain sole power here. A bill merely created and submitted by earnest, intelligent citizens is no good on its face.

A presentation of the basic tenets of Creation Science and Evolutionary Science follows in the transcript, setting the two in opposition to each other. An attack is made on this method of presentation as follows and the "true" definition of science is arrived at so that Creation Science can quickly be excluded entirely from serious consideration. The statement that "in a free society, knowledge does not require the imprimatur of legislation in order to become science" is almost laughable if it weren't such a lie. This whole case is about legislating what is and isn't Science.

In addition to the fallacious pedagogy of the two model approach, Section 4(a) lacks legitimate educational value because "creation-science" as defined in that section is simply not science. Several witnesses suggested definitions of science. A descriptive definition was said to be that science is what is "accepted by the scientific community" and is "what scientists do." The obvious implication of this description is that, in a free society, knowledge does not require the imprimatur of legislation in order to become science.

More precisely, the essential characteristics of science are:(1) It is guided by natural law;

(2) It has to be explanatory by reference to nature law;(3) It is testable against the empirical world;(4) Its conclusions are tentative, i.e. are not necessarily the final word; and (5) It is falsifiable. (Ruse and other science witnesses).

The term "Natural Law" comes from Plato and Aristotle. Aristotle acknowledged the possibility of an "unmoved mover," but Plato is famous for having thrown "the gods" (and the true God) out of his perfect society thousands of years ago. This court has taken an adversarial position carefully devised to exclude the possibility of Creation and set its own position up as the only possible fact. It's not fact, it's philosophy. The entire "definition" of Science presented here is Naturalism, a philosophy designed to exclude God, not true Science at all but a way to set up the worship of man's intellect as an extension of nature.

As many times as the transcript argues that Creation Science proofs don't prove anything, you would think that it would become clear that this premise as a definition of Science doesn't prove anything. About the only thing true about "Science" as defined here is that its conclusions certainly are tentative. Yet the position taken is that they are the final word. This is the dogma of a belief, a religion, not Science.

Note the folksy statements that Science is "what scientists do." Naturally that excludes Creationists, even though most of these proponents of Creation Science hold advanced degrees from accredited institutions in recognized scientific fields. Unless you presuppose that a Creationist can't be a scientist you would have to grant that these people really are scientists and therefore they also do what scientists do.

Creation science as described in Section 4(a) fails to meet these essential characteristics. First, the section revolves around 4(a)(1) which asserts a sudden creation "from nothing." Such a concept is not science because it depends upon a supernatural intervention which is not guided by natural law. It is not explanatory by reference to natural law, is not testable and is not falsifiable.

The same arguments are applicable to Evolution, or would be if Evolution were forced to justify its tenets by actually coming up with a viable theory to cover origins. Instead it is allowed to slide by with the explanation that it doesn't deal with origins. Actually, it does, but more along the lines of Eastern religions which allow for an endless cycle of time, progressively more billions of years. How can the statement that it presupposes the existence of life be satisfactory? It allows for all of Evolutionary theory to be based on presuppositions, and indeed that's all it is, suppositions based on the founding premise that we suppose there isn't any God who started everything.

Creation science as defined in Section 4(a), not only fails to follow the canons of dealing with scientific theory, it also fails to fit the more general descriptions of "what scientists think" and "what scientists do." The scientific community consists of individuals and groups, nationally and internationally, who work independently in such varied fields as biology, paleontology, geology, and astronomy. Their work is published and subject to review and testing by their peers. The journals for publication are both numerous and varied. There is, however, not one recognized scientific journal which has published an article espousing the creation science theory described in Section 4(a). Some of the State's witnesses suggested that the scientific community was "close-minded" on the subject of creationism and that explained the lack of acceptance of the creation science arguments. Yet no witness produced a scientific article for which publication has been refused. Perhaps some members of the scientific community are resistant to new ideas. It is, however, inconceivable that such a loose knit group of independent thinkers in all the varied fields of science could, or would, so effectively censor new scientific thought.

The reader is directed to Dr. Richard Sternberg's discussion of what happened to him when he published an article by Dr. Stephen Meyer which contained material related to Intelligent Design, not even espousing Creationism. (See the Section Three Appendix for specific examples of attacks on recognized members of the scientific community because of a connection with Intelligent Design.)

The trial transcript simply dismisses the possibility that the scientific community could be narrow minded. No doubt thousands of articles and books which have been refused publication could have been produced as evidence of this narrow-mindedness. The transcript later brings up the fact that a woman who was charged with developing curriculum materials was unable to find any that met her criteria for inclusion. In other words, her fruitless search proves one of two points, either that reputable scientists cannot get creationist material published or that her criteria is narrow-minded and exclusive of this material.

The defendants' argument would be more persuasive if, in fact, there were only two theories or idea about the origins of life and the world. That there are a number of theories was acknowledge by the State's witnesses, Dr. Wickramasinghe and Dr. Geisler. Dr. Wickramasinghe testified at length in support of a theory that life on earth was "seeded" by comets which delivered genetic material and perhaps organisms to the earth's surface from interstellar dust far outside the solar system. The "seeding" theory further hypothesizes that the earth remains under the continuing influence of genetic material from space which continues to affect life. While Wickramasinghe's theory about the origins of life on earth has not received general acceptance within the scientific community, he has, at least, used scientific methodology to produce a theory of origins which meets the essential characteristics of science.

It is a logical fallacy to create a definition and then make it the only definition anybody can use to prove anything. The preceding exposition of the theory of "genetic seeding" by Dr. Wickramasinghe is presented to prove that creation science isn't allowed to set itself off against Evolution because Evolution isn't the only theory of how things are the way they are. There's this one, which the Scientific community doesn't recognize and won't even fund further study about. Excellent choice. A theory with a completely unprovable, unexaminable and already generally discarded premise is at least good Science.

Robert Gentry's discovery of radioactive polonium haloes in granite and coalified woods is, perhaps, the most recent scientific work which the creationists use as argument for a "relatively recent inception" of the earth and a "worldwide flood." The existence of polonium haloes in granite and coalified wood is thought to be inconsistent with radiometric dating methods based upon constant radioactive decay rates. Mr. Gentry's findings were published almost ten years ago and have been the subject of some discussion in the scientific community. The discoveries have not, however, led to the formulation of any scientific hypothesis or theory which would explain a relatively recent inception of the earth or a worldwide flood. Gentry's discovery has been treated as a minor mystery which will eventually be explained. It may deserve further investigation, but the National Science Foundation has not deemed it to be of sufficient import to support further funding.

The National Science Foundation has decided not to fund this promising area of research for only one reason: It might disprove a few presuppositions Evolutionists cling to. If ever there was an example of narrow-mindedness in the scientific community, here it is. Demanding that Creationists must produce something "new" before they will get a hearing is a humorous thought coming from someone who resurrects Plato to craft a definition of Science. This is a common dismissal of Creationist evidence, that it's old so it isn't valid. How is age a worthy criteria for judging evidentiary value? If you can prove you were born in the United States thirty years ago is that evidence too old to be admitted as proof of citizenship?

In any event, if Act 590 is implemented, many teachers will be required to teach materials in support of creation science which they do not consider academically sound. Many teachers will simply forego teaching subjects which might trigger the "balanced treatment" aspects of Act 590 even though they think the subjects are important to a proper presentation of a course.

Implementation of Act 580 will have serious and untoward consequences for students, particularly those planning to attend college. Evolution is the cornerstone of modern biology, and many courses in public schools contain subject matter relating to such varied topics as the age of the earth, geology and relationships among living things. Any student who is deprived of instruction as to the prevailing scientific thought on these topics will be denied a significant part of science education. Such a deprivation through the high school level would undoubtedly have an impact upon the quality of education in the State's colleges and universities, especially including the pre-professional and professional programs in the health sciences.

"Evolution is the cornerstone of modern biology," certainly gives enormous weight to a theoretical teaching that is not supposed to be presented as dogma. While it's true that eliminating evolution from the curriculum would severely limit what can be taught, this bill did not ask for that to be done. It asked for balance, for equal time, to present the opposing viewpoint. This transcript direly predicts that instead teachers will live n fear of reprisals from wild-eyed religionists and children's education will suffer. They will be denied a full preparation and have stunted opportunities and a blighted future. Who would not fear the possibility that their children might fail to learn important things, things they need to go on in their education?

The defendants argue in their brief that evolution is, in effect, a religion, and that by teaching a religion which is contrary to some students' religious views, the State is infringing upon the student's free exercise rights under the First Amendment. Mr. Ellwanger's legislative findings, which were adopted as a finding of fact by the Arkansas Legislature in Act 590, provides:

Evolution-science is contrary to the religious convictions or moral values or philosophical beliefs of many students and parents, including individuals of many different religious faiths and with diverse moral and philosophical beliefs. Act 590, &7(d).

The defendants argue that the teaching of evolution alone presents both a free exercise problem and an establishment problem which can only be redressed by giving balanced treatment to creation science, which is admittedly consistent with some religious beliefs. This argument appears to have its genesis in a student note written by Mr. Wendell Bird, "Freedom of Religion and Science Instruction in Public Schools," 87 Yale L.J. 515 (1978). The argument has no legal merit.

If creation science is, in fact, science and not religion, as the defendants claim, it is difficult to see how the teaching of such a science could "neutralize" the religious nature of evolution.

Assuming for the purposes of argument, however, that evolution is a religion or religious tenet, the remedy is to stop the teaching of evolution, not establish another religion in opposition to it. Yet it is clearly established in the case law, and perhaps also in common sense, that evolution is not a religion and that teaching evolution does not violate the Establishment Clause, Epperson v. Arkansas, supra, Willoughby v. Stever, No. 15574-75 (D.D.C. May 18, 1973); aff'd. 504 F.2d 271 (D.C. Cir. 1974), cert. denied , 420 U.S. 924 (1975); Wright v. Houston Indep. School Dist., 366 F. Supp. 1208 (S.D. Tex 1978), aff.d. 486 F.2d 137 (5th Cir. 1973), cert. denied 417 U.S. 969 (1974).

As proof that Evolution is not a religion, the transcript cites precedent, case law. This is circular reasoning if there ever was such a thing. The court rules that Evolution is not a religion because another court has already ruled that Evolution is not a religion. Case closed.

The Court closes this opinion with a thought expressed eloquently by the great Justice Frankfurter:

We renew our conviction that "we have at stake the very existence of our country on the faith that complete separation between the state and religion is best for the state and best for religion." Everson v. Board of Education, 330 U.S. at 59. If nowhere else, in the relation between Church and State, "good fences make good neighbors." [McCollum v. Board of Education, 333 U.S. 203, 232 (1948)]

Once again Justice Frankfurter claims for the state the sole right to educate, and to dictate what shall and shall not be allowed in the scope of that education.

The quote from Robert Frost's 1914 poem "Mending Wall" is extremely significant in this context. The narrator of the poem objects to the metaphorical walls dividing people from one another. If the state is that neighbor on the other side, I feel the same as the narrator of Frost's poem:

*Before I built a wall I'd ask to know*
*What I was walling in or walling out,*
*And to whom I was like to give offense.*
*Something there is that doesn't love a wall,*
*That wants it down.'*
*I could say 'Elves' to him,*
*But it's not elves exactly, and I'd rather*
*He said it for himself. I see him there*
*Bringing a stone grasped firmly by the top*
*In each hand, like an old-stone savage armed.*
*He moves in darkness as it seems to me,*
*Not of woods only and the shade of trees.*
*He will not go behind his father's saying,*
*And he likes having thought of it so well*
*He says again,*
*'Good fences make good neighbors.'*

*Edwards v. Aguillard, U.S. Supreme Court, 1987*

(Author's Note: Italicized material represents direct quotations.

Material in regular type represents the author's comments.)

(The following paragraph is not part of a trial transcript, but is quoted from the website Voices For Evolution)

In 1987, in Edwards v. Aguillard, the U.S. Supreme Court held unconstitutional Louisiana's "Creationism Act." This statute prohibited the teaching of evolution in public schools, except when it was accompanied by instruction in "creation science." The Court found that, by advancing the religious belief that a supernatural being created humankind, which is embraced by the term creation science, the act impermissibly endorses religion. In addition, the Court found that the provision of a comprehensive science education is undermined when it is forbidden to teach evolution except when creation science is also taught. (Segraves v. State of California (1981) Sacramento Superior Court #278978)

Instead of excerpts from the full trial transcript, which is essentially the same issue as that treated in the case of McLean v. Arkansas Board of Education, 1982, what follows is Justice Antonin Scalia's dissenting opinion, which was shared by the Chief Justice William Rehnquist. This material is taken from www.talkorigins.org/faqs/ edwards-v-aguillard. It is lengthy and includes many notes and references but his statement is in vocabulary easy to understand and well worth reading. It is possible to get through the notes and references with patient effort. There is no inserted commentary because the justice's statements are those of a straightforward, honest man honestly frustrated by his inability to stop an injustice. They need no real explanation and would be difficult to improve upon.

Even if I agreed with the questionable premise that legislation can be invalidated under the Establishment Clause on the basis of its motivation alone, without regard to its effects, I would still find no justification for today's decision. The Louisiana legislators who passed the "Balanced Treatment for Creation-Science and Evolution-Science Act" (Balanced Treatment Act), La. Rev. Stat. Ann. 17:286.1-17:286.7 (West 1982), each of whom had sworn to support the Constitution were well aware of the potential Establishment Clause problems and considered that aspect of the legislation with great care. After seven hearings and several months of study, resulting in substantial revision of the original proposal, they approved the Act overwhelmingly and specifically articulated the secular purpose they meant it to serve.

Although the record contains abundant evidence of the sincerity of that purpose (the only issue pertinent to this case), the Court today holds, essentially on the basis of "its visceral knowledge regarding what must have motivated the legislators," 778 F.2d 225, 227 (CA5 1985) (Gee, J., dissenting) (emphasis added), that the members of the Louisiana Legislature knowingly violated their oaths and then lied about it. I dissent. Had requirements of the Balanced Treatment Act that are not apparent on its face been clarified by an interpretation of the Louisiana Supreme Court, or by the manner of its implementation, the Act might well be found unconstitutional; but the question of its constitutionality cannot rightly be disposed of on the gallop, by impugning the motives of its supporters.

I

This case arrives here in the following posture: The Louisiana Supreme Court has never been given an opportunity to interpret the Balanced Treatment Act, State officials have never attempted to implement it, and it has never been the subject of a full evidentiary hearing. We can only guess at its meaning. We know that it forbids instruction in either "creation-science" or "evolution-science" without instruction in the other, @ 17:286.4A, but the parties are sharply divided over what creation science consists of. Appellants insist that it is a collection of educationally valuable scientific data that has been censored from classrooms by an embarrassed scientific establishment. Appellees insist it is not science at all but thinly veiled religious doctrine. Both interpretations of the intended meaning of that phrase find considerable support in the legislative history.

At least at this stage in the litigation, it is plain to me that we must accept appellants' view of what the statute means. To begin with, the statute itself defines "creation-science" as "the scientific evidences for creation and inferences from those scientific evidences." @ 17:286.3(2) (emphasis added). If, however, that definition is not thought sufficiently helpful, the means by which the Louisiana Supreme Court will give the term more precise content is quite clear -- and again, at this stage in the litigation, favors the appellants' view. "Creation science" is unquestionably a "term of art," see Brief for 72 Nobel Laureates et al. as Amici Curiae 20, and thus, under Louisiana law, is "to be interpreted according to [its] received meaning and acceptation with the learned in the art, trade or profession to which [it] refer[s]." La. Civ. Code Ann., Art. 15 (West 1952). The only evidence in the record of the "received meaning and acceptation" of "creation science" is found in five affidavits filed by appellants. In those affidavits, two scientists, a philosopher, a theologian, and an educator, all of whom claim extensive knowledge of creation science, swear that it is essentially a collection of scientific data supporting the theory that the physical universe and life within it appeared suddenly and have not changed substantially since appearing. See App. to Juris. Statement A-19 (Kenyon); id., at A-36 (Morrow); id., at A-41 (Miethe). These experts insist that creation science is a strictly scientific concept that can be presented without religious reference. See id., at A-19 -- A-20, A-35 (Kenyon); id., at A-36 -- A-38 (Morrow); id., at A-40, A-41, A-43 (Miethe); id., at A-47, A-48 (Most); id., at A-49 (Clinkert). At this point, then, we must assume that the Balanced Treatment Act does not require the presentation of religious doctrine.

Nothing in today's opinion is plainly to the contrary, but what the statute means and what it requires are of rather little concern to the Court. Like the Court of Appeals, 765 F.2d 1251, 1253, 1254 (CA5 1985), the Court finds it necessary to consider only the motives of the legislators who supported the Balanced Treatment Act, ante, at 586, 593-594, 596. After examining the statute, its legislative history, and its historical and social context, the Court holds that the Louisiana Legislature acted without "a secular legislative purpose" and that the Act therefore fails the "purpose" prong of the three-part test set forth in Lemon v. Kurtzman, 403 U.S. 602, 612 (1971). As I explain below, infra, at 636-640, I doubt whether that "purpose" requirement of Lemon is a proper interpretation of the Constitution; but even if it were, I could not agree with the Court's assessment that the requirement was not satisfied here.

This Court has said little about the first component of the Lemon test. Almost invariably, we have effortlessly discovered a secular purpose for measures challenged under the Establishment Clause, typically devoting no more than a sentence or two to the matter. See, e. g., Witters v. Washington Dept. of Services for Blind, 474 U.S. 481, 485-486 (1986); Grand Rapids School District v. Ball, 473 U.S. 373, 383 (1985); Mueller v. Allen, 463 U.S. 388, 394-395 (1983); Larkin v. Grendel's Den, Inc., 459 U.S. 116, 123-124 (1982); Widmar v. Vincent, 454 U.S. 263, 271 (1981); Committee for Public Education & Religious Liberty v. Regan, 444 U.S. 646, 654, 657 (1980); Wolman v. Walter, 433 U.S. 229, 236 (1977) (plurality opinion); Meek v. Pittenger, 421 U.S. 349, 363 (1975); Committee for Public Education & Religious Liberty v. Nyquist, 413 U.S. 756, 773 (1973); Levitt v. Committee for Public Education & Religious Liberty, 413 U.S. 472, 479-480, n. 7 (1973); Tilton v. Richardson, 403 U.S. 672, 678-679 (1971) (plurality opinion); Lemon v.

Kurtzman, supra, at 613. In fact, only once before deciding Lemon, and twice since, have we invalidated a law for lack of a secular purpose. See Wallace v. Jaffree, 472 U.S. 38 (1985); Stone v. Graham, 449 U.S. 39 (1980) (per curiam); Epperson v. Arkansas, 393 U.S. 97 (1968).

Nevertheless, a few principles have emerged from our cases, principles which should, but to an unfortunately large extent do not, guide the Court's application of Lemon today. It is clear, first of all, that regardless of what "legislative purpose" may mean in other contexts, for the purpose of the Lemon test it means the "actual" motives of those responsible for the challenged action. The Court recognizes this, see ante, at 585, as it has in the past, see, e. g., Witters v. Washington Dept. of Services for Blind, supra, at 486; Wallace v. Jaffree, supra, at 56. Thus, if those legislators who supported the Balanced Treatment Act in fact acted with a "sincere" secular purpose, ante, at 587, the Act survives the first component of the Lemon test, regardless of whether that purpose is likely to be achieved by the provisions they enacted.

Our cases have also confirmed that when the Lemon Court referred to "a secular . . . purpose," 403 U.S., at 612, it meant "a secular purpose." The author of Lemon, writing for the Court, has said that invalidation under the purpose prong is appropriate when "there [is] no question that the statute or activity was motivated wholly by religious considerations." Lynch v. Donnelly, 465 U.S. 668, 680 (1984) (Burger, C. J.) (emphasis added); see also id., at 681, n. 6; Wallace v. Jaffree, supra, at 56 ("The First Amendment requires that a statute must be invalidated if it is entirely motivated by a purpose to advance religion") (emphasis added; footnote omitted). In all three cases in which we struck down laws under the Establishment Clause for lack of a secular purpose, we found that the legislature's sole motive was to promote religion. See Wallace v. Jaffree, supra, at 56, 57, 60; Stone v. Graham, supra, at 41, 43, n. 5; Epperson v.

Arkansas, supra, at 103, 107-108; see also Lynch v. Donnelly, supra, at 680 (describing Stone and Epperson as cases in which we invalidated laws "motivated wholly by religious considerations"). Thus, the majority's invalidation of the Balanced Treatment Act is defensible only if the record indicates that the Louisiana Legislature had no secular purpose.

It is important to stress that the purpose forbidden by Lemon is the purpose to "advance religion." 403 U.S., at 613; accord, ante, at 585 ( "promote" religion); Witters v. Washington Dept. of Services for Blind, supra, at 486 ( "endorse religion"); Wallace v. Jaffree, 472 U.S., at 56 ( "advance religion"); ibid. ( "endorse . . . religion"); Committee for Public Education & Religious Liberty v. Nyquist, supra, at 788 ( "'advancing' . . . religion"); Levitt v. Committee for Public Education & Religious Liberty, supra, at 481 ( "advancing religion"); Walz v. Tax Comm'n of New York City, 397 U.S. 664, 674 (1970) ( "establishing, sponsoring, or supporting religion"); Board of Education v. Allen, 392 U.S. 236, 243 (1968) ( "'advancement or inhibition of religion'") (quoting Abington School Dist. v. Schempp, 374 U.S. 203, 222 (1963)). Our cases in no way imply that the Establishment Clause forbids legislators merely to act upon their religious convictions. We surely would not strike down a law providing money to feed the hungry or shelter the homeless if it could be demonstrated that, but for the religious beliefs of the legislators, the funds would not have been approved. Also, political activism by the religiously motivated is part of our heritage. Notwithstanding the majority's implication to the contrary, ante, at 589-591, we do not presume that the sole purpose of a law is to advance religion merely because it was supported strongly by organized religions or by adherents of particular faiths. See Walz v. Tax Comm'n of New York City, supra, at 670; cf. Harris v. McRae, 448 U.S. 297, 319-320 (1980). To do so would deprive religious men and women of their right to participate in the political process. Today's religious activism may give us the Balanced Treatment Act, but yesterday's resulted in the abolition of slavery, and tomorrow's may bring relief for famine victims. Similarly, we will not presume that a law's purpose is to advance religion merely because it "'happens to coincide or harmonize with the tenets of some or all religions,'" Harris v. McRae, supra, at 319 (quoting McGowan v. Maryland, 366 U.S. 420, 442 (1961)), or because it benefits religion, even substantially. We have, for example, turned back Establishment Clause challenges to restrictions on abortion funding, Harris v. McRae, supra, and to Sunday closing laws, McGowan v. Maryland, supra, despite the fact that both "agre[e] with the dictates of [some] Judaeo-Christian religions," id., at 442. "In many instances, the Congress or state legislatures conclude that the general welfare of society, wholly apart from any religious considerations, demands such regulation." Ibid. On many past occasions we have had no difficulty finding a secular purpose for governmental action far more likely to advance religion than the Balanced Treatment Act. See, e. g., Mueller v. Allen, 463 U.S., at 394-395 (tax deduction for expenses of religious education); Wolman v. Walter, 433 U.S., at 236 (plurality opinion) (aid to religious schools); Meek v. Pittenger, 421 U.S., at 363 (same); Committee for Public Education & Religious Liberty v. Nyquist, 413 U.S., at 773 (same); Lemon v. Kurtzman, 403 U.S., at 613 (same); Walz v. Tax Comm'n of New York City, supra, at 672 (tax exemption for church property); Board of Education v. Allen, supra, at 243 (textbook loans to students in religious schools). Thus, the fact that creation science coincides with the beliefs of certain religions, a fact upon which the majority relies heavily, does not itself justify invalidation of the Act.

Finally, our cases indicate that even certain kinds of governmental actions undertaken with the specific intention of improving the position of religion do not “advance religion” as that term is used in Lemon. 403 U.S., at 613. Rather, we have said that in at least two circumstances government must act to advance religion, and that in a third it may do so.

First, since we have consistently described the Establishment Clause as forbidding not only state action motivated by the desire to advance religion, but also that intended to “disapprove,” “inhibit,” or evince “hostility” toward religion, see, e. g., ante, at 585 ( “‘disapprove’”) (quoting Lynch v. Donnelly, supra, at 690 (O’CONNOR, J., concurring)); Lynch v. Donnelly, supra, at 673 ( “hostility”); Committee for Public Education & Religious Liberty v. Nyquist, supra, at 788 ( “‘inhibi[t]’”); and since we have said that governmental “neutrality” toward religion is the preeminent goal of the First Amendment, see, e. g., Grand Rapids School District v. Ball, 473 U.S., at 382; Roemer v. Maryland Public Works Bd., 426 U.S. 736, 747 (1976) (plurality opinion); Committee for Public Education & Religious Liberty v. Nyquist, supra, at 792-793; a State which discovers that its employees are inhibiting religion must take steps to prevent them from doing so, even though its purpose would clearly be to advance religion. Cf. Walz v. Tax Comm’n of New York City, supra, at 673. Thus, if the Louisiana Legislature sincerely believed that the State’s science teachers were being hostile to religion, our cases indicate that it could act to eliminate that hostility without running afoul of Lemon’s purpose test.

Second, we have held that intentional governmental advancement of religion is sometimes required by the Free Exercise Clause. For example, in Hobbie v. Unemployment Appeals Comm’n of Fla., 480 U.S. 136 (1987); Thomas v. Review Bd., Indiana Employment Security Div., 450 U.S. 707 (1981); Wisconsin v. Yoder, 406 U.S. 205 (1972); and Sherbert v. Verner, 374 U.S. 398 (1963), we held that in some circumstances States must accommodate the beliefs of religious citizens by exempting them from generally applicable regulations.

We have not yet come close to reconciling Lemon and our Free Exercise cases, and typically we do not really try. See, e. g., Hobbie v. Unemployment Appeals Comm'n of Fla., supra, at 144-145; Thomas v. Review Bd., Indiana Employment Security Div., supra, at 719-720. It is clear, however, that members of the Louisiana Legislature were not impermissibly motivated for purposes of the Lemon test if they believed that approval of the Balanced Treatment Act was required by the Free Exercise Clause.

We have also held that in some circumstances government may act to accommodate religion, even if that action is not required by the First Amendment. See Hobbie v. Unemployment Appeals Comm'n of Fla., supra, at 144-145. It is well established that "the limits of permissible state accommodation to religion are by no means co-extensive with the noninterference mandated by the Free Exercise Clause." Walz v. Tax Comm'n of New York City, supra, at 673; see also Gillette v. United States, 401 U.S. 437, 453 (1971). We have implied that voluntary governmental accommodation of religion is not only permissible, but desirable. See, e. g., ibid. Thus, few would contend that Title VII of the Civil Rights Act of 1964, which both forbids religious discrimination by private-sector employers, 78 Stat. 255, 42 U. S. C. @ 2000e-2(a)(1), and requires them reasonably to accommodate the religious practices of their employees, @ 2000e(j), violates the Establishment Clause, even though its "purpose" is, of course, to advance religion, and even though it is almost certainly not required by the Free Exercise Clause. While we have warned that at some point, accommodation may devolve into "an unlawful fostering of religion," Hobbie v. Unemployment Appeals Comm'n of Fla., supra, at 145, we have not suggested precisely (or even roughly) where that point might be. It is possible, then, that even if the sole motive of those voting for the Balanced Treatment Act was to advance religion, and its passage was not actually required, or even believed to be required, by either the Free Exercise or Establishment Clauses, the Act would nonetheless survive scrutiny under Lemon's purpose test.

One final observation about the application of that test: Although the Court's opinion gives no hint of it, in the past we have repeatedly affirmed "our reluctance to attribute unconstitutional motives to the States." Mueller v. Allen, supra, at 394; see also Lynch v. Donnelly, 465 U.S., at 699 (BRENNAN, J., dissenting). We "presume that legislatures act in a constitutional manner." Illinois v. Krull, 480 U.S. 340, 351 (1987); see also Clements v. Fashing, 457 U.S. 957, 963 (1982) (plurality opinion); Rostker v. Goldberg, 453 U.S. 57, 64

(1981); McDonald v. Board of Election Comm'rs of Chicago, 394 U.S. 802, 809 (1969). Whenever we are called upon to judge the constitutionality of an act of a state legislature, "we must have 'due regard to the fact that this Court is not exercising a primary judgment but is sitting in judgment upon those who also have taken the oath to observe the Constitution and who have the responsibility for carrying on government.'" Rostker v. Goldberg, supra, at 64 (quoting Joint Anti-Fascist Refugee Committee v. McGrath, 341 U.S. 123, 164 (1951) (Frankfurter, J., concurring)). This is particularly true, we have said, where the legislature has specifically considered the question of a law's constitutionality. Ibid.

With the foregoing in mind, I now turn to the purposes underlying adoption of the Balanced Treatment Act.

II

II A

We have relatively little information upon which to judge the motives of those who supported the Act. About the only direct evidence is the statute itself and transcripts of the seven committee hearings at which it was considered. Unfortunately, several of those hearings were sparsely attended, and the legislators who were present revealed little about their motives. We have no committee reports, no floor debates, no remarks inserted into the legislative history, no statement from the Governor, and no postenactment statements or testimony from the bill's sponsor or any other legislators. Cf. Wallace v. Jaffree, 472 U.S., at 43, 56-57. Nevertheless, there is ample evidence that the majority is wrong in holding that the Balanced Treatment Act is without secular purpose.

At the outset, it is important to note that the Balanced Treatment Act did not fly through the Louisiana Legislature on wings of fundamentalist religious fervor -- which would be unlikely, in any event, since only a small minority of the State's citizens belong to fundamentalist religious denominations. See B. Quinn, H. Anderson, M. Bradley, P. Goetting, & P. Shriver, Churches and Church Membership in the United States 16 (1982). The Act had its genesis (so to speak) in legislation introduced by Senator Bill Keith in June 1980. After two hearings before the Senate Committee on Education, Senator Keith asked that his bill be referred to a study commission composed of members of both Houses of the Louisiana Legislature. He expressed hope that the joint committee would give the bill careful consideration and determine whether his arguments were "legitimate." 1 App. E-29

-- E-30. The committee met twice during the interim, heard testimony (both for and against the bill) from several witnesses, and received staff reports. Senator Keith introduced his bill again when the legislature reconvened. The Senate Committee on Education held two more hearings and approved the bill after substantially amending it (in part over Senator Keith's objection). After approval by the full Senate, the bill was referred to the House Committee on Education. That committee conducted a lengthy hearing, adopted further amendments, and sent the bill on to the full House, where it received favorable consideration. The Senate concurred in the House amendments and on July 20, 1981, the Governor signed the bill into law.

Senator Keith's statements before the various committees that considered the bill hardly reflect the confidence of a man preaching to the converted. He asked his colleagues to "keep an open mind" and not to be "biased" by misleading characterizations of creation science. Id., at E-33. He also urged them to "look at this subject on its merits and not on some preconceived idea." Id., at E-34; see also 2 id., at E-491. Senator Keith's reception was not especially warm. Over his strenuous objection, the Senate Committee on Education voted 5-1 to amend his bill to deprive it of any force; as amended, the bill merely gave teachers permission to balance the teaching of creation science or evolution with the other. 1 id., at E-442 -- E-461. The House Committee restored the "mandatory" language to the bill by a vote of only 6-5, 2 id., at E-626 -- E-627, and both the full House (by vote of 52-35), id., at E-700 -- E-706, and full Senate (23-15), id., at E-735 -- E-738, had to repel further efforts to gut the bill.

The legislators understood that Senator Keith's bill involved a "unique" subject, 1 id., at E-106 (Rep. M. Thompson), and they were repeatedly made aware of its potential constitutional problems, see, e. g., id., at E-26 -- E-28 (McGehee); id., at E-38 -- E-39 (Sen. Keith); id., at E-241 -- E-242 (Rossman); id., at E-257 (Probst); id., at E-261 (Beck); id., at E-282 (Sen. Keith). Although the Establishment Clause, including its secular purpose requirement, was of substantial concern to the legislators, they eventually voted overwhelmingly in favor of the Balanced Treatment Act: The House approved it 71-19 (with 15 members absent), 2 id., at E-716 -- E-722; the Senate 26-12 (with all members present), id., at E-741 -- E-744. The legislators specifically designated the protection of "academic freedom" as the purpose of the Act. La. Rev. Stat. Ann. @

17:286.2 (West 1982). We cannot accurately assess whether this purpose is a "sham," ante, at 587, until we first examine the evidence presented to the legislature far more carefully than the Court has done.

Before summarizing the testimony of Senator Keith and his supporters, I wish to make clear that I by no means intend to endorse its accuracy. But my views (and the views of this Court) about creation science and evolution are (or should be) beside the point. Our task is not to judge the debate about teaching the origins of life, but to ascertain what the members of the Louisiana Legislature believed. The vast majority of them voted to approve a bill which explicitly stated a secular purpose; what is crucial is not their wisdom in believing that purpose would be achieved by the bill, but their sincerity in believing it would be.

Most of the testimony in support of Senator Keith's bill came from the Senator himself and from scientists and educators he presented, many of whom enjoyed academic credentials that may have been regarded as quite impressive by members of the Louisiana Legislature. To a substantial extent, their testimony was devoted to lengthy, and, to the layman, seemingly expert scientific expositions on the origin of life. See, e. g., 1 App. E-11 -- E-18 (Sunderland); id., at E-50 -- E-60 (Boudreaux); id., at E-86 -- E-89 (Ward); id., at E-130 -- E-153 (Boudreaux paper); id., at E-321 -- E-326 (Boudreaux); id., at E-423 -- E-428 (Sen. Keith). These scientific lectures touched upon, inter alia, biology, paleontology, genetics, astronomy, astrophysics, probability analysis, and biochemistry. The witnesses repeatedly assured committee members that "hundreds and hundreds" of highly respected, internationally renowned scientists believed in creation science and would support their testimony. See, e. g., id., at E-5 (Sunderland); id., at E-76 (Sen. Keith); id., at E-100 -- E-101 (Reiboldt); id., at E-327 -- E-328 (Boudreaux); 2 id., at E-503 -- E-504 (Boudreaux).

Senator Keith and his witnesses testified essentially as set forth in the following numbered paragraphs:

(1) There are two and only two scientific explanations for the beginning of life -- evolution and creation science. 1 id., at E-6 (Sunderland); id., at E-34 (Sen. Keith); id., at E-280 (Sen. Keith); id., at E-417 -- E-418 (Sen. Keith). Both are bona fide "sciences." Id., at E-6 -- E-7 (Sunderland); id., at E-12 (Sunderland); id., at E-416 (Sen. Keith); id., at E-427 (Sen. Keith); 2 id., at E-491 -- E-492 (Sen. Keith); id., at E-497 -- E-498 (Sen. Keith). Both posit a theory of the origin of life and subject that theory to empirical testing. Evolution posits that life arose out of inanimate chemical compounds and has gradually evolved over millions of years. Creation science posits that all life forms now on earth appeared suddenly and relatively recently and have changed little. Since there are only two possible explanations of the origin of life, any evidence that tends to disprove the theory of evolution necessarily tends to prove the theory of creation science, and vice versa. For example, the abrupt appearance in the fossil record of complex life, and the extreme rarity of transitional life forms in that record, are evidence for creation science. 1 id., at E-7 (Sunderland); id., at E-12 -- E-18 (Sunderland); id., at E-45 -- E-60 (Boudreaux); id., at E-67 (Harlow); id., at E-130 -- E-153 (Boudreaux paper); id., at E-423 -- E-428 (Sen. Keith).

(2) The body of scientific evidence supporting creation science is as strong as that supporting evolution. In fact, it may be stronger. Id., at E-214 (Young statement); id., at E-310 (Sen. Keith); id., at E-416 (Sen. Keith); 2 id., at E-492 (Sen. Keith). The evidence for evolution is far less compelling than we have been led to believe. Evolution is not a scientific "fact," since it cannot actually be observed in a laboratory. Rather, evolution is merely a scientific theory or "guess." 1 id., at E-20 -- E-21 (Morris); id., at E-85 (Ward); id., at E-100 (Reiboldt); id., at E-328 -- E-329 (Boudreaux); 2 id., at E-506

(Boudreaux). It is a very bad guess at that. The scientific problems with evolution are so serious that it could accurately be termed a "myth." 1 id., at E-85 (Ward); id., at E-92 -- E-93 (Kalivoda); id., at E-95 -- E-97 (Sen. Keith); id., at E-154 (Boudreaux paper); id., at E-329 (Boudreaux); id., at E-453 (Sen. Keith); 2 id., at E-505 -- E-506 (Boudreaux); id., at E-516 (Young).

(3) Creation science is educationally valuable. Students exposed to it better understand the current state of scientific evidence about the origin of life. 1 id., at E-19 (Sunderland); id., at E-39 (Sen. Keith); id., at E-79 (Kalivoda); id., at E-308 (Sen. Keith); 2 id., at E-513 -- E-514 (Morris). Those students even have a better understanding of evolution. 1 id., at E-19 (Sunderland). Creation science can and should be presented to children without any religious content. Id., at E-12 (Sunderland); id., at E-22 (Sanderford); id., at E-35 -- E-36 (Sen. Keith); id., at E-101 (Reiboldt); id., at E-279 -- E-280 (Sen. Keith); id., at E-282 (Sen. Keith).

(4) Although creation science is educationally valuable and strictly scientific, it is now being censored from or misrepresented in the public schools. Id., at E-19 (Sunderland); id., at E-21 (Morris); id., at E-34 (Sen. Keith); id., at E-37 (Sen. Keith); id., at E-42 (Sen. Keith); id., at E-92 (Kalivoda); id., at E-97 -- E-98 (Reiboldt); id., at E-214 (Young statement); id., at E-218 (Young statement); id., at E-280 (Sen. Keith); id., at E-309 (Sen. Keith); 2 id., at E-513 (Morris). Evolution, in turn, is misrepresented as an absolute truth. 1 id., at E-63 (Harlow); id., at E-74 (Sen. Keith); id., at E-81 (Kalivoda); id., at E-214 (Young statement); 2 id., at E-507 (Harlow); id., at E-513 (Morris); id., at E-516 (Young). Teachers have been brainwashed by an entrenched scientific establishment composed almost exclusively of scientists to whom evolution is like a "religion." These scientists discriminate against creation scientists so as to prevent evolution's weaknesses from being exposed. 1 id., at E-61 (Boudreaux); id., at E-63 --

E-64 (Harlow); id., at E-78 -- E-79 (Kalivoda); id., at E-80 (Kalivoda); id., at E-95 -- E-97 (Sen. Keith); id., at E-129 (Boudreaux paper); id., at E-218 (Young statement); id., at E-357 (Sen. Keith); id., at E-430 (Boudreaux).

(5) The censorship of creation science has at least two harmful effects. First, it deprives students of knowledge of one of the two scientific explanations for the origin of life and leads them to believe that evolution is proven fact; thus, their education suffers and they are wrongly taught that science has proved their religious beliefs false. Second, it violates the Establishment Clause. The United States Supreme Court has held that secular humanism is a religion. Id., at E-36 (Sen. Keith) (referring to Torcaso v. Watkins, 367 U.S. 488, 495, n. 11 (1961)); 1 App. E-418 (Sen. Keith); 2 id., at E-499 (Sen. Keith). Belief in evolution is a central tenet of that religion. 1 id., at E-282 (Sen. Keith); id., at E-312 -- E-313 (Sen. Keith); id., at E-317 (Sen. Keith); id., at E-418 (Sen. Keith); 2 id., at E-499 (Sen. Keith). Thus, by censoring creation science and instructing students that evolution is fact, public school teachers are now advancing religion in violation of the Establishment Clause. 1 id., at E-2 -- E-4 (Sen. Keith); id., at E-36 -- E-37, E-39 (Sen. Keith); id., at E-154 -- E-155 (Boudreaux paper); id., at E-281 -- E-282 (Sen. Keith); id., at E-313 (Sen. Keith); id., at E-315 -- E-316 (Sen. Keith); id., at E-317 (Sen. Keith); 2 id., at E-499 -- E-500 (Sen. Keith).

Senator Keith repeatedly and vehemently denied that his purpose was to advance a particular religious doctrine. At the outset of the first hearing on the legislation, he testified: "We are not going to say today that you should have some kind of religious instructions in our schools. . . . We are not talking about religion today. . . . I am not proposing that we take the Bible in each science class and read the first chapter of Genesis." 1 id., at E-35. At a later hearing, Senator Keith stressed: "To . . . teach religion and disguise it as creationism . . . is not my intent. My intent is to see to it that our textbooks are not censored." Id., at E-280. He made many similar statements throughout the hearings. See, e. g., id., at E-41; id., at E-282; id., at E-310; id., at E-417; see also id., at E-44 (Boudreaux); id., at E-80 (Kalivoda).

We have no way of knowing, of course, how many legislators believed the testimony of Senator Keith and his witnesses. But in the absence of evidence to the contrary (4), we have to assume that many of them did. Given that assumption, the Court today plainly errs in holding that the Louisiana Legislature passed the Balanced Treatment Act for exclusively religious purposes.

II B

Even with nothing more than this legislative history to go on, I think it would be extraordinary to invalidate the Balanced Treatment Act for lack of a valid secular purpose. Striking down a law approved by the democratically elected representatives of the people is no minor matter. "The cardinal principle of statutory construction is to save and not to destroy. We have repeatedly held that as between two possible interpretations of a statute, by one of which it would be unconstitutional and by the other valid, our plain duty is to adopt that which will save the act." NLRB v. Jones & Laughlin Steel Corp., 301 U.S. 1, 30 (1937). So, too, it seems to me, with discerning statutory purpose. Even if the legislative history were silent or ambiguous about the existence of a secular purpose -- and here it is not -- the statute should survive Lemon's purpose test. But even more validation than mere legislative history is present here. The Louisiana Legislature explicitly set forth its secular purpose ( "protecting academic freedom") in the very text of the Act. La. Rev. Stat. @ 17:286.2 (West 1982). We have in the past repeatedly relied upon or deferred to such expressions, see, e. g., Committee for Public Education & Religious Liberty v. Regan, 444 U.S., at 654; Meek v. Pittenger, 421 U.S., at 363, 367-368;

Committee for Public Education & Religious Liberty v. Nyquist, 413 U.S., at 773; Levitt v. Committee for Public Education & Religious Liberty, 413 U.S., at 479-480, n. 7; Tilton v. Richardson, 403 U.S., at 678-679 (plurality opinion); Lemon v. Kurtzman, 403 U.S., at 613; Board of Education v. Allen, 392 U.S., at 243.

The Court seeks to evade the force of this expression of purpose by stubbornly misinterpreting it, and then finding that the provisions of the Act do not advance that misinterpreted purpose, thereby showing it to be a sham. The Court first surmises that "academic freedom" means "enhancing the freedom of teachers to teach what they will," ante, at 586 -- even though "academic freedom" in that sense has little scope in the structured elementary and secondary curriculums with which the Act is concerned. Alternatively, the Court suggests that it might mean "maximiz[ing] the comprehensiveness and effectiveness of science instruction," ante, at 588 -- though that is an exceedingly strange interpretation of the words, and one that is refuted on the very face of the statute. See @ 17:286.5. Had the Court devoted to this central question of the meaning of the legislatively expressed purpose a small fraction of the research into legislative history that produced its quotations of religiously motivated statements by individual legislators, it would have discerned quite readily what "academic freedom" meant: students' freedom from indoctrination. The legislature wanted to ensure that students would be free to decide for themselves how life began, based upon a fair and balanced presentation of the scientific evidence -- that is, to protect "the right of each [student] voluntarily to determine what to believe (and what not to believe) free of any coercive pressures from the State." Grand Rapids School District v. Ball, 473 U.S., at 385. The legislature did not care whether the topic of origins was taught; it simply wished to ensure that when the topic was taught, students would receive "'all of the evidence.'" Ante, at 586 (quoting Tr. of Oral Arg. 60).

As originally introduced, the "purpose" section of the Balanced Treatment Act read: "This Chapter is enacted for the purposes of protecting academic freedom . . . of students . . . and assisting students in their search for truth." 1 App. E-292 (emphasis added). Among the proposed findings of fact contained in the original version of the bill was the following: "Public school instruction in only evolution-science . . . violates the principle of academic freedom because it denies students a choice between scientific models and instead indoctrinates them in evolution science alone." Id., at E-295 (emphasis added). Senator Keith unquestionably understood "academic freedom" to mean "freedom from indoctrination." See id., at E-36 (purpose of bill is "to protect academic freedom by providing student choice"); id., at E-283 (purpose of bill is to protect "academic freedom" by giving students a "choice" rather than subjecting them to "indoctrination on origins")

If one adopts the obviously intended meaning of the statutory term "academic freedom," there is no basis whatever for concluding that the purpose they express is a "sham." Ante, at 587. To the contrary, the Act pursues that purpose plainly and consistently. It requires that, whenever the subject of origins is covered, evolution be "taught as a theory, rather than as proven scientific fact" and that scientific evidence inconsistent with the theory of evolution (viz., "creation science") be taught as well. La. Rev. Stat. Ann. @ 17:286.4A (West 1982). Living up to its title of "Balanced Treatment for Creation-Science and Evolution-Science Act," @ 17.286.1, it treats the teaching of creation the same way. It does not mandate instruction in creation science, @ 17:286.5; forbids teachers to present creation science "as proven scientific fact," @ 17:286.4A; and bans the teaching of creation science unless the theory is (to use the Court's terminology) "discredit[ed] '. . . at every turn'" with the teaching of evolution. Ante, at 589 (quoting 765 F.2d, at 1257). It surpasses understanding how the Court can see in this a purpose "to restructure the science curriculum to conform with a particular religious viewpoint," ante, at 593,"to provide a persuasive advantage to a particular religious doctrine," ante, at 592,"to promote the theory of creation science which embodies a particular religious tenet," ante, at 593, and "to endorse a particular religious doctrine," ante, at 594.

The Act's reference to "creation" is not convincing evidence of religious purpose. The Act defines creation science as "scientific evidenc[e]," @ 17:286.3(2) (emphasis added), and Senator Keith and his witnesses repeatedly stressed that the subject can and should be presented without religious content. See supra, at 623. We have no basis on the record to conclude that creation science need be anything other than a collection of scientific data supporting the theory that life abruptly appeared on earth. See n. 4, supra. Creation science, its proponents insist, no more must explain whence life came than evolution must explain whence came the inanimate materials from which it says life evolved. But even if that were not so, to posit a past creator is not to posit the eternal and personal God who is the object of religious veneration. Indeed, it is not even to posit the "unmoved mover" hypothesized by Aristotle and other notably nonfundamentalist philosophers. Senator Keith suggested this when he referred to "a creator however you define a creator." 1 App. E-280 (emphasis added).

The Court cites three provisions of the Act which, it argues, demonstrate a "discriminatory preference for the teaching of creation science" and no interest in "academic freedom." Ante, at 588. First, the Act prohibits discrimination only against creation scientists and those who teach creation science. @ 17:286.4C. Second, the Act requires local school boards to develop and provide to science teachers "a curriculum guide on presentation of creation-science." @ 17:286.7A. Finally, the Act requires the Governor to designate seven creation scientists who shall, upon request, assist local school boards in developing the curriculum guides. @ 17:286.7B. But none of these provisions casts doubt upon the sincerity of the legislators' articulated purpose of "academic freedom" -- unless, of course, one gives that term the obviously erroneous meanings preferred by the Court. The Louisiana legislators had been told repeatedly that creation scientists were scorned by most educators and scientists, who themselves had an almost religious faith in evolution. It is hardly surprising, then, that in seeking to achieve a balanced,"nonindoctrinating" curriculum, the legislators protected from discrimination only those teachers whom they thought were suffering from discrimination. (Also, the legislators were undoubtedly aware of Epperson v. Arkansas, 393 U.S. 97 (1968), and thus could quite reasonably have concluded that discrimination against evolutionists was already prohibited.) The two provisions respecting the development of curriculum guides are also consistent with "academic freedom" as the Louisiana Legislature understood the term. Witnesses had informed the legislators that, because of the hostility of most scientists and educators to creation science, the topic had been censored from or badly misrepresented in elementary and secondary school texts. In light of the unavailability of works on creation science suitable for classroom use (a fact appellees concede, see Brief for Appellees 27, 40) and the existence of ample materials on evolution, it was entirely reasonable for the legislature to conclude that science teachers attempting to implement the Act would need a curriculum guide on creation science, but not on evolution, and that those charged with developing the guide would need an easily accessible group of creation scientists. Thus, the provisions of the Act of so much concern to the Court support the conclusion that the legislature acted to advance "academic freedom."

The legislative history gives ample evidence of the sincerity of the Balanced Treatment Act's articulated purpose. Witness after witness urged the legislators to support the Act so that students would not be "indoctrinated" but would instead be free to decide for themselves, based upon a fair presentation of the scientific evidence, about the origin of life. See, e. g., 1 App. E-18 (Sunderland) ( "all that we are advocating" is presenting "scientific data" to students and "letting [them] make up their own mind[s]"); id., at E-19 -- E-20 (Sunderland) (Students are now being "indoctrinated" in evolution through the use of "censored school books. . . . All that we are asking for is [the] open unbiased education in the classroom . . . your students deserve"); id., at E-21 (Morris) ( "A student cannot [make an intelligent decision about the origin of life] unless he is well informed about both [evolution and creation science]"); id., at E-22 (Sanderford) ( "We are asking very simply [that] . . . creationism [be presented] alongside . . . evolution and let people make their own mind[s] up"); id., at E-23 (Young) (the bill would require teachers to live up to their "obligation to present all theories" and thereby enable "students to make judgments themselves"); id., at E-44 (Boudreaux) ( "Our intention is truth and as a scientist, I am interested in truth"); id., at E-60 -- E-61 (Boudreaux) ( "We [teachers] are guilty of a lot of brainwashing. . . . We have a duty to . . . [present the] truth" to students "at all levels from gradeschool on through the college level"); id., at E-79 (Kalivoda) ( "This [hearing] is being held I think to determine whether children will benefit from freedom of information or if they will be handicapped educationally by having little or no information about creation"); id., at E-80 (Kalivoda) ( "I am not interested in teaching religion in schools. . . . I am interested in the truth and [students] having the opportunity to hear more than one side"); id., at E-98 (Reiboldt) ( "The students have a right to know there is an alternate creationist point of view. They have a right to know the scientific evidences which suppor[t] that alternative"); id., at E-218 (Young statement) (passage of the bill will ensure that "communication of scientific ideas and discoveries may be unhindered"); 2 id., at E-514 (Morris) ( "Are we going to allow [students] to look at evolution, to look at creationism, and to let one or the other stand or fall on its own merits, or will we by failing to pass this bill . . . deny students an opportunity to hear another viewpoint?"); id., at E-516 -- E-517 (Young) ( "We want to give the children here in this state an equal opportunity to see both sides of the theories"). Senator Keith expressed similar views. See, e. g., 1 id., at E-36; id., at E-41; id., at E-280; id., at E-283.

Legislators other than Senator Keith made only a few statements providing insight into their motives, but those statements cast no doubt upon the sincerity of the Act's articulated purpose. The legislators were concerned primarily about the manner in which the subject of origins was presented in Louisiana schools -- specifically, about whether scientifically valuable information was being censored and students misled about evolution. Representatives Cain, Jenkins, and F. Thompson seemed impressed by the scientific evidence presented in support of creation science. See 2 id., at E-530 (Rep. F. Thompson); id., at E-533 (Rep. Cain); id., at E-613 (Rep. Jenkins). At the first study commission hearing, Senator Picard and Representative M. Thompson questioned Senator Keith about Louisiana teachers' treatment of evolution and creation science. See 1 id., at E-71 -- E-74. At the close of the hearing, Representative M. Thompson told the audience:

"We as members of the committee will also receive from the staff information of what is currently being taught in the Louisiana public schools. We really want to see [it]. I . . . have no idea in what manner [biology] is presented and in what manner the creationist theories [are] excluded in the public school[s]. We want to look at what the status of the situation is." Id., at E-104.

Legislators made other comments suggesting a concern about censorship and misrepresentation of scientific information. See, e. g., id., at E-386 (Sen. McLeod); 2 id., at E-527 (Rep. Jenkins); id., at E-528 (Rep. M. Thompson); id., at E-534 (Rep. Fair).

It is undoubtedly true that what prompted the legislature to direct its attention to the misrepresentation of evolution in the schools (rather than the inaccurate presentation of other topics) was its awareness of the tension between evolution and the religious beliefs of many children. But even appellees concede that a valid secular purpose is not rendered impermissible simply because its pursuit is prompted by concern for religious sensitivities. Tr. of Oral Arg. 43, 56. If a history teacher falsely told her students that the bones of Jesus Christ had been discovered, or a physics teacher that the Shroud of Turin had been conclusively established to be inexplicable on the basis of natural causes, I cannot believe (despite the majority's implication to the contrary, see ante, at 592-593) that legislators or school board members would be constitutionally prohibited from taking corrective action, simply because that action was prompted by concern for the religious beliefs of the misinstructed students.

In sum, even if one concedes, for the sake of argument, that a majority of the Louisiana Legislature voted for the Balanced Treatment Act partly in order to foster (rather than merely eliminate discrimination against) Christian fundamentalist beliefs, our cases establish that that alone would not suffice to invalidate the Act, so long as there was a genuine secular purpose as well. We have, moreover, no adequate basis for disbelieving the secular purpose set forth in the Act itself, or for concluding that it is a sham enacted to conceal the legislators' violation of their oaths of office. I am astonished by the Court's unprecedented readiness to reach such a conclusion, which I can only attribute to an intellectual predisposition created by the facts and the legend of

Scopes v. State, 154 Tenn. 105, 289 S. W. 363 (1927) -- an instinctive reaction that any governmentally imposed requirements bearing upon the teaching of evolution must be a manifestation of Christian fundamentalist repression. In this case, however, it seems to me the Court's position is the repressive one. The people of Louisiana, including those who are Christian fundamentalists, are quite entitled, as a secular matter, to have whatever scientific evidence there may be against evolution presented in their schools, just as Mr. Scopes was entitled to present whatever scientific evidence there was for it. Perhaps what the Louisiana Legislature has done is unconstitutional because there is no such evidence, and the scheme they have established will amount to no more than a presentation of the Book of Genesis. But we cannot say that on the evidence before us in this summary judgment context, which includes ample uncontradicted testimony that "creation science" is a body of scientific knowledge rather than revealed belief. Infinitely less can we say (or should we say) that the scientific evidence for evolution is so conclusive that no one could be gullible enough to believe that there is any real scientific evidence to the contrary, so that the legislation's stated purpose must be a lie. Yet that illiberal judgment, that Scopes-in-reverse, is ultimately the basis on which the Court's facile rejection of the Louisiana Legislature's purpose must rest.

Since the existence of secular purpose is so entirely clear, and thus dispositive, I will not go on to discuss the fact that, even if the Louisiana Legislature's purpose were exclusively to advance religion, some of the well-established exceptions to the impermissibility of that purpose might be applicable -- the validating intent to eliminate a perceived discrimination against a particular religion, to facilitate its free exercise, or to accommodate it. See supra, at 617-618. I am not in any case enamored of those amorphous exceptions, since I think them no more than unpredictable correctives to what is (as the next Part of this opinion will discuss) a fundamentally unsound rule. It is surprising, however, that the Court does not address these exceptions, since the context of the legislature's action gives some reason to believe they may be applicable. (6)

Because I believe that the Balanced Treatment Act had a secular purpose, which is all the first component of the Lemon test requires, I would reverse the judgment of the Court of Appeals and remand for further consideration.

III

I have to this point assumed the validity of the Lemon "purpose" test. In fact, however, I think the pessimistic evaluation that THE CHIEF JUSTICE made of the totality of Lemon is particularly applicable to the "purpose" prong: it is "a constitutional theory [that] has no basis in the history of the amendment it seeks to interpret, is difficult to apply and yields unprincipled results ..." Wallace v. Jaffree, 472 U.S., at 112 (REHNQUIST, J., dissenting).

Our cases interpreting and applying the purpose test have made such a maze of the Establishment Clause that even the most conscientious governmental officials can only guess what motives will be held unconstitutional. We have said essentially the following: Government may not act with the purpose of advancing religion, except when forced to do so by the Free Exercise Clause (which is now and then); or when eliminating existing governmental hostility to religion (which exists sometimes); or even when merely accommodating governmentally uninhibited religious practices, except that at some point (it is unclear where) intentional accommodation results in the fostering of religion, which is of course unconstitutional. See supra, at 614-618.

But the difficulty of knowing what vitiating purpose one is looking for is as nothing compared with the difficulty of knowing how or where to find it. For while it is possible to discern the objective "purpose" of a statute (i. e., the public good at which its provisions appear to be directed), or even the formal motivation for a statute where that is explicitly set forth (as it was, to no avail, here), discerning the subjective motivation of those enacting the statute is, to be honest, almost always an impossible task. The number of possible motivations, to begin with, is not binary, or indeed even finite. In the present case, for example, a particular legislator need not have voted for the Act either because he wanted to foster religion or because he wanted to improve education. He may have thought the bill would provide jobs for his district, or may have wanted to make amends with a faction of his party he had alienated on another vote, or he may have been a close friend of the bill's sponsor, or he may have been repaying a favor he owed the Majority Leader, or he may have hoped the Governor would appreciate his vote and make a fundraising appearance for him, or he may have been pressured to vote for a bill he disliked by a wealthy contributor or by a flood of constituent mail, or he may have been seeking favorable publicity, or he may have been reluctant to hurt the feelings of a loyal staff member who worked on the bill, or he may have been settling an old score with a legislator who opposed the bill, or he may have been mad at his wife who opposed the bill, or he may have been intoxicated and utterly unmotivated when the vote was called, or he may have accidentally voted "yes" instead of "no," or, of course, he may have had (and very likely did have) a combination of some of the above and many other motivations. To look for the sole purpose of even a single legislator is probably to look for something that does not exist.

Putting that problem aside, however, where ought we to look for the individual legislator's purpose? We cannot of course assume that every member present (if, as is unlikely, we know who or even how many they were) agreed with the motivation expressed in a particular legislator's preenactment floor or committee statement. Quite obviously, "what motivates one legislator to make a speech about a statute is not necessarily what motivates scores of others to enact it." United States v. O'Brien, 391 U.S. 367, 384 (1968). Can we assume, then, that they all agree with the motivation expressed in the staff-prepared committee reports they might have read -- even though we are unwilling to assume that they agreed with the motivation expressed in the very statute that they voted for? Should we consider postenactment floor statements? Or postenactment testimony from legislators, obtained expressly for the lawsuit? Should we consider media reports on the realities of the legislative bargaining? All of these sources, of course, are eminently manipulable. Legislative histories can be contrived and sanitized, favorable media coverage orchestrated, and postenactment recollections conveniently distorted. Perhaps most valuable of all would be more objective indications -- for example, evidence regarding the individual legislators' religious affiliations. And if that, why not evidence regarding the fervor or tepidity of their beliefs?

Having achieved, through these simple means, an assessment of what individual legislators intended, we must still confront the question (yet to be addressed in any of our cases) how many of them must have the invalidating intent. If a state senate approves a bill by vote of 26 to 25, and only one of the 26 intended solely to advance religion, is the law unconstitutional? What if 13 of the 26 had that intent? What if 3 of the 26 had the impermissible intent, but 3 of the 25 voting against the bill were motivated by religious hostility or were simply attempting to "balance" the votes of their impermissibly motivated colleagues? Or is it possible that the intent of the bill's sponsor is alone enough to invalidate it -- on a theory, perhaps, that even though everyone else's intent was pure, what they produced was the fruit of a forbidden tree?

Because there are no good answers to these questions, this Court has recognized from Chief Justice Marshall, see Fletcher v. Peck, 6 Cranch 87, 130 (1810), to Chief Justice Warren, United States v. O'Brien, supra, at 383-384, that determining the subjective intent of legislators is a perilous enterprise. See also Palmer v. Thompson, 403 U.S. 217, 224-225 (1971); Epperson v. Arkansas, 393 U.S., at 113 (Black, J., concurring). It is perilous, I might note, not just for the judges who will very likely reach the wrong result, but also for the legislators who find that they must assess the validity of proposed legislation -- and risk the condemnation of having voted for an unconstitutional measure -- not on the basis of what the legislation contains, nor even on the basis of what they themselves intend, but on the basis of what others have in mind.

Given the many hazards involved in assessing the subjective intent of governmental decision makers, the first prong of Lemon is defensible, I think, only if the text of the Establishment Clause demands it. That is surely not the case. The Clause states that "Congress shall make no law respecting an establishment of religion." One could argue, I suppose, that any time Congress acts with the intent of advancing religion, it has enacted a "law respecting an establishment of religion"; but far from being an unavoidable reading, it is quite an unnatural one. I doubt, for example, that the Clayton Act, 38 Stat. 730, as amended, 15 U. S. C. @ 12 et seq., could reasonably be described as a "law respecting an establishment of religion" if bizarre new historical evidence revealed that it lacked a secular purpose, even though it has no discernible nonsecular effect. It is, in short, far from an inevitable reading of the Establishment Clause that it forbids all governmental action intended to advance religion; and if not inevitable, any reading with such untoward consequences must be wrong.

In the past we have attempted to justify our embarrassing Establishment Clause jurisprudence (7) on the ground that it "sacrifices clarity and predictability for flexibility. " Committee for Public Education & Religious Liberty v. Regan, 444 U.S., at 662. One commentator has aptly characterized this as "a euphemism . . . for . . . the absence of any principled rationale." Choper, supra n. 7, at 681. I think it time that we sacrifice some "flexibility" for "clarity and predictability." Abandoning Lemon's purpose test -- a test which exacerbates the tension between the Free Exercise and Establishment Clauses, has no basis in the language or history of the Amendment, and, as today's decision shows, has wonderfully flexible consequences -- would be a good place to start.

Notes:

1. Article VI, cl. 3, of the Constitution provides that "the Members of the several State Legislatures . . . shall be bound by Oath or Affirmation, to support this Constitution."

2. Thus the popular dictionary definitions cited by JUSTICE POWELL, ante, at 598-599 (concurring opinion), and appellees, see Brief for Appellees 25, 26; Tr. of Oral Arg. 32, 34, are utterly irrelevant, as are the views of the school superintendents cited by the majority, ante, at 595, n. 18. Three-quarters of those surveyed had "no" or "limited" knowledge of "creation-science theory," and not a single superintendent claimed "extensive" knowledge of the subject. 2 App. E-798.

3. Although creation scientists and evolutionists also disagree about the origin of the physical universe, both proponents and opponents of Senator Keith's bill focused on the question of the beginning of life.

4. Although appellees and amici dismiss the testimony of Senator Keith and his witnesses as pure fantasy, they did not bother to submit evidence of that to the District

Court, making it difficult for us to agree with them. The State, by contrast, submitted the affidavits of two scientists, a philosopher, a theologian, and an educator, whose academic credentials are rather impressive. See App. to Juris. Statement A-17 -- A-18 (Kenyon); id., at A-36 (Morrow); id., at A-39 -- A-40 (Miethe); id., at A-46 -- A-47 (Most); id., at A-49 (Clinkert). Like Senator Keith and his witnesses, the affiants swear that evolution and creation science are the only two scientific explanations for the origin of life, see id., at A-19 -- A-20 (Kenyon); id., at A-38 (Morrow); id., at A-41 (Miethe); that creation science is strictly scientific, see id., at A-18 (Kenyon); id., at A-36 (Morrow); id., at A-40 -- A-41 (Miethe); id., at A-49 (Clinkert); that creation science is simply a collection of scientific data that supports the hypothesis that life appeared on earth suddenly and has changed little, see id., at A-19 (Kenyon); id., at A-36 (Morrow); id., at A-41 (Miethe); that hundreds of respected scientists believe in creation science, see id., at A-20 (Kenyon); that evidence for creation science is as strong as evidence for evolution, see id., at A-21 (Kenyon); id., at A-34 -- A-35 (Kenyon); id., at A-37 -- A-38 (Morrow); that creation science is educationally valuable, see id., at A-19 (Kenyon); id., at A-36 (Morrow); id., at A-38 -- A-39 (Morrow); id., at A-49 (Clinkert); that creation science can be presented without religious content, see id., at A-19 (Kenyon); id., at A-35 (Kenyon); id., at A-36 (Morrow); id., at A-40 (Miethe); id., at A-43 -- A-44 (Miethe); id., at A-47 (Most); id., at A-49 (Clinkert); and that creation science is now censored from classrooms while evolution is misrepresented as proven fact, see id., at A-20 (Kenyon); id., at A-35 (Kenyon); id., at A-39 (Morrow); id., at A-50 (Clinkert). It is difficult to conclude on the basis of these affidavits -- the only substantive evidence in the record -- that the laymen serving in the Louisiana Legislature must have disbelieved Senator Keith or his witnesses.

5. The majority finds it "astonishing" that I would cite a portion of Senator Keith's original bill that was later deleted as evidence of the legislature's understanding of the phrase "academic freedom." Ante, at 589, n. 8. What is astonishing is the majority's implication that the deletion of that section deprives it of value as a clear indication of what the phrase meant -- there and in the other, retained, sections of the bill. The Senate Committee on Education deleted most of the lengthy "purpose" section of the bill (with Senator Keith's consent) because it resembled legislative "findings of fact," which, committee members felt, should generally not be incorporated in legislation. The deletion had absolutely nothing to do with the manner in which the section described "academic freedom." See 1 App. E-314 -- E-320; id., at E-440 -- E-442.

6. As the majority recognizes, ante, at 592, Senator Keith sincerely believed that "secular humanism is a bona fide religion," 1 App. E-36; see also id., at E-418; 2 id., at E-499, and that "evolution is the cornerstone of that religion," 1 id., at E-418; see also id., at E-282; id., at E-312 -- E-313; id., at E-317; 2 id., at E-499. The Senator even told his colleagues that this Court had "held" that secular humanism was a religion. See 1 id., at E-36, id., at E-418; 2 id., at E-499. (In Torcaso v. Watkins, 367 U.S. 488, 495, n. 11 (1961), we did indeed refer to "Secular Humanism" as a "religio[n].") Senator Keith and his supporters raised the "religion" of secular humanism not, as the majority suggests, to explain the source of their "disdain for the theory of evolution," ante, at 592, but to convince the legislature that the State of Louisiana was violating the Establishment Clause because its teachers were misrepresenting evolution as fact and depriving students of the information necessary to question that theory. 1 App. E-2 -- E-4 (Sen. Keith); id., at E-36 -- E-37, E-39 (Sen. Keith); id., at E-154 -- E-155 (Boudreaux paper); id., at E-281 -- E-282 (Sen. Keith); id., at E-317 (Sen. Keith); 2 id., at E-499 -- E-500

(Sen. Keith). The Senator repeatedly urged his colleagues to pass his bill to remedy this Establishment Clause violation by ensuring state neutrality in religious matters, see, e. g., 1 id., at E-36; id., at E-39; id., at E-313, surely a permissible purpose under Lemon. Senator Keith's argument may be questionable, but nothing in the statute or its legislative history gives us reason to doubt his sincerity or that of his supporters.

7. Professor Choper summarized our school aid cases thusly:

"[A] provision for therapeutic and diagnostic health services to parochial school pupils by public employees is invalid if provided in the parochial school, but not if offered at a neutral site, even if in a mobile unit adjacent to the parochial school. Reimbursement to parochial schools for the expense of administering teacher-prepared tests required by state law is invalid, but the state may reimburse parochial schools for the expense of administering state-prepared tests. The state may lend school textbooks to parochial school pupils because, the Court has explained, the books can be checked in advance for religious content and are 'self-policing'; but the state may not lend other seemingly self-policing instructional items such as tape recorders and maps. The state may pay the cost of bus transportation to parochial schools, which the Court has ruled are 'permeated' with religion; but the state is forbidden to pay for field trip transportation visits 'to governmental, industrial, cultural, and scientific centers designed to enrich the secular studies of students.'" Choper, The Religion Clauses of the First Amendment: Reconciling the Conflict, 41 U. Pitt. L. Rev. 673, 680-681 (1980) (footnotes omitted).

Since that was written, more decisions on the subject have been rendered, but they leave the theme of chaos securely unimpaired. See, e. g., Aguilar v.Felton, 473 U.S.

402 (1985); Grand Rapids School District v. Ball, 473 U.S. 373 (1985).

*Webster v. New Lenox School District,* 1990, the Seventh Circuit Court of Appeals

(Author's Note: Italicized material represents direct quotations. Material in regular type represents the author's comments.)

(The following paragraph is not part of a trial transcript, but is quoted from the website Voices For Evolution)

In 1990, in Webster v. New Lenox School District, the Seventh Circuit Court of Appeals found that a school district may prohibit a teacher from teaching creation science, in fulfilling its responsibility to ensure that the First Amendment's establishment clause is not violated, and religious beliefs are not injected into the public school curriculum. The court upheld a district court finding that the school district had not violated Webster's free speech rights when it prohibited him from teaching "creation science," since it is a form of religious advocacy. (Webster v. New Lenox School District #122, 917 F. 2d 1004)

This case stands out among the others because it does not deal directly with Science teaching. The plaintiff in this case was a junior-high Social Studies teacher. As shown in the background section of the transcript, Webster's classroom textbook contained a statement that the world was more than four billion years old. It didn't propose it as a theory. It didn't say there was a possibility it might not be four billion years old. It just made a statement without qualification.

The one thing that ought to be noticed here is, in the case of Segrave vs State of California, 1981, that state had an anti-dogmatism law. This should mean, in simplest terms, that theories can't be taught as facts. Yet if you look at the thousands of textbooks and millions of even quasi-educational materials on every possible subject available to children, from post-graduate doctoral material to preschool "world explorer" cartoons, this is the way they always state their dogma. Not "studies suggest an age of four billion years for the earth," or "Scientists have said the earth may be more than four billion years old." It's stated as a fact. Our eyes run right past it now because it's so common. History books begin with Cro-Magnon and Neanderthal man, or maybe even Australopithecus Afarensis, the so-called "Lucy" fossil. Literature survey books cover "prehistory" such as cave paintings and attribute them to an earlier link to modern man. And the information is presented as factual, not theoretical.

Author's Note: The format of this transcript is somewhat unusual so the following should help to clarify its presentation here. The transcript is presented in its original format. Structure and headings (such as the Roman numeral I and the heading entitled Background) are part of the original document. All quoted material appears in italic type. Commentary by the author appears in regular type, in various places throughout. Occasionally the author picks up a quote to repeat, and this material also appears in italic type. The heading information from the very beginning of the original document, with the title of the case and various legal listings has been omitted. The transcript reproduced here begins with the name of the presiding judge and a statement of the case.

Ripple, Circuit Judge. Ray Webster sought injunctive and declaratory relief based on his claim that the New Lenox School District violated his first and fourteenth amendment rights by prohibiting him from teaching a nonevolutionary theory of creation in the classroom. He appeals the dismissal of his complaint for failure to state a claim. For the following reasons, we affirm the judgment of the district court.

I

Background

The district court dismissed Mr. Webster's suit for failure to state a claim upon which relief can be granted. See Fed. R. Civ. P. 12(b)(6). The grant of a motion to dismiss is, of course, reviewed de novo. Villegas v. Princeton Farms, Inc., 893 F.2d 919, 924 (7th Cir. 1990); Corcoran v. Chicago Park Dist., 875 F2d 609, 611 (7th Cir. 1989). It is well settled that, when reviewing the grant of a motion to dismiss, we must assume the truth of all well-pleaded factual allegations and make all possible inferences in favor of the plaintiff. Janowsky v. United States, No. 89-2219, slip op. at 4 (7th Cir. Sept. 17, 1990); Rogers v. United States, 902, F.2d 1268, 1269 (7th Cir. 1990).

A complaint should not be dismissed "unless it appears beyond doubt that the plaintiff can prove no set of facts in support of his claim which would entitle him to relief." Conley v. Gibson, 355 U. S. 41, 45-46 (1957). This obligation is especially serious when, as here, we deal with allegations involving the freedom of expression protected by the first amendment. See Stewart v. District of Columbia Armory Bd., 863 F.2d 1013, 1017-18 (D.C. Cir. 1988) ( "where government action is challenged on first amendment grounds, a court should be especially 'unwilling to decide the legal questions posed by the parties without a more thoroughly developed record of proceedings in which the parties have an opportunity to prove those disputed factual assertions upon which they rely'") (quoting City of Los Angeles v. Preferred Communications, 476 U.S. 488, 494 (1986)). Courts may, however, consider exhibits attached to the complaint as part of the pleadings. Beam v. IPCO Corp., 838 F.2d 242, 244 (1988). With these constraints in mind, we set forth the pertinent facts.

A. Facts

Ray Webster teaches social studies at the Oster-Oakview Junior High School in New Lenox, Illinois. In the spring of 1987, a student in Mr. Webster's social studies class complained that Mr. Webster's teaching methods violated principles of separation between church and state. In addition to the student, both the American Civil Liberties Union and the Americans United for the Separation of Church and State objected to Mr. Webster's teaching practices. Mr. Webster denied the allegations. On July 31, 1987, the New Lenox school board (school board), through its superintendent, advised Mr. Webster by letter that he should restrict his classroom instruction to the curriculum and refrain from advocating a particular religious viewpoint.

Believing the superintendent's letter vague, Mr. Webster asked for further clarification in a letter dated September 4, 1987. In this letter, Mr. Webster also set forth his teaching methods and philosophy. Mr. Webster stated that the discussion of religious issues in his class was only for the purpose of developing an open mind in his students. For example, Mr. Webster explained that he taught nonevolutionary theories of creation to rebut a statement in the social studies textbook indicating that the world is over four billion years old. Therefore, his teaching methods in no way violated the doctrine of separation between church and state. Mr. Webster contended that, at most, he encouraged students to explore alternative viewpoints.

The superintendent responded to Mr. Webster's letter on October 13, 1987. The superintendent reiterated that advocacy of a Christian viewpoint was prohibited, although Mr. Webster could discuss objectively the historical relationship between church and state when such discussions were an appropriate part of the curriculum. Mr. Webster was specifically instructed not to teach creation science, because the teaching of this theory had been held by the federal courts to be religious advocacy.

Mr. Webster brought suit, principally arguing that the school board's prohibitions constituted censorship in violation of the first and fourteenth amendments. In particular, Mr. Webster argued that the school board should permit him to teach a nonevolutionary theory of creation in his social studies class.

Unfortunately the actual correspondence that preceded this case is not available, only summaries which in themselves seem biased in favor the school district. It would also be interesting to know exactly what the student's original complaint was and how all of this got started. It would seem necessary to know how Webster worded his letters or even how he presented his material in the classroom. But these facts are not deemed important enough to be included, apparently. We only know that Webster said he only wished to present a "nonevolutionary" theory (not a fact, not a religious belief, only a theory) to balance the statement in the textbook, which was not presented as a theory, but as a fact. The students would logically assume their textbook taught them facts, unless it told them it was presenting a theory.

B. The District Court

The district court concluded that Mr. Webster did not have a first amendment right to teach creation science in a public school. The district court began by noting that, in deciding whether to grant the school district's motion to dismiss, the court was entitled to consider the letters between the superintendent and Mr. Webster because Mr. Webster had attached these letters to his complaint as exhibits. In particular, the district court determined that the October 13, 1987 letter was critical; this letter clearly indicated exactly what conduct the school district sought to proscribe. Specifically, the October 13 letter directed that Mr. Webster was prohibited from teaching creation science and was admonished not to engage in religious advocacy. Furthermore, the superintendent's letter explicitly stated that Mr. Webster could discuss objectively the historical relationship between church and state.

The case here rests on whether Webster was denied the freedom to teach what he as an educator thought was right for his students to know. He thought it was right for his students to know that determining the age of the earth is theoretical. He taught them that there was more than one theory used to determine this information and that more than one conclusion could be reached. That is his statement of what he did and why he did it. Unless he committed perjury and lied about what he taught, it is necessary to accept his statement as fact.

In order to explain how it is possible that the factual statement in the textbook might not in fact be a fact, it was necessary to bring up an alternate theory for determining the age of the earth. It should be significant to note that it was apparently not sufficient for Webster to say, "this statement about the age of the earth is part of a theory, the theory of evolution. There are other theories about how to determine how old the earth is, but you already know all about them, so we'll just leave it at that."

He was unable to do that, because it's extremely likely that the students in his classroom had no idea that statement wasn't a fact or what any other theories that challenge it might be. We are not privy to the discussion in the classroom. It wasn't drawn out in interviews and made part of the case writings. It is possible, however, to speculate based on the modern teaching texts and quasi-educational materials available that students are not being given more than one theory to consider. They are being presented with statements of fact about things that are in reality still theories. It was therefore necessary for Webster to spell out another theory that encompasses how to determine the age of the earth. It was necessary to point out that the textbook had a fact that wasn't a fact. It was then necessary to explain why it wasn't a fact. He was a teacher. It was his job to tell students things they didn't know, even if those things weren't part of the curriculum.

The letter Webster got from the school district, the one considered critical to the disposition of the case, tells him he was prohibited from teaching creation science and was admonished not to engage in religious advocacy. Furthermore, the superintendent's letter explicitly stated that Mr. Webster could discuss objectively the historical relationship between church and state. Propping itself up on the crutch of previous court decisions, the school district considered teaching creation science teaching religion. Apparently it was not just teaching religion, but advocating it. It must not be possible to teach a concept without advocating it. Webster presented creation science as a concept in his classroom. Therefore he advocated it. Therefore he must be proscribed from it. Of course he was permitted to deal with historic church and state relationships. He was permitted to teach something, even though it really had nothing to do with correcting the error in his textbook. Because he was allowed to teach something about religion, his free speech wasn't infringed upon. Case dismissed.

The district court noted that a school board generally has wide latitude in setting the curriculum, provided the school board remains within the boundaries established by the constitution. Because the establishment clause prohibits the enactment of any law "respecting an establishment of religion," the school board could not enact a curriculum that would inject religion into the public schools. U.S. Const. amend. I. Moreover, the district court determined that the school board had the responsibility to ensure that the establishment clause was not violated.

The district court then framed the issue as whether Mr. Webster had the right to teach creation science. Relying on Edwards v. Aguillard, 482 U.S. 578 (1987), the district court determined that teaching creation science would constitute religious advocacy in violation of the first amendment and that the school board correctly prohibited Mr. Webster from teaching such material. The court further noted:

Webster has not been prohibited from teaching any nonevolutionary theories or from teaching anything regarding the historical relationship between church and state. Martino's [the superintendent] letter of October 13, 1987 makes it clear that the religious advocacy of Webster's teaching is prohibited and nothing else. Since no other constraints were placed on Webster's teaching, he had no basis for his complaint and it must fail.

Webster v. New Lenox School Dist., Mem. op, at 4-5 (N.D. Ill. May 25 1989). Accordingly, the district court dismissed the complaint.

II

Analysis

At the outset, we note that a narrow issue confronts us: Mr. Webster asserts that he has a first amendment right to determine the curriculum content of his junior high school class. He does not, however, contest the general authority of the school board, acting through its executive agent, the superintendent, to set the curriculum.

This case does not present a novel issue. We have already confirmed the right of those authorities charged by state law with curriculum development to require the obedience of subordinate employees, including the classroom teacher. Judge Wood expressed the controlling principle succinctly in Palmer v. Board of Educ., 603 F.2d 1271, 1274 (7th Cir. 1979), cert. denied, 444 U.S. 1026 (1980), when he wrote:

Parents have a vital interest in what their children are taught. Their representatives have in general prescribed a curriculum. There is a compelling state interest in the choice and adherence to a suitable curriculum for the benefit of our young citizens and society. It cannot be left to individual teachers to teach what they please.

Yet Mr. Webster, in effect, argues that the school board must permit him to teach what he pleases. The first amendment is "not a teacher license for uncontrolled expression at variance with established curricular content." Id. at 1273. See also Clard v. Holmes, 474 F.2d 928 (7th Cir.) (holding that individual teacher has no constitutional prerogative to override the judgment of his superiors as to proper course content), cert. denied, 411 U.S. 972 (1973). Clearly, the school board had the authority and the responsibility to ensure that Mr. Webster did not stray from the established curriculum by injecting religious advocacy into the classroom. "Families entrust public schools with the education of their children, but condition their trust on the understanding that the classroom will not purposely be used to advance religious views that may conflict with the private beliefs of the student and his or her family." Edwards v. Aguillard, 482 U.S. 578, 584 (1987).

There is no indication that Webster said he had a right to determine the curriculum content of his junior high school class, nor that Mr. Webster, in effect, argues that the school board must permit him to teach what he pleases. (already cited) The court acknowledges that he accepted the authority of the board. He had the required textbook and was teaching from it, or he wouldn't have run across the passage in question. He would have saved himself from a great deal of trouble if he had simply not assigned his class to read that part of the book. Yet Webster was not interested in stifling even what he considered to be a lie, or at least not a fact. He presented the statement, and then he offered an alternative. It seems extreme to state that he was guilty of "uncontrolled expression at variance with established curricular content." He also was not guilty of betraying the trust of the School District families by abusing his position to advance conflicting religious views. The key word is "advancing." It implies putting something forward as superior, similar to the idea of "advocacy." A teacher presents a concept in his class, and the board and the court assumes he is in favor of it, that he wants his students to believe it, not just listen to it. But it seems that is only the case if the teacher presents Creation Science. He can objectively present anything else. Not that.

A teacher may say, "the 'Final Solution' for dealing with the Jews was to put them in concentration camps and kill them." Is the teacher advocating death camps for Jews? Of course not. He is presenting to his class a historical position. Unless the teacher is insane, his position is quite opposite from advocating what he states. Surely other "solutions" were possible for Hitler (granting that there was a problem of the nature under discussion, which, again, no sane person would agree with) and may even have been presented to Hitler at the time of this historical event. But Hitler wanted this one. Only this one. He may even have proscribed his advisors from bringing any other theories up. He certainly would not have been interested in possible solutions that appeared to advocate or advance a religious position.

If we ever would have wanted a government to permit the presentation of an alternate theory to deal with an issue, even a religious-based theory, that would have been the time. Alternate theories were apparently stifled, because, ironically enough, survival of the fittest, one of Evolution's foundational tenets, one upon which Hitler based many of his actions, couldn't survive on its own. It had to be protected then, and it has to be protected by the American justice system now.

A junior high school student's immature stage of intellectual development imposes a heightened responsibility upon the school board to control the curriculum. See Zykan v. Warsaw Community School Corp., 631 F.2d 1300, 1304 (7th Cir. 1980). We have noted that secondary school teachers occupy a unique position for influencing secondary school students, thus creating a concomitant power in school authorities to choose the teachers and regulate their pedagogical methods. Id. "The state exerts great authority and coercive power through mandatory attendance requirements, and because of the students' emulation of teachers as role models and the children's susceptibility to peer pressure." Edwards, 482 U.S. at 584 (footnote omitted).

It is true that the discretion lodged in school boards is not completely unfettered. For example, school boards may not fire teachers for random classroom comments. Zykan, 631 F.2d at 1305. Moreover, school boards may not require instruction in a religiously inspired dogma to the exclusion of other points of view. Epperson v. Arkansas, 393 U.S. 97, 106 (1968).

Interesting that Epperson v. Arkansas is brought up to support exactly the opposite of what it accomplished. Creation Science, another point of view, was squashed and the religious dogma of Evolution was exclusively preferred.

This complaint contains no allegation that school authorities have imposed "a pall of orthodoxy" on the offerings of the entire public school curriculum, Keyishian v. Board of Regents, 385 U.S. 589, 603 (1967)," which might either implicate the state in the propagation of an identifiable religious creed or otherwise impair permanently the student's ability to investigate matters that arise in the natural course of intellectual inquiry." Zykan, 631 F2d at 1306. Therefore, this case does not present the issue of whether, or under what circumstances, a school board may completely eliminate material from the curriculum. Cf. Zykan, 631 F.2d at 1305-06 (school may not flatly prohibit teachers from mentioning relevant material). Rather, the principle that an individual teacher has no right to ignore the directives of duly appointed education authorities is dispositive of this case. Today, we decide only that, given the allegations of the complaint, the school board has successfully navigated the narrow channel between impairing intellectual inquire and propagating a religious creed.

The wording of the previous opinion implies that the school board must be guilty of promoting a religion throughout the entire curriculum before it can be said to be in violation of the separation principle or infringing upon an individual teacher's free expression right. A teacher, however, can be denied the right to express one idea, apparently. Never mind that the entire curriculum required by the state and the school board is riddled with evolutionary language. This case is a perfect example of that. Who would have thought evolution would be an issue in a social studies class?

This is a concept appearing absolutely everywhere in curriculum. It can't be repeated often enough that it exists in every subject, often in incidental but purposeful references, as a fact, not as a theory. The state and the school boards absolutely are guilty of promoting this dogma exclusive of any other, in every subject. Try to find a state-approved textbook in any academic subject that does not bring up the subject of billions of years of earth age, or discuss man as being at first entirely primitive and gradually becoming civilized, or note that the extinction of certain types of animals or plants also indicates that more adaptable types replaced them. These are evolutionary concepts.

Here, the superintendent concluded that the subject matter taught by Mr. Webster created serious establishment clause concerns. Cf. Edwards, 482 U.S. at 583-84 ("The Court has been particularly vigilant in monitoring compliance with the Establishment Clause in elementary and secondary schools."); Epperson, 393 U.S at 106 (school may not adopt programs that aid or oppose any religion). As the district court noted, the superintendent's letter is directed to this concern. "[E]ducators do not offend the First Amendment so long as their actions are reasonably related to legitimate pedagogical concerns." Hazelwood School Dist. v. Kuhlmier, 484 U.S 260, 278 (1988). Given the school board's important pedagogical interest in establishing the curriculum and legitimate concern with possible establishment clause violations, the school board's prohibition on the teaching of creation science to junior high students was appropriate. See Palmer v. Board of Educ., 603 F.2d 1274 (7th Cir. 1979) (school board has "compelling" interest in setting the curriculum). Accordingly, the district court properly dismissed Mr. Webster's complaint.

The school in this case adopted a program that both aided one religion and opposed another. The dogma of evolution was once again aided, and the truth was opposed.

*Peloza v. Capistrano School District,* 1994

(Author's Note: Italicized material represents direct quotations. Material in regular type represents the author's comments. This section also has material from the website Vine & Fig Tree.)

(The following paragraph is not part of a trial transcript, but is quoted from the website Voices For Evolution)

In 1994, in Peloza v. Capistrano School District, the Ninth Circuit Court of Appeals upheld a district court finding that a teacher's First Amendment right to free exercise of religion is not violated by a school district's requirement that evolution be taught in biology classes.

Rejecting plaintiff Peloza's definition of a "religion" of "evolutionism", the Court found that the district had simply and appropriately required a science teacher to teach a scientific theory in biology class. (John E. Peloza v. Capistrano Unified School District, (1994) 917 F. 2d 1004)

A summary of the case follows, taken from the transcript appearing on the website *www.talkorigins.org*.

SUMMARY

High school biology teacher brought action against school district, its board of trustees, and various personnel at high school, challenging school district's requirement that he teach evolutionism, as well as school district order barring him from discussing his religious beliefs with students. The United States District Court, Central District of California, David W. Williams, J., 782 F.Supp. 1412, dismissed and awarded attorney fees to school district. Teacher appealed. The Court of Appeals held that: (1) teacher failed to state claim for violation of establishment clause of First Amendment in connection with school district's requiring him to teach evolution, i.e., that higher life forms evolved from lower ones; (2) school district's restriction on teacher's right of free speech in prohibiting teacher from talking with students about religion during school day, including times when he was not actually teaching class, was justified by school district's interest in avoiding establishment clause violation; (3) teacher's allegations of injury to his reputation as result of allegedly defamatory statements made to and about him were insufficient to support claim for deprivation of liberty interest under § 1983; but (4) teacher's complaint was not entirely frivolous, precluding award of costs and attorney fees under Rule 11 and § 1988.

The case disposition almost entirely ruled against every point the teacher Peloza brought up. One judge, Pole, offered a partial dissenting opinion, of which an excerpt follows.

I am in agreement with the majority's resolution of John Peloza's Establishment Clause and Due Process Clause claims. However, because I believe we can dismiss Peloza's free speech claims only by turning a deaf ear to the procedural posture of this case, I respectfully dissent from parts I. B and II of the majority opinion.

I

Schoolteacher John Peloza seeks a declaratory judgment permitting him to "respond to student-initiated inquiries ... regarding religion" during contract time. The majority opinion concludes that if Peloza's discussions would constitute an establishment of religion, the District may permissibly limit those discussions, even though such limitations restrict Peloza's free speech. With this I have no quarrel. But the majority's premise is that any discussions Peloza might have do constitute such an establishment, and I am unpersuaded that we may reach such a conclusion in the case's present posture.

This is an appeal from the granting of a Rule 12(b)(6) motion. As such, we are not permitted to affirm dismissal of the complaint "unless it appears beyond doubt that plaintiff can prove no set of facts in support of his claim which would entitle him to relief." Love V. United States, 915 F.2d 1242, 1245 (9th Cir.1989). At this stage, we know almost nothing about what past or future discussions might involve. I can imagine a wide range of circumstances and questions "regarding religion" which Peloza could permissibly answer without violating the Establishment Clause. For example, a student might come to a teacher during lunch and ask about Malcolm X or Martin Luther King's religious beliefs, and how and why they evolved, or about the origins of Islam, or what the seven great religions of the world were. Such questions would certainly be "regarding religion," student-initiated, and during contract time. As such, they fall within the class of discussions Peloza seeks to be permitted, yet it is hard to see how the descriptive role a teacher would have in responding to these questions would work any violation of the Establishment Clause.

The majority holding only makes sense if we presume that we know what kinds of questions are being asked and what kinds of answers Peloza would give. In the posture of this case, where we must reverse if there are any facts Peloza could conceivably prove which would entitle him to relief, this is a presumption we are forbidden from making. As a result, the majority holding means that any response to a student-initiated inquiry "regarding religion" during contract time, other than "Ask someone else," works a violation of the Establishment Clause. I cannot join in such a broad legal holding, and indeed the case law forbids it:

In each case, the inquiry calls for line-drawing; no fixed, per se rule can be framed. The Establishment Clause like the Due Process Clauses is not a precise, detailed provision in a legal code capable of ready application.... The line between permissible relationships and those barred by the Clause can no more be straight and unwavering than due process can be defined in a single stroke or phrase or test. The Clause erects a "blurred, indistinct, and variable barrier depending on all the circumstances of a particular relationship." Lemon V. Kurtzman, 403 U.S. [602, 614, 91 S.Ct. 2105, 2112, 29 L.Ed.2d 745 (1971)]. Lynch V. Donnelly, 465 U.S. 668, 678-79, 104 S.Ct. 1355,1362, 79 L.Ed.2d 604 (1984).

Roberts V. Madigan, 921 F.2d 1047 (10th Cir.1990), upon which the majority relies, is not to the contrary. There, the court had before it a host of particulars: the conduct at issue involved a teacher displaying religious books and a poster reading "You have only to open your eyes to see the hand of God" in the classroom. Id. at 1049. That court also had the benefit of a district court factual determination that the conduct "created the appearance that [the teacher] was seeking to advance his religious views." Id. As this case stands, we know far less.

The majority impermissibly attempts to narrow the scope of Peloza's complaint by relying on a written warning from the school district which Peloza has incorporated into the complaint. The letter forbids Peloza from "attempt[ing] to convert students to Christianity or initiating conversations about your religious beliefs." Complaint at 45. Were this all that the complaint said, I would have little trouble joining the majority. But the complaint alleges more; it contends that "the school district ... has directed Plaintiff not to discuss any religious matters during any of this 'instructional time,' including student-initiated conversations regarding religion during lunch, class breaks, and before and after school hours." Complaint at 3. This allegation we must take as true. If all that lies behind it is the far narrower warning the majority cites, then Peloza's case will not be long for this world. But we may not presume that this is so.

I believe that, in a broad range of cases, the majority and I could agree about what would or would not constitute a violation of the Establishment Clause. But the majority errs in presuming to know that what is at stake here is Peloza's right to "discuss his religious beliefs" with students. In doing so, it ignores the fact that this is a Rule 12(b)(6) case. More generally, it gives short shrift to the possibility that we may well be limiting free speech more broadly than the state's compelling interest in avoiding an establishment of religion would warrant.

II

I join in the majority's part II insofar as it dismisses Peloza's § 1985(3) due process and Establishment Clause claims based on his failure to properly allege a violation of these rights. However, because I conclude that Peloza's free speech claim should not have been dismissed, I would also remand, rather than dismiss, his 1985(3) claim based on alleged free speech violations.

III

Religion has been used to justify the suppression of speech for centuries. See Everson V. Board of Ed,, 330 U.S. 1, 8-10, 67 S.Ct. 504, 5074)9, 91 L.Ed. 711 (1947). With the development of a vigorous First Amendment jurisprudence, we have quelled some of the worst abuses. But points of tension remain. We must thus remain vigilant to ensure that in our rush to preserve certain fundamental rights, we do not trample others. Caution is of the essence; only through a methodical and fact-specific jurisprudence can we hope to achieve a proper accommodation.

For the reasons stated above, I respectfully dissent.

1. On appeal, Peloza abandoned his equal protection argument.

2. The Establishment Clause of the First Amendment provides that "Congress shall make no law respecting an establishment of religion..." The Fourteenth Amendment incorporates the Establishment Clause's prohibitions against offending state action as well. Board of Education v. Pico, 457 U.S. 853, 864, 102 S.Ct.2799, 2806-07, 73 L.Ed.2d 435 (1982).

3. See Webster's Third New Int'l Dictionary (G. & C. Merriam Co. Springfield, MA. 1969). p.789 ("evolutionism: 1: a theory of evolution (as in philosophy, biology, or sociology) - See Darwinism 2: adherence to or belief in evolution esp. of living beings").

4. According to Webster's, religion is the "belief in and reverence for a supernatural power accepted as the creator and governor of the universe." Webster's II New Riverside University Dictionary 993.

5. See Smith v. Board of School Com'rs of Mobile County, 827 F.2d 684, 690-95 (11th Cir.1987) (refusing

to adopt district court's holding that "secular humanism" is a religion for Establishment Clause purposes; deciding case on other grounds); United States v. Allen, 760 F.2d 447, 450-51 (2d Cir.1985) (quoting Tribe, American Constitutional Law 827-28 (1987), for the proposition that, while "religion" should be broadly interpreted for Free Exercise Clause purposes, "anything 'arguably non-religious' should not be considered religious in applying the establishment clause").

6. The dissent claims this interpretation impermissibly narrows the scope of Peloza's complaint. However, the very sentence quoted by the dissent, Dissent at p.12064, focuses not on the definition of "religious matters," but on the definition of "instructional time." We agree with the dissent that a complaint must be read charitably at the Rule 12(b)(6) stage. However, a reviewing court need not go so far as to invent claims not within the reasonable intendment of the complaint.

7. As with his equal protection claim under section 1983, Peloza appears to have dropped his equal protection claim from his appeal to this court.

8. See United Brotherhood of Carpenters & Joiners of America, Local 610, AFL-CIO v. Scott, 463 U.S. 825, 830, 103 S.Ct. 3352,3357, 77 L.Ed.2d 1049 (1983) (hate speech rights protected by section 1985 so long as the State is involved in the conspiracy alleged). As to due process rights, there appears to be some confusion within this circuit. Older cases have stated that section 1985(3) provides no remedy for violation of due process rights, Cohen V. Norris, 300 F.2d 24, 28 (9th Cir. 1962) (dicta); Mitchell V. Greenough, 100 F.2d 184, 187 (9th Cir.1938) (holding), cert. denied. 306 U.S. 659, 59 S.Ct. 788, 83 L.Ed. 1056 (1939). In some more recent cases, we have allowed claims of due process violations to proceed under section 1985(3) without comment. See Judie V. Hamilton. 872 F.2d 919,924 (9th Cir.1989); Padway V. Palches. 665 F.2d 965, 969 (9th Cir. 1982).

See Taylor V. Gilmartin, 686 F.2d 1346, 1358 (10th Cir.1982) (First Amendment freedom of religion protected by section 1985(3)). cert. denied, 459 U.S. 1147, 103 S.Ct. 788,74 L.Ed.2d 994 and cert. denied, 463 U.S. 1229, 103 S.Ct. 3570, 77 L.Ed.2d 1411 (1983); Action V. Gannon. 450 F.2d 1227, 1234 (8th Cir.1971) (satne); Cooper V. Molko, 512 F.Supp. 563, 570 (N.D.Cal.1981) (same); but see Africa V. Anderson, 510 F.Supp. 28, 30 (E.D.Penn.1980) (freedom of religion not protected by section 1985(3)).

The dissenting judge touches on the key point of the whole argument all of these evolution-related court case have shared. Opposition to the teaching of Evolution can only be on religious grounds and all religious talk must be stifled. Only in that way can Evolution opposition be stifled.

The judge properly questioned how a school district could make a blanket order forbidding the teacher such a wide range of activities. First, they prohibited any discussion of religion at all. Second, they forbade conversations outside the classroom and class time. Third, they forbade even student-initiated conversations.

With the development of a vigorous First Amendment jurisprudence, we have quelled some of the worst abuses. But points of tension remain. We must thus remain vigilant to ensure that in our rush to preserve certain fundamental rights, we do not trample others. Caution is of the essence; only through a methodical and fact-specific jurisprudence can we hope to achieve a proper accommodation.

This is a well-spoken statement, but it is too little, too late. The damage is done. The fundamental right to teach truth and reject error has been trampled repeatedly by court decisions designed solely to protect the State religion of Secular Humanism and its Bible of Evolution Dogma. For a judge to stop now and think of how the judicial system might have gone too far is sad. To date, judges have fervently served as the High Priests of Humanism and defended the dogma against all comers.

In an earlier court case Justice Black was quoted as having brought up Thomas Jefferson's "wall of separation" concept. That non-constitutional statement has since been solidly welded into place and given rise to a host of misinterpretations and abuses of intent and power.

A later case chose to quote Robert Frost's "Mending Wall," as if that were proof of the need for separation when its point is really the opposite. Is it possible that judges do not at all understand the intention of the founding fathers in the Constitution and documents of the same time period? And is it possible that even the United States Supreme Court had a different interpretation of the "separation principle" long after the days of the founding (see the 1844 quotation below) but before Secular Humanism became the law of the land?

The following comes from the website Vine & Fig Tree, which describes itself as Supporting: love, joy, peace, patience, gentleness, goodness, faith, meekness, sobriety [and] Opposing: Secularism, Humanism, Anti-Family Sex, Hedonism, Autonomy, Totalitarianism, and Mass Death.

In stark contrast to the myth of separation, the Founders believed that schools should positively and affirmatively teach religion. Every single person who signed the Constitution believed that religious and moral inculcation was the purpose of schools. Peloza is light-years away from the original intent of the Constitution. Consider Samuel Adams:

As piety, religion, and morality have a happy influence on the minds of men, in their public as well as private transactions, you will not think it unseasonable, although I have frequently done it, to bring to your remembrance the great importance of encouraging our

University, town schools, and other seminaries of education, that our children and youth while they are engaged in the pursuit of useful science, may have their minds impressed with a strong sense of the duties they owe to God. If we continue to be a happy people, that happiness must be assured by the enacting and executing of the reasonable and wise laws expressed in the plainest language and by establishing such modes of education as tend to inculcate in the minds of youth the feelings and habits of "piety, religion and morality." (Addressing the Legislature of Mass., 1/16/1795)

Let divines and philosophers, statesmen and patriots, unite their endeavors to renovate the age, by impressing the minds of men with the importance of educating their little boys and girls, of inculcating in the minds of youth the fear and love of the Deity. . . and, in subordination to these great principles, the love of their country. . . . In short, of leading them in the study and practice of the exalted virtues of the Christian system. Letter to John Adams, 1790, who wrote back: "You and I agree." Four Letters: Being an Interesting Correspondence Between Those Eminently Distinguished Characters, John Adams, Late President of the United States; and Samuel Adams, Late Governor of Massachusetts. On the Important Subject of Government (Boston: Adams and Rhoades, 1802) pp. 9-10

It has been observed that "education has a greater influence on manners than human laws can have." [A] virtuous education is calculated to reach and influence the heart and to prevent crimes. . . . Such an education, which leads the youth beyond mere outside show, will impress their minds with a profound reverence of the Deity [and] . . . will excite in them a just regard to Divine revelation. The Life and Public Services of Samuel Adams, Wm.Wells., ed. (Boston: Little, Brown, & Co., 1865) Vol.III, p. 327.

Art. 3. Religion, morality, and knowledge, being necessary to good government and the happiness of mankind, schools and the means of education shall forever be encouraged. Northwest Ordinance, 1787

In my view, the Christian religion is the most important and one of the first things in which all children, under a free government, ought to be instructed. . . . No truth is more evident to my mind than that the Christian religion must be the basis of any government intended to secure the rights and privileges of a free people. The opinion that human reason left without the constant control of Divine laws and commands will preserve a just administration, secure freedom and other rights, restrain men from violations of laws and constitutions, and give duration to a popular government is as chimerical as the most extravagant ideas that enter the head of a maniac . . . . Where will you find any code of laws among civilized men in which the commands and prohibitions are not founded on Christian principles? I need not specify the prohibition of murder, robbery, theft [and] trespass. Noah Webster, Letters, Harry A Warfel, ed., (NY: Library Publishers, 1953) pp. 453-454, to David McClure, Oct. 25, 1836.

Thomas Jefferson's good friend Benjamin Rush, after he signed the Declaration of Independence, was the first Founding Father to call for free public schools. He said:

[T]he only foundation for a useful education in a republic is to be laid in religion. Without this there can be no virtue, and without virtue there can be no liberty, and liberty is the object and life of all republican governments. Without religion, I believe that learning does real mischief to the morals and principles of mankind.(Benjamin Rush, Essays, Literary, Moral, and Philosophical, 1798, p.6 [ "On the Mode of Education Proper in a Republic"])

Rush was clearly a Christian, but no "fundamentalist nut." In his paper entitled, "A Defense of the Use of the Bible as a Schoolbook," Rush argued,

[T]he only means of establishing and perpetuating our republican forms of government . . . is the universal education of our youth in the principles of Christianity by means of the Bible. For this Divine book, above all others, favors that equality among mankind, that respect for just laws, and those sober and frugal virtues, which constitute the soul of republicanism.

Daniel Webster reflected the views of every single Signer of the Constitution:

We regard it [public instruction] as a wise and liberal system of police by which property and life and the peace of society are secured. We seek to prevent in some measure the extension of the penal code by inspiring a salutary and conservative principle of virtue and of knowledge. [1]

[However, t]he attainment of knowledge does not comprise all which is contained in the larger term of education. The feelings are to be disciplined; the passions are to be restrained; true and worthy motives are to be inspired; a profound religious feeling is to be instilled, and pure morality inculcated. [Four years later, the U.S. Supreme Court would agree that this could only be done by having the government teach the Bible.] [2]

The cultivation of the religious sentiment represses licentiousness . . . inspires respect for law and order, and gives strength to the whole social fabric.[3]

[1] Works of Daniel Webster (Boston: Little, Brown, and Co., 1853) vol I, pp 41-42, Dec 22., 1820.[2] vol II, pp 107-108, Oct 5: 1840[3] vol II, p 615, July 4, 1851

The Father of his Country warned:

And let us with caution indulge the supposition that morality can be maintained without religion. Whatever may be conceded to the influence of refined education on minds of peculiar structure, reason and experience both forbid us to expect that national morality can prevail in exclusion of religious principle And secularists would be quick to point out that Washington was less Biblically-oriented than the most influential educators in the nation, such as Benjamin Rush and Noah Webster.

All the scholars are required to live a religious and blameless life according to the rules of God's Word, diligently reading the holy Scriptures, that fountain of Divine light and truth, and constantly attending all the duties of religion . . . . All the scholars are obliged to attend Divine worship in the College Chapel on the Lord's Day and on Days of Fasting and Thanksgiving appointed by public Authority. The Laws of Yale College in New Haven in Connecticut (New Haven: Josiah Meigs, 1787) p. 5-6, ch II, art. 1,4

William Samuel Johnson, signer of the Constitution, was appointed Columbia's first president. Under him, It is expected that all students attend public worship on Sundays. Columbia Rules (NY: Samuel Loudon, 1785) 5-8

Johnson's views on public education were similar to those of every other signer of the Constitution. In his commencement address, he told the graduates:

You this day, gentlemen, . . . have . . . received a public education, the purpose whereof hath been to qualify you the better to serve your Creator and your country . . . . Your first great duties, you are sensible, are those you owe to Heaven, to your Creator and Redeemer. Let these be ever present to your minds, and exemplified in your lives and conduct. Imprint deep upon your minds the principles of piety towards God and a reverence and fear of His holy name. The fear of God is the beginning of wisdom [Proverbs 9:10]. Remember too, that you are the redeemed of the Lord, that you are bought with a price, even the inestimable price of the precious blood of the

Son of God. . . . Love, fear and serve Him as your Creator, Redeemer, and Sanctifier. Acquaint yourselves with Him in His Word and holy ordinances. Make Him your friend and protector and your felicity is secured both here and hereafter.

Early US Supreme Court decisions agreed that in a Christian nation such as America, the Bible must be taught in all government-run schools.

In 1844, the Court was asked, Can the state enforce a will which creates a government-operated school which will not teach the Bible? The Supreme Court said that the very idea of a school which will not teach the Bible is contrary to the legal foundations of this Christian nation.

It is unnecessary for us, however, to consider what would be the legal effect of a devise in Pennsylvania for the establishment of a school or college, for the propagation of . . . Deism, or any other form of infidelity. Such a case is not to be presumed to exist in a Christian country; and therefore it must be made out by clear and indisputable proof.

The government made firm assurances that the Bible would be taught in the school, and the will was approved. (Vidal v. Girard's Executors)

The Vidal Court, as it talks about Christianity and the Bible, sounds more like David Barton than anything one would hear from the post-1947 Court. The Vidal Court said that the government in its school "may, nay must impart to their youthful pupils . . . the Bible, and especially the New Testament," which must "be read and taught as a divine revelation in the college -- its general precepts expounded, its evidences explained, and its glorious principles of morality inculcated." The Court asked rhetorically:

Where can the purest principles of morality be learned so clearly or so perfectly as from the New Testament? Where are benevolence, the love of truth, sobriety, and industry, so powerfully and irresistibly inculcated as in the sacred volume?

The Bible MUST be taught in government schools, the 1844 US Supreme Court declared.

You would NEVER EVER hear language like this from the modern secularist Court. But you ALWAYS heard language like this from the Founding Fathers.

The "separation of church and state" is a myth.

# Appendix Three: Supplementary Material for Section Two

Higher Criticism

*For the prophecy came not in old time by the will of man: but holy men of God spake as they were moved by the Holy Ghost.* (2 Peter 1:21).

*All Scripture is given by inspiration of God, and is profitable for doctrine, for reproof, for correction, for instruction in righteousness.* (2 Timothy 3:16).

Until well after the American Civil War, biblical scholars in the United States accepted these verses as truth. Everyone, conservative or liberal, acknowledges that human beings wrote down the words of the Scriptures. After that admission, two positions are possible to answer the question of who wrote the Bible. Either it was written by the people who claim to have written it, or it was written much later, by unknown authors or editors. If it was written much later, by unknown authors or editors, it does not contain truth, but is a patchwork of mythologies and lies and not worthy of serious study.

The Bible itself makes claims as to its authorship. For example, Moses wrote the first five books, with later minor additions by Joshua and Samuel. Ezra performed major editorial work on most of the Old Testament to bring it into its present form. Samuel and the School of the Prophets are responsible for the books through II Samuel, Ezra was responsible for Chronicles, Kings, and the book bearing his name, and many other books bear the names of their authors, continuing into the New Testament with the gospels and General Epistles. There is no evidence of an editor of the New Testament with the possible exception of the book of Hebrews. Works acknowledged to be written by Paul bear the names of the cities or churches he wrote to but also have his statement of authorship. Luke wrote the Gospel bearing his name and Acts and John the Beloved Disciple the Gospel and epistles bearing his name as well as the book of Revelation.

A few books are of uncertain authorship, Esther and Hebrews, for example. Honest disagreement about these matters does not mean the scholars do not believe in the Inspiration of the Scriptures. Textual Critics are another form of legitimate scholars who seek to find the best ancient manuscripts and discover the most accurate meaning of the Scriptures.

By contrast, "Higher Criticism" of the Bible compares ancient documents of many cultures with Scriptures as if the Bible were no different from any other writing. "Higher Criticism treats the Bible as a text created by human beings at a particular historical time and for various human motives, in contrast with the treatment of the Bible as the inerrant word of God," says Wikipedia. Wikipedia's article on the subject contains much confusion between Higher and Textual Criticism and even calls Higher Criticism "Historical" Criticism. For instance, it claims that Desiderus Erasmus (1466?-1536), publisher of the Greek New Testament Martin Luther used in his translation work, was a Higher Critic. In fact he was a textual critic, simply seeking to find the best biblical manuscripts to obtain the most accurate meanings of the texts. His work was essential to translators like Luther, Calvin and the KJV scholars.

"The School of Higher Criticism" questioned the authorship of most books of the Bible and rejected many as being not part of the Scriptures. They believed all the supernatural events could be explained by natural means and interpreted Scriptures in the light of cultural superstitions of the surrounding nations. They actually held these cultural superstitions of the surrounding nations superior to the Bible because there are archaeological artifacts supporting the fact that these nations believed these superstitions. The lack of artifacts to support Israel's culture lessens the authenticity of Israel's culture in the eyes of these "higher critics." They had no use for any of the Old Testament as spiritual truth but only for what historical information it might contain. Higher Critics included Jean Astruc (mid-18th cent.), a French Physician and the first to begin formulating the JEDP or Documentary Hypothesis (see below). Johann Salomo Semler (1725-91) questioned the equality of authority of the Old and New Testaments, the authorship of most of the books of the Bible, and any true revelation or inspiration by God. Johann Gottfried Eichhorn (1752-1827), a Professor of Oriental Languages, was sometimes called the "founder of modern Old Testament criticism."

Ferdinand Christian Baur (1792-1860) was a member of the Tübingen School. He argued that "Jewish Christianity" and "Pauline Christianity" were opposing viewpoints in the New Testament and placed the writings of the pastoral epistles much later than conservative scholars.

Julius Wellhausen (1844-1918) was best known for refining the JEDP Documentary Theory. He demanded a much later time period for the writing of the Pentateuch. He dismissed the possibility of early Jewish monotheism and their status as "God's chosen people." Some of his works are believed to have encouraged anti-Semitism and formed the justification for later Nazi beliefs and practices. Friedrich Schleiermacher (1768–1834) made an early confession in a letter to his father about his religious doubts, no doubt speaking for many of the Higher Critics.

"Faith is the regalia of the Godhead, you say. Alas! dearest father, if you believe that without this faith no one can attain to salvation in the next world, nor to tranquility in this - and such, I know, is your belief - oh! then pray to God to grant it to me, for to me it is now lost. I cannot believe that he who called himself the Son of Man was the true, eternal God; I cannot believe that his death was a vicarious atonement."

In his later work, Addresses on Religion (1799), Schleiermacher makes clear his position as one based simply on feelings, with no Scriptural truth or doctrine involved. This is in strange contrast to the fact that he was supposedly a great lecturer and scholar on Hermeneutics, the attempt to examine and arrive at the true meaning of Scriptural texts.

David Friedrich Strauss (1808–74) wrote The Life of Jesus, Historically Examined. It dismissed all possibility that Jesus Christ was the Son of God. It treated the gospels as mythology and claimed they were written by recreating a Jewish Messianic tradition of teaching folklore. Ludwig Feuerbach (1804–72) studied external manuscripts in what he claimed was a quest to confirm events related in the Bible. His works were later translated by George Eliot [see below] in England and taught that man and God are essentially the same, since nature is all that exists and man is a part of nature. Attributes of the Divine are just projections from man himself. He is considered to be a primary inspiration for the Marxist Dialectic. Higher Critics in these later times were inspired by Enlightenment and Rationalist thinkers like John Locke, David Hume, Immanuel Kant, Gotthold Lessing, Gottlieb Fichte, Georg Hegel and the French rationalists. (See the appendix on Natural Law to examine whether some of these writers would have agreed with the position of the Higher Critics on the Scriptures.)

Samuel Taylor Coleridge brought Higher Criticism to England along with George Eliot, who translated Strauss's The Life of Jesus (1846) and Feuerbach's The Essence of Christianity (1854). (Note that George Elliot, or Mary Anne Evans, wrote Silas Marner, a bitter attack on organized religion and staunch advocacy for humanism.) Seven Anglican theologians began in 1860 to make this criticism a part of Christian doctrine in Essays and Reviews. Dealing with this work was considered more important by the Church of that time than the publication of Origin of Species by Darwin and absorbed five years in a fiery battle for the truth. Two authors of Essays and Reviews were charged with heresy and fired in 1862. By 1864 the judgment was reversed on appeal. La Vie de Jésus (1863), by Ernest Renan (1823–92), followed in the footsteps of Strauss and Feuerbachin, stripping Jesus Christ of His divinity. In Catholicism, Alfred Loisy wrote L'Evangile et l'Eglise (1902), opposing Essence of Christianity of Adolf von Harnack, who questioned early Christian church doctrines, rejected John's Gospel because of the differences with the Synoptic Gospels and promoted the social gospel, saying that man's relationship with God was personal and needed no organized church. Alfred Loisy, however, believed that Jesus Christ did not consciously know He was one with God. La Vie de Jesus by Ernest Renan once again attempted to make Jesus a "real person" while robbing Him of His Divine Nature. Albert Schweitzer criticized the "human only" view of Jesus, but replaced it with the idea that Jesus and his disciples thought an immediate fulfillment of the prophecies of judgment was going to occur, in His lifetime, and only when they didn't occur did He realize He had to die for sin. Schweitzer was still a humanist and apparently reasoned that Jesus' great sacrifice made the fulfillment of the prophecies unnecessary. Rudolf Bultmann, among others, claimed higher criticism was needed to "demythologize" the Bible.

The "Documentary Hypothesis" of Wellhausen, also called the "J, E, D, P Hypothesis," claims to identify supposed writers of the respective portions of the Pentateuch (Genesis-Deuteronomy) especially, and also much of the Old Testament. The "Jehovist Document," supposedly dates from about 850 B.C., used Jehovah for God; the "Elohist Document," about 750 B.C., used Elohim; the "Deuteronomist Document," was supposed to be an editor of the first two, dated about 620 B.C., containing especially most of the Book of Deuteronomy; and, finally, the "Priestly Document," supposed editorial revisions by Jewish priests around 500 B.C.

It was necessary to attribute the Bible to different or unknown authors, especially to place the writings into later time periods, because these "scholars" came to their work presupposing that all ancient manuscripts were equal, that they probably had an even more ancient common source in the "oral tradition," and that the world couldn't be only six to ten thousand years old and have an advanced civilization as described in Genesis four and six when they didn't even credit people from Moses' time with the ability to write. It was also essential to discredit prophecy in the later books of the Old Testament, so their dates of writing were placed after the fulfillment of the prophecy. The Bible can't be reduced to the level of any other book if it accurately predicts the future, so the prophecies can't be allowed to remain in the time period where they were actually made.

Higher Critics can produce a chart showing each Book of the Bible and assigning it an unknown or post-period author/editor. They consign some of the acknowledged epistles to the category of the pseudepigrapha, the non-scriptural writings, like the Apocrypha. The key is the Higher Critics' presuppositions. They were presupposing that there was no God who gave His words to Man. They were presupposing that culture and religion evolved as man evolved, because they were evolutionists, of course, and all cultures and religions were equally mythological.

The first eleven chapters of Genesis must have been rehashed and modified from the Babylonian myths, which had to be older than the Bible. The truth is that writing is older than Moses who lived thirty-five hundred years ago, as proved by archaeological finds, and Abraham lived when the Bible says he lived. But the Higher Critics couldn't have Monotheism and metallurgy and city-building and musical instruments where there should be nomadic hunter-gatherers scratching paintings on cave walls.

Christ Himself quoted the Old Testament extensively and credited its acknowledged authors as true prophets: "And beginning at Moses and all the prophets, he expounded unto them in all the scriptures the things concerning himself. . . These are the words which I spake unto you, while I was yet with you, that all things must be fulfilled, which were written in the law of Moses, and in the prophets, and in the psalms, concerning me" (Luke 24:27, 44).

There are still questions about the writings describing creation and events before Moses' birth and after his death. Possibly God taught Moses these directly. It is also possible that manuscripts of earlier writers whom God inspired were collected and preserved, by Noah on the Ark, and others, and handed over to Moses to work from. Possibly Samuel was given an account of Moses' death written by Joshua. The Scriptures do not say, but these theories do not rob the Scriptures of their uniqueness and their truth as Higher Criticism does.

Higher critics, on the other hand, do not believe that any of the books of Old Testament were written in form we have them now before about 250 BC. They believe that the New Testament was not complete until the council of Nicene in 325 AD. One solid example of the stark contrast between conservatives and higher critics is found in the synoptic gospels. Conservatives point out that Church tradition has always held that the Gospel of

Matthew was written first, probably from Aramaic sources, maybe as early as 35 AD, certainly no later than 45 AD. Matthew was written to Jewish believers and he expected his readers to have a solid knowledge of the Old Testament. Luke was written soon after Matthew to a Gentile believer who needed some explanations of Jewish traditions. The Gospel of Mark is traditionally known as Peter's Gospel, written when Peter was an old man in Rome, with Mark as transcriber and possibly editor.

The Roman culture did not allow a great deal of leisure time, so Mark's Gospel is cut to about half the size of Matthew or Luke and includes many words to emphasize action, such as immediately and straightway. Higher Critics say that the Gospel of Mark was written first simply because it is the shortest. Without the slightest evidence, higher critics believe that the Gospel of Mark was written from some smaller document which they call "Q." Material was made up and added to make the Gospel of Mark. Still later, more material was added to the Gospel of Mark to create the Gospels of Matthew, Luke and John. According to Higher Critics, "Q" could have been written as late as 45 AD, the Gospel of Mark maybe around 65 AD and the other Gospels as late as the Nicene Council 325 AD. Though this is accepted throughout the academic world and has sold millions of books, this is all without any evidence.

[Some of the material on the Documentary Theory, archaeological proofs and authorships is adapted from The Genesis Record: a Scientific and Devotional Commentary on the Book of Beginnings, by Henry M. Morris, Baker Book House, Grand Rapids, MI.]

Problems with Calendars

Almost everyone on planet Earth works with more than one calendar every single day. The United States of America officially uses the Gregorian calendar. A budget calendar, the one that determines a company or other business entity's working year, is called a Fiscal calendar. The federal budget uses a calendar which begins October 1. The vast majority of school systems or school districts use a calendar which begins around the first of September. Employees of NASA or the US military use an Ordinal calendar which starts approximately the first week of January on a Gregorian calendar and numbers each week without naming months. This type of calendar is very useful for imputing computer data, since the week number determines where you are in the calendar year, not the month. This system has international application as well. Because companies can operate on any calendar they want, the different possible calendar combinations are nearly infinite.

It is quite normal for an American family to use one calendar for the husband's job, a different calendar for the wife's job, different calendars for each school-aged child, a different calendar for taxes, plus an attempt to synchronize these different calendars with a Gregorian calendar. To add to the confusion, it is also normal for every one of these families to know families with completely different calendars. So why do so many people fail to understand the difficulty of synchronizing a modern Gregorian calendar with an ancient calendar?

Modern calendars began with Julius Caesar. When he began collecting taxes throughout his empire, the lack of a common calendar was a serious difficulty. He issued a new calendar to aid in tax collection. Though it was very good, it was not perfect and has been corrected many times throughout the centuries. The standard throughout the Western world today is a Julian calendar revised by Pope Gregory known as a Gregorian calendar. In the middle ages a mathematician developed the Ordinal calendar which is also called a Julian calendar but is not related to Julius Caesar's Julian calendar. A Revised Julian calendar was adopted by the Orthodox Churches of Constantinople, Alexandria, Antioch, Greece, Cyprus, Romania, Poland, and Bulgaria by 1963.

This is distinct from previous Julian calendar revisions or the Gregorian calendar. Confused yet?

Realizing how difficult our daily lives are with all of these various calendars, the real question is how do we even come close to matching ancient dates to our Gregorian calendar? Prior to Julius Caesar, each country and often every city had its own calendar. Each new king would introduce his own new calendar. Sometimes two kings would reign at the same time, especially father and son, and two different calendars would overlap. Sometimes the beginning or the end of a king's reign would count a partial year as a full year. Each culture also had civil and religious calendars which started at different times of the year and often had a different number of days in the year. Israel still functions this way today. The book The Mysterious Numbers of the Hebrew Kings by Edwin Thiele does a good job of reconciling the many pieces of information contained in the Bible concerning the dates of the kings from Saul to the Babylonian captivity.

Our position is that modern historians do not do a very good job of synchronizing modern calendars with ancient events before Alexander the Great. Since Alexander, writers throughout the Mediterranean world have used common events to synchronize their calendars, so synchronizing their writings with our calendars is much easier. From the time period of Alexander the Great back to the founding of the Chaldean or Babylonian Empire at the battle of Carchemish under Nabopolasser, Nebuchadnezzer's father, the many common events still allow for a very high degree of synchronization. Before the Battle of Carchemish, however, the calendars of different nations have few common events to synchronize. Since mainstream historians rely on the highly flawed Egyptian timeline popularized by James Breasted in his Ancient Records of Egypt and supplement that timeline with artifacts which are either radiocarbon dated or simply assigned an assumed date, there are plenty of opportunities for massive errors. Immanuel Velikovsky, for instance, in his book Ages In Chaos, believes that synchronization of Egyptian history with Hebrew history at the time of King Saul has Hebrew history too young by about 200 years and Egyptian history at this point too old by about 300 years for a total error of at least 500 years.

Prejudice against the Bible influences often influences objectivity. To avoid this prejudice, we will examine the founding of Carthage as an example. The founding of Carthage is an example of archaeological dating unrelated to biblical records. Many ancient writings reference the founding of Carthage, such as Virgil's Aeneid and The Antiquities of the Jews by Flavius Josephus. Timaeus of Tauromenion , Dionysius of Halicarnassus and Velleius Paterculus date the founding of Carthage in the same general time period. The number of references to Carthage as a city are staggering, so we can be certain that Carthage was founded sometime. All of the ancient sources date the founding of Carthage in the mid to late ninth century BC (853-814 BC). Carthage was, however, so thoroughly destroyed, first by the Romans in 146 BC and later by the Muslims in 698 AD, that there is almost no physical evidence that Carthage as a Phoenician capital ever existed. The scanty remains which modern archeologists have unearthed are never dated anywhere near the recorded late ninth century date, usually no earlier than 725 BC.

And this is the problem. Modern historians, knowing that the city of Carthage was destroyed many times, place more faith in a few remaining artifacts than the written records. Just because we no longer have any physical evidence that Carthage was founded in the ninth century, modern historians are completely discounting all ancient written records and claiming that Carthage was founded much later. This nonsense has actually become mainstream. Reliance upon physical objects from an archaeological dig as the sole means of dating a site's true age, origin and beginning is neither good science nor good sense. Dating methods can produce flawed results. Artifacts might be from later periods of time than the first settlers. They might be from other cultures, imported in trade or left by invaders.

This is a case where a staggering weight of written evidence is being ignored in favor of a very few artifacts with no certain connection to the founding of Carthage. Scholars around the ancient world acknowledged the founding of Carthage. Archaeologists use the evidence of broken pots or pieces of charcoal instead of written records.

An example of this prevailing prejudice is found in a brief article on the founding of Carthage at varchive.org, a scholarly archive of Immanuel Velikovsky's unpublished works. "The Date of Carthage's Founding," from a supplementary section called, New Light on the Dark Age of Greece by Jan Sammer. Jan Sammer (b. Plzen, Czechoslovakia, 1953) was an assistant to Immanuel Velikovsky (1976-1979), an archivist and editor for the Velikovsky Estate, 1980-1983. He has a Bachelor of Arts from SGWU, Montreal, 1975, and a Master of International Affairs, Columbia University, NYC, 1986. He has also made contributions to Kronos and Aeon journals.

"Archaeology, however, does not support a mid- or late-ninth century date for Carthage's founding. After many years of digging archaeologists have succeeded to penetrate to the most ancient of Carthage's buildings. P. Cintas, excavating a chapel dedicated to the goddess Tanit, found in the lowest levels a small rectangular structure with a foundation deposit of Greek orientalizing vases datable to the last quarter of the eighth century. These are still the earliest signs of human habitation at the site; although Cintas originally held out hope that there would be found remains of the earliest settlers of the end of the ninth century, the years have not substantiated such expectation. Scholars are now for the most part ready to admit that the ancient chronographers' estimate of the date of the city's founding was exaggerated."

These rejected written records do not even include the Hebrew Scriptures. The bias of archeologists against written records added to the bias against the Bible make a synchronization of calendars impossible.

Even Conservatives who start with the position that the Biblical record is factually accurate have extreme difficulty synchronizing the dates of ancient events with our modern Gregorian calendar. The most important date and the starting point looking backwards from the present is the dating of the Fall of Jerusalem. Since the campaigns of Nebuchadnezzar are recorded in multiple places, the Fall of Jerusalem to the Babylonians in the early sixth century BC is universally accepted. Since the campaign against Jerusalem took several years and we have that campaign mentioned from several points of view, a disagreement over the exact date is almost inevitable. This does not mean, however, that these conservatives disagree about the facts. One conservative might believe the evidence concludes that the final fall of Jerusalem took place in 584 BC of our calendar. Someone else might believe the evidence concludes the final fall of Jerusalem took place in 587 BC. These men have no disagreement over the facts. The only thing they disagree about is method of synchronizing the calendars.

As we go back in time, these minor disagreements over calendar synchronization will grow greater. The correct dating of the Fall of Jerusalem determines the correct dating of the founding of Solomon's temple, which determines the correct dating of the Exodus of Egypt, which determines the correct dating of the call of Abraham, which determines the correct dating of the flood of Noah, which determines the correct dating of the creation of the world.

Specific examples of attacks on recognized members of the scientific community because of a connection with Intelligent Design

Dr. Richard Sternberg, on his website RichardSternberg.org, describes himself as an evolutionary biologist with interests in the relation between genes and morphological homologies, and the nature of genomic 'information.' I hold a Ph.D. in Biology (Molecular Evolution) from Florida International University and a Ph.D. in Systems Science (Theoretical Biology) from Binghamton University.

His position of respect and influence in the mainstream scientific community is undeniable. From 2001-2007, I served as a staff scientist at the National Center for Biotechnology Information, and from 2001-2007 I was a Research Associate at the Smithsonian's National Museum of Natural History. I am presently a research scientist at the Biologic Institute, supported by a research fellowship from the Center for Science and Culture at Discovery Institute. I am also a Research Collaborator at the National Museum of Natural History.

Dr. Sternberg goes on to say that, In 2004, in my capacity as editor of The Proceedings of the Biological Society of Washington, I authorized "The Origin of Biological Information and the Higher Taxonomic Categories" by Dr. Stephen Meyer to be published in the journal after passing peer-review. Because Dr. Meyer's article presented scientific evidence for intelligent design in biology, I faced retaliation, defamation, harassment, and a hostile work environment at the Smithsonian's National Museum of Natural History that was designed to force me out as a Research Associate there. Federal government employees acting in concert with an outside advocacy group, the National Center for Science Education, took these actions. Efforts were also made to get me fired from my job as a staff scientist at the National Center for Biotechnology Information.

Subsequently, there were two federal investigations of my mistreatment, one by the U.S. Office of Special Counsel in 2005, and the other by subcommittee staff of the U.S. House Committee on Government Reform in 2006. Both investigations unearthed clear evidence that my rights had been repeatedly violated.

The author of the article Dr. Sternberg approved for publication in the above reference is Dr. Stephen C. Meyer. His credentials are as follows, taken from the website of the Access Research Network (ARN.org).

Dr. Stephen C. Meyer received his Ph.D. in the History and Philosophy of Science from the University of Cambridge in 1991 for a dissertation on origin-of-life biology and the methodology of the historical sciences. Formerly a geophysicist with the Atlantic Richfield Company, he is currently Director of the Center for Renewal of Science and Culture at Discovery Institute and an Associate Professor of Philosophy at Whitworth College. He is a past recipient of a Rotary International Scholarship, the American Friends of Cambridge scholarship (administered by the Cambridge Commonwealth Trust) and a Templeton Foundation science-religion teaching grant. He has contributed articles to several scholarly books and anthologies including "The History of Science and Religion in the Western Tradition: An Encyclopedia, Darwinism: Science or Philosophy," "Of Pandas and People: The Central Question of Biological Origins," "The Creation Hypothesis: Scientific Evidence for An Intelligent Designer" and "Facets of Faith and Science: Interpreting God's Action in the World." In addition to technical articles on the philosophy of science, he has published many editorial features in newspapers and magazines such as The Wall Street Journal, The Los Angeles Times, The Chicago Tribune and National Review. He has also recently appeared as a guest on several national television programs including PBS's Freedom Speaks and TechnoPolitics, and CNBC's Hardball with Chris

Matthews. He is currently working on a book formulating a scientific theory of biological design, which looks specifically at the evidence for design in the encoded information in DNA.

As a proponent of Intelligent Design, Dr. Meyer and the Center for Science and Culture were featured in an article in The American Prospect, Liberal Intelligence, a web magazine describing itself in part as follows:

The American Prospect was founded in 1990 as an authoritative magazine of liberal ideas, committed to a just society, an enriched democracy, and effective liberal politics. ... Our mission, simply put, is to rise to the momentous occasion that confronts all Americans who seek a just society built on our greatest traditions. Contemporary conservatism stands to thwart those traditions; it advances its agenda by way of stealth, fear-mongering, and a massive propaganda apparatus. It is our mission to expose that agenda and the lies that support it. ... We founded the Prospect out of a conviction that the conservative undertow in American political life is profoundly influenced by the dominance of conservative media and think tanks. Our conservative counterparts have played a critical role in pulling the entire national debate to the right. We intend to take it back.

Chris Mooney is, according to the magazine's website, a Prospect senior correspondent and a freelance writer living in Washington, D.C. He focuses on issues at the intersection of science and politics, and has been praised as a "revolutionary mind" by Seed Magazine, which recently commended his "trenchant brand of science-centered commentary." His most recent articles include a Columbia Journalism Review feature story about the problem with "balance" in science coverage and a Boston Globe commentary.

In an article written December 2, 2002, entitled "Survival of the Slickest: How Anti-Evolutionists are Mutating Their Message," Mooney says,

These "Intelligent Design" (ID) theorists, as they call themselves, are epitomized by Stephen C. Meyer, an anti-Darwinian philosopher who made the following appeal to The American Prospect: "People with liberal credentials ought to understand what we're up against. This is an entrenched establishment."

ID theorists posit that living things, due to their organizational complexity and magnificent design, simply must be the creations of some form of intelligence. Where evolutionary biologists see species evolving through a blind process of natural selection acting over millions of years, ID theorists assert that life as we know it simply could not have arisen in such a manner. Furthermore, they claim that this is a scientific observation. ID advocates don't always articulate precisely what sort of intelligence they think should stand in lieu of evolution on textbook pages, but God -- defined in a very nebulous way -- generally outpolls extraterrestrials as the leading candidate.

ID's home base is the Center for Science and Culture at Seattle's conservative Discovery Institute. Meyer directs the center; former Reagan adviser Bruce Chapman heads the larger institute, with input from the Christian supply-sider and former American Spectator owner George Gilder (also a Discovery senior fellow). From this perch, the ID crowd has pushed a "teach the controversy" approach to evolution that closely influenced the Ohio State Board of Education's recently proposed science standards, which would require students to learn how scientists "continue to investigate and critically analyze" aspects of Darwin's theory.

This language may seem innocuous enough, but it clearly allows teachers room to bring up ID if they choose. Moreover, the proposal is insidious because the standards don't ask for the critical analysis of any other bedrock scientific theories, such as plate tectonics or quantum mechanics. Unless there's a shift in the political winds, however, Ohio will finalize the troubling new standards in December.

Mooney does not seem to want anybody to be able to bring up ID, ever. His publication claims that conservative ideals are overcoming liberal ideals. His solution is to stifle the "opposition" by mockery, arousing fear of invasion by religionists posing as scientists, and complaining that they're going to take over if they're not stopped. It is also interesting to compare Dr. Meyer's list of credentials against Christopher Mooney's. Mr. Mooney, however, doesn't list any credentials, just some publication credits. (He is also mentioned below in the *Blogspot* of Professor Jeffrey Shallit, in connection with one of his books and complimented for his researching ability.) Mooney can apparently enjoy the freedom to write and publish his beliefs even without years of study and productivity in recognized scientific circles. This is the freedom enjoyed in America. Yet he would deny the same rights to Dr. Meyer. Note that what he writes are beliefs, as fervently held and staunchly defended as any organized dogma.

*Expelled Exposed: Why Expelled Flunks* is a website self-described as "created and maintained by the National Center for Science Education." It goes through the movie item by item and tries to disprove all of its claims. The following is an example of the website's treatment of the content of the movie.

Expelled claims that Iowa State University astronomy professor Guillermo Gonzalez was denied tenure because of his views on intelligent design. However, this shows a naïve and distorted understanding of the tenure process at a major research university. The tenure process involves intense scrutiny of a candidate's accomplishments in order to assess his future potential;

the beliefs or extra-academic opinions held by the candidate are not a factor.

According to ISU, Gonzalez's tenure decision was based on "refereed publications, his level of success in attracting research funding and grants, the amount of telescope observing time he had been granted, the number of graduate students he had supervised, and most importantly, the overall evidence of future career promise in the field of astronomy." As documented below, the university had grounds to conclude that the early promise of Gonzalez's career was not being met.

In other words, Professor Guillermo Gonzalez failed to measure up to his university's scrutiny of his present work and future prospects. Unfortunately, all of the factors presented as criteria for evaluation are completely controlled by the university and it is circular reasoning to blame failure on the man when the university didn't grant him the means. "Refereed publications" means the university has to approve what you write. Failing in "attracting funding and grants" means his ideas for research didn't meet with the approval of the powers that control the purse strings. Who allots the amount of telescope time granted? The university. Again, not his choice. Who assigns graduate students? And how can a man have future promise if he is not permitted to pursue the work he deems to have the most future promise? These so-called proofs certainly admit of more than one interpretation. It is easy to stall a man's career when you control his access to publication, equipment, and students and then accuse him of failing to live up to his promise if his promise doesn't fit in with your dogma.

Also, while teaching at ISU, Gonzalez had 17 articles published. Tenure was withheld not because he failed to publish, but because those in authority did not like what he published. In other words, tenure was withheld from Professor Guillermo Gonzalez because of censorship.

Guillermo Gonzalez - publication record (at ISU)

From the Web of Science (Formerly Science Citation Index)

1. Vanture AD, Smith VV, Lutz J, et al.Correlations between lithium and technetium absorption lines in the spectra of galactic S starsPUBLICATIONS OF THE ASTRONOMICAL SOCIETY OF THE PACIFIC 119 (852): 147-155 FEB 2007Times Cited: 02. Gonzalez GThe chemical compositions of stars with planets: A review PUBLICATIONS OF THE ASTRONOMICAL SOCIETY OF THE PACIFIC 118 (849): 1494-1505 NOV 2006Times Cited: 0

3. Tautvaisiene G, Wallerstein G, Geisler D, et al.Chemical abundances in the Sagittarius galaxy: Terzan 7IAU SYMPOSIA 13: 210-210 2005Times Cited: 04. Gonzalez GIndium abundance trends among sun-like starsMONTHLY NOTICES OF THE ROYAL ASTRONOMICAL SOCIETY 371 (2): 781-785 SEP 11 2006Times Cited: 05. Gonzalez GCondensation temperature trends among stars with planetsMONTHLY NOTICES OF THE ROYAL ASTRONOMICAL SOCIETY 367 (1): L37-L41 MAR 21 2006Times Cited: 56. Gonzalez GHabitable zones in the universeORIGINS OF LIFE AND EVOLUTION OF THE BIOSPHERE 35 (6): 555-606 DEC 2005Times Cited: 07. Gonzalez GMisrepresenting intelligent designSCIENTIST 19 (16): 8-8 AUG 29 2005Times Cited: 0

8. Giridhar S, Lambert DL, Reddy BE, et al.

Abundance analyses of field RV Tauri stars. VI. An extended sampleASTROPHYSICAL JOURNAL 627 (1): 432-445 Part 1 JUL 1 2005Times Cited: 89. Geisler D, Smith VV, Wallerstein G, et al. “Sculptoring” the galaxy? The chemical compositions of red giants in the Sculptor dwarf spheroidal galaxyASTRONOMICAL JOURNAL 129 (3): 1428-1442 MAR 2005Times Cited: 1610. Laws C, Gonzalez GA reevaluation of the super-lithium-rich star in NGC 6633ASTROPHYSICAL JOURNAL 595 (2): 1148-1153 Part 1 OCT 1 2003Times Cited: 511. Laws C, Gonzalez G, Walker KM, et al.Parent stars of extrasolar planets. VII. New abundance analyses of 30 systemsASTRONOMICAL JOURNAL 125 (5): 2664-2677 MAY 2003Times Cited: 4812. Wells LE, Armstrong JC, Gonzalez GReseeding of early Earth by impacts of returning ejecta during the late heavy bombardmentICARUS 162 (1): 38-46 MAR 2003Times Cited: 1313. Gonzalez GColloquium: Stars, planets, and metalsREVIEWS OF MODERN PHYSICS 75 (1): 101-120 JAN 2003Times Cited: 2714. Candia P, Krisciunas K, Suntzeff NB, et al.Optical and infrared photometry of the unusual Type Ia supernova 2000cxPUBLICATIONS OF THE ASTRONOMICAL SOCIETY OF THE PACIFIC 115 (805): 277-294 MAR 2003Times Cited: 2315. Armstrong JC, Wells LE, Gonzalez GRummaging through Earth's attic for remains of ancient life ICARUS 160 (1): 183-196 NOV 2002Times Cited: 1216. Reddy BE, Lambert DL, Laws C, et al.A search for Li-6 in stars with planetsMONTHLY NOTICES OF THE ROYAL ASTRONOMICAL SOCIETY 335 (4): 1005-1016 OCT 1 2002Times Cited: 2617. Gonzalez G, Brownlee D, Ward PDRefugees for life in a hostile universeSCIENTIFIC AMERICANTimes Cited: 1

Pamela Winnick, a former writer for the Pittsburgh Post-Gazette, is interviewed in Expelled because she wrote a piece mentioning Intelligent Design and claimed that she was blacklisted as a journalist because of it. Jeffrey Shallitt, a Canadian professor, gives space in his "Blogspot" to discussing Winnick.

Monday, July 10, 2006 "Pamela Winnick's Science Envy"

Pamela Winnick is an attorney and former reporter for the Pittsburgh Post-Gazette who has written several articles that lean against evolution and in favor of intelligent design. I recently forced myself to read her 2005 book, A Jealous God: Science's Crusade Against

Religion. It wasn't a pleasant experience. Winnick's book covers a variety of topics: abortion, population control, eugenics, medical experimentation, the Scopes trial, the theory of evolution, intelligent design, and fetal tissue research. Her thesis -- if this rambling, disjointed book can be said to have one -- is contained in the book's final paragraph ... "The Galileo prototype of the scientist martyred by religion is now purely a myth. Science long ago won its war against religion, not just traditional religion, but any faith in a power outside the human mind. Now it wants more.

"Throughout the book, scientists are depicted as crazed, power-hungry, and immoral. Only religion, Winnick implies, can rein in these dangerous nuts who threaten society. Winnick's claim that "science long ago won its war against religion" is far too glib. Ironically, 2005 also saw the publication of Chris Mooney's The Republican War on Science, a far-better-documented book that shows in depressing detail how American science has been subjugated to the political and especially religious goals of the Christian right. Winnick's reporting is sloppy. Incidents are slanted to support her thesis, names are misspelled (Stanislaw Ulam's last name is comically morphed into "Ulsam"; Richard Lewontin's middle initial is given incorrectly), quotes are mined (sometimes incorrectly), and some "facts" are just plain made up.

Detractors claim that Winnick hasn't been blacklisted. She has continued to write for pay and was in no way harmed by those who object to her giving space to ID.

Certainly she has written for publication since this blacklisting. But consider that a person in an occupation needs to make a full-time living at that occupation. He or she must be able to sell enough writing to live from the proceeds. Listing a handful of works she has sold, including a book, does not prove that she has not been censured. It seems to prove the opposite.

If this were a Marxist, totalitarian regime she would of course have published nothing. As it is, she has probably managed to find a smaller voice and no doubt a smaller living. The attacks in the foregoing quote represent one voice among many who have risen to censure her for daring to give a voice to ID thinking. Note the condescending tone, the insults, the insertion of a plug for the "right" (or is it "left"?) kind of writing. He accuses Winnick of being sloppy, slanted, picking at minor errors, which may not even have been her doing, but editorial responsibilities, "mining quotes," as if a person can afford to include every nuance of every scholar's perspective on a topic between the covers of a book that isn't his work, and even calls her a liar. He provides documentation for many of his claims, of course, but as was pointed out in the Professor Guillermo Gonzalez situation, there are multiple perspectives to consider when presenting evidence, and if anybody's perspective is slanted, it is Professor Jeffrey Shallit's.

Discovery Institute Background, Positions and Membership

(Author's Note: All of the material following comes directly from the Discovery Institute website, www.discovery.org, relating to the PBS series Evolution which aired in 2001. This material is included in its entirety to explain what the Discovery Institute is, to make clear who its members and associates are, and what they do and do not believe, in their own words. Special notice should be taken of the Zogby Poll released at the same time as this report and its conclusions about what Americans think about the teaching of Evolution or the introduction of Intelligent Design evidence in the classroom. The complete poll is available for review on Discovery Institute's website.) Discovery Institute is a non-profit, non-partisan public policy center for national and international affairs. The Institute's mission is to make a positive vision of the future practical. The Institute discovers and promotes ideas in the common sense tradition of representative government, the free market and individual liberty. Its mission is promoted through books, reports, legislative testimony, articles, public conferences and debates, plus media coverage and the Institute's own publications and website. Current projects explore the fields of technology, science and culture, reform of the law, national defense, the environment and the economy, the future of democratic institutions, transportation, religion and public life, government entitlement spending, foreign affairs and cooperation within the bi-national region of "Cascadia". Discovery Institute 1511 Third Ave Suite 808 Seattle, WA 98101 (206) 292-0401 fax (206) 682-5320 *http://www.discovery.org*

Discovery Institute's Critique of the PBS 2001 series Evolution:

SEATTLE--In an ironic greeting to the seven-part public television series "Evolution" that begins tonight, 100 scientists have declared that they "are skeptical of claims for the ability of random mutation and natural selection to account for the complexity of life." The signers say, "Careful examination of the evidence for Darwinian theory should be encouraged."

Discovery Institute, a Seattle-based public policy center, compiled the list of statement signers (attached). Among other things, the long list may help to answer the contention of designated spokespeople for the series "Evolution" that "virtually all reputable scientists in the world" support Darwin's theory. Institute officials charge that officials of WGBH/Clear Blue Sky Productions have used that contention to keep any scientific criticism of Darwinism from being acknowledged or examined in the eight-hour series. "They want people to think that the only criticism of Darwin's theory today is from religious fundamentalists," said Discovery president Bruce Chapman. "They routinely try to stigmatize scientists who question Darwin as 'creationists'. "Chemist and five time Nobel nominee, Henry "Fritz" Schaefer of the University of Georgia, commented on the need to encourage debate on Darwin's theory of evolution. "Some defenders of Darwinism," says Schaefer, "embrace standards of evidence for evolution that as scientists they would never accept in other circumstances." Schaefer was on the roster of signers of the statement, termed "A Scientific Dissent on Darwinism." Meanwhile, a Zogby Poll released today shows overwhelming public support--81 percent--for the position that "When public broadcasting networks discuss Darwin's theory of evolution, they should present the scientific evidence for it, but also the scientific evidence against it." Only 10 percent support presenting "only the scientific evidence that supports" Darwin's theory. (Less than 10 percent said "Neither" or "Not sure.") "Public television producers are clearly at odds with overwhelming public sentiment in favor of hearing all scientific sides of the debate," said Chapman, a former Director of the US Census Bureau. "The huge majorities in the poll cross every demographic, regional and political line in America." The national sample of 1,202 adults was conducted by Zogby International from August 25-29. The margin of error is +/-3.0%. Discovery Institute commissioned the Zogby poll, though the survey itself was designed by the Zogby organization. It also included questions on education and "intelligent design," a theory that some scientific critics of Darwin support. (That theory makes no religious claims, but says that the best natural evidence for life's origins points to design rather than a process of random mutation and natural selection.) Discovery Institute last week also opened a special website (www.reviewevolution.org) to critique the WGBH/Clear Blue Sky series in a scholarly "Viewer's Guide." Discovery officials say that the website analyzes all program segments in the series and has uncovered numerous scientific and historical errors, exaggerations and omissions. Full results of the Zogby poll also are available on the website. "The numbers of scientists who question Darwinism is a minority, but it is growing fast," said Stephen Meyer, a Cambridge-educated philosopher of science who directs the Center for the Renewal of Science and Culture at Discovery Institute. "This is happening in the face of fierce attempts to intimidate and suppress legitimate dissent. Young scientists are threatened with deprivation of tenure. Others have seen a consistent pattern of answering scientific arguments with ad hominem attacks. In particular, the series' attempt to stigmatize all critics--including scientists--as religious 'creationists' is an excellent example of viewpoint discrimination." Signers of the statement questioning Darwinism came from throughout the US and from several other countries, representing biology, physics, chemistry, mathematics, geology, anthropology and other scientific fields. Professors and researchers at such universities as Princeton, MIT, U Penn, and Yale, as well as smaller colleges and the National Laboratories at Livermore, CA and Los Alamos, N.M., are included. A number of the signers have authored or contributed to books on issues related to evolution, or have books underway. Despite repeated requests, the series' producers refused to cover scientific objections to Darwinism. Instead, the producers offered only to let scientific dissenters go on camera to tell their "personal faith stories" in the last program of the series, "What About God?" According to Discovery's Chapman, "This was almost an insult to serious scientists. Some of these dissenting scientists are not even religious. When you watch that last program, you realize they were wise to refuse to take part in it." Jed Macosko, a young research molecular biologist at the University of California, Berkeley, and a statement signer, said, "It is time for defenders of Darwin to engage in serious dialogue and debate with their scientific critics. Science can't grow where institutional gatekeepers try to prevent new challengers from being heard."

A Scientific Dissent on Darwinism "I am skeptical of claims for the ability of random mutation and natural selection to account for the complexity of life. Careful examination of the evidence for Darwinian theory should be encouraged." Henry F.Schaefer: Director, Center for Computational Quantum Chemistry: U. of Georgia • Fred Sigworth: Prof. of Cellular & Molecular Physiology-Grad. School: Yale U. • Philip S. Skell: Emeritus Prof. Of Chemistry: NAS member • Frank Tipler: Prof. of Mathematical Physics: Tulane U. • Robert Kaita: Plasma Physics Lab: Princeton U. • Michael Behe: Prof. of Biological Science: Lehigh U. • Walter Hearn: PhD Biochemistry-U of Illinois • Tony Mega: Assoc. Prof. of Chemistry: Whitworth College • Dean Kenyon: Prof. Emeritus of Biology: San Francisco State U. • Marko Horb: Researcher, Dept. of Biology & Biochemistry: U. of Bath, UK • Daniel Kubler: Asst. Prof. of Biology: Franciscan U. of Steubenville • David Keller: Assoc. Prof. of Chemistry: U. of New Mexico • James Keesling: Prof. of Mathematics: U. of Florida • Roland F. Hirsch: PhD Analytical Chemistry-U. of Michigan • Robert Newman: PhD Astrophysics-Cornell U. • Carl Koval: Prof., Chemistry & Biochemistry: U. of Colorado, Boulder • Tony Jelsma: Prof. of Biology: Dordt College • William A.Dembski: PhD Mathematics-U. of Chicago: • George Lebo: Assoc. Prof. of Astronomy: U. of Florida • Timothy G. Standish: PhD Environmental Biology-George Mason U. • James Keener: Prof. of Mathematics & Adjunct of Bioengineering: U. of Utah • Robert J. Marks: Prof. of Signal & Image Processing: U. of Washington • Carl Poppe: Senior Fellow: Lawrence Livermore Laboratories • Siegfried Scherer: Prof. of Microbial Ecology: Technische Universitaet Muenchen • Gregory Shearer: Internal Medicine, Research: U. of California, Davis • Joseph Atkinson: PhD Organic Chemistry-M.I.T.: American Chemical Society, member • Lawrence H. Johnston: Emeritus Prof. of Physics: U. of Idaho • Scott Minnich: Prof., Dept of Microbiology, Molecular Biology & Biochem: U. of Idaho • David A. DeWitt: PhD

Neuroscience-Case Western U. • Theodor Liss: PhD Chemistry-M.I.T. • Braxton Alfred: Emeritus Prof. of Anthropology: U. of British Columbia • Walter Bradley: Prof. Emeritus of Mechanical Engineering: Texas A & M •

Paul D. Brown: Asst. Prof. of Environmental Studies: Trinity Western U. (Canada) • Marvin Fritzler: Prof. of Biochemistry & Molecular Biology: U. of Calgary, Medical School • Theodore Saito: Project Manager: Lawrence Livermore Laboratories • Muzaffar Iqbal: PhD Chemistry-U. of Saskatchewan: Center for Theology the Natural Sciences • William S. Pelletier: Emeritus Distinguished Prof. of Chemistry: U. of Georgia, Athens • Keith Delaplane: Prof. of Entomology: U. of Georgia • Ken Smith: Prof. of Mathematics: Central Michigan U. • Clarence Fouche: Prof. of Biology: Virginia Intermont College • Thomas Milner: Asst. Prof. of Biomedical Engineering: U. of Texas, Austin • Brian J.Miller: PhD Physics-Duke U. • Paul Nesselroade: Assoc. Prof. of Psychology: Simpson College • Donald F.Calbreath: Prof. of Chemistry: Whitworth College • William P. Purcell: PhD Physical Chemistry-Princeton U. • Wesley Allen: Prof. of Computational Quantum Chemistry: U. of Georgia • Jeanne Drisko: Asst. Prof., Kansas Medical Center: U. of Kansas, School of Medicine • Chris Grace: Assoc. Prof. of Psychology: Biola U. • Wolfgang Smith: Prof. Emeritus-Mathematics: Oregon State U. • Rosalind Picard: Assoc. Prof. Computer Science: M.I.T. • Garrick Little: Senior Scientist, Li-Cor: Li-Cor • John L. Omdahl: Prof. of Biochemistry & Molecular Biology: U. of New Mexico • Martin Poenie: Assoc. Prof. of Molecular Cell & Developmental Bio: U. of Texas, Austin • Russell W.Carlson: Prof. of Biochemistry & Molecular Biology: U. of Georgia • Hugh Nutley: Prof. Emeritus of Physics & Engineering: Seattle Pacific U. • David Berlinski: PhD Philosophy-Princeton: Mathematician, Author • Neil Broom: Assoc. Prof., Chemical & Materials Engineeering: U. of Auckland • John Bloom: Assoc.

Prof., Physics: Biola U. • James Graham: Professional Geologist, Sr. Program Manager: National Environmental Consulting Firm • John Baumgardner: Technical Staff, Theoretical Division: Los Alamos National Laboratory • Fred Skiff: Prof. of Physics: U. of Iowa • Paul Kuld: Assoc. Prof., Biological Science: Biola U. • Yongsoon Park: Senior Research Scientist: St. Luke's Hospital, Kansas City • Moorad Alexanian: Prof. of Physics: U. of North Carolina, Wilmington • Donald Ewert: Director of Research Administration: Wistar Institute • Joseph W. Francis: Assoc. Prof. of Biology: Cedarville U. • Thomas Saleska: Prof. of Biology: Concordia U. • Ralph W. Seelke: Prof. & Chair of Dept. of Biology & Earth Sciences: U. of Wisconsin, Superior • James G. Harman: Assoc. Chair, Dept. of Chemistry & Biochemistry: Texas Tech U. • Lennart Moller: Prof. of Environmental Medicine, Karolinska Institute: U. of Stockholm • Raymond G. Bohlin: PhD

Molecular & Cell Biology-U. of Texas: • Fazale R. Rana: PhD Chemistry-Ohio U. • Michael Atchison: Prof. of Biochemistry: U. of Pennsylvania, Vet School • William S. Harris: Prof. of Basic Medical Sciences: U. of Missouri, Kansas City • Rebecca W. Keller: Research Prof., Dept. of Chemistry: U. of New Mexico • Terry Morrison: PhD Chemistry-Syracuse U. • Robert F. DeHaan: PhD Human Development-U. of Chicago • Matti Lesola: Prof., Laboratory of Bioprocess Engineering: Helsinki U. of Technology • Bruce Evans: Assoc. Prof. of Biology: Huntington College • Jim Gibson: PhD Biology-Loma Linda U. • David Ness: PhD Anthropology-Temple U. • Bijan Nemati: Senior Engineer: Jet Propulsion Lab (NASA) • Edward T. Peltzer: Senior Research Specialist: Monterey Bay Research Institute • Stan E. Lennard: Clinical Assoc. Prof. of Surgery: U. of Washington • Rafe Payne: Prof. & Chair, Biola Dept. of Biological Sciences: Biola U. • Phillip Savage: Prof. of Chemical Engineering: U. of Michigan • Pattle Pun: Prof. of Biology: Wheaton College • Jed Macosko: Postdoctoral Researcher-

Molecular Biology: U. of California, Berkeley • Daniel Dix: Assoc. Prof. of Mathematics: U. of South Carolina • Ed Karlow: Chair, Dept. of Physics: LaSierra U. • James Harbrecht: Clinical Assoc. Prof.: U. of Kansas Medical Center • Robert W. Smith: Prof. of Chemistry: U. of Nebraska, Omaha • Robert DiSilvestro: PhD Biochemistry-Texas A & M U., Professor, Human Nutrition, Ohio State University • David Prentice: Prof., Dept. of Life Sciences: Indiana State U. • Walt Stangl: Assoc. Prof. of Mathematics: Biola U. • Jonathan Wells: PhD Molecular & Cell Biology-U. of California, Berkeley: • James Tour: Chao Prof. of Chemistry: Rice U. • Todd Watson: Asst. Prof. of Urban & Community Forestry: Texas A & M U. • Robert Waltzer: Assoc. Prof. of Biology: Belhaven College • Vincente Villa: Prof. of Biology: Southwestern U. • Richard Sternberg: Pstdoctoral Fellow, Invertebrate Biology: Smithsonian Institute • James Tumlin: Assoc. Prof. of Medicine: Emory U. Charles Thaxton: PhD Physical Chemistry-Iowa State U.

Lunar Recession

PUBLIC INFORMATION OFFICE

JET PROPULSION LABORATORY

CALIFORNIA INSTITUTE OF TECHNOLOGY

NATIONAL AERONAUTICS AND SPACE ADMINISTRATION

PASADENA, CALIF. 911909. TELEPHONE (818) 354-5011

Contact: Diane Ainsworth

FOR IMMEDIATE RELEASE July 21, 1994

During their brief moon walk 25 years ago, the Apollo 11 astronauts deployed a variety of scientific experiments, including a reflector array left in the fine powder of the Sea of Tranquility that continues to measure the moon's orbit around Earth to unprecedented accuracy.

Scientist who analyze data from the Lunar Laser Ranging Experiment have reported some watershed results from these long-term experiments, said Jet Propulsion Laboratory team investigator Dr. Jean Dickey. The team's findings appear in this week's issue of Science magazine, which commemorates the silver anniversary of the Apollo 11 lunar landing.

"Using the Lunar Laser Ranging Experiment, we have been able to improve, by orders of magnitude, measurements of the moon's rotation," Dickey said. "We also have strong evidence that the moon has a liquid core, and laser ranging has allowed us to determine with great accuracy the rate at which the moon is gradually receding from the Earth."

The laser ranging retroreflector was positioned on the moon in 1969 by the Apollo 11 astronauts so that it would point toward Earth and be able to reflect pulses of laser light fired from the ground. By beaming laser pulses at the reflector, scientists have been able to determine the round-trip travel time of a laser pulse and provide the distance between these two bodies at any given time down to an accuracy of about 3 centimeters (about 1 inch).

The laser reflector consists of 100 fused silica half-cubes, called corner cubes, mounted in a 46-centimeter (18-inch) square aluminum panel.

Each corner cube is 3.8 centimeters (1.5 inches) in diameter. Corner cubes reflect a beam of light directly back toward the point of origin and, thus, allow scientists to measure the Earth-moon separation and study the dynamics of the Earth, the moon and the Earth-moon system.

Once the laser ranging experiments bean to yield valuable results, more reflectors were left on the moon. A reflector identical to the Apollo 11 mission reflector was left the Apollo 14 crew, and a larger reflector using 300 corner cubes was placed on the moon by the Apollo 15 astronauts. French-built reflectors were also left on the moon by the unmanned Russian Lunakhod 2 mission.

Several observatories have regularly ranged the moon with these reflectors: one is located at McDonald Observatory near Fort Davis, Texas; another is located atop the extinct Haleakala volcano on the island of Maui in Hawaii; another is located in southern France near Grasse.

The Lick Observatory in northern California also has been used in the past for the lunar laser ranging experiments and ranging programs have been carried out in Australia, Russia and Germany. Despite the difficulty of detecting reflected laser light from the moon, Dickey said, more than 8,300 ranges have been measured over the last 25 years.

Lunar ranging involves sending a laser beam through an optical telescope," Dickey said. "The beam enters the telescope where the eye piece would be, and the transmitted beam is expanded to become the diameter of the main mirror, then bounced off the surface toward the reflector on the moon."

The reflectors are too small to be seen from Earth, so even when the beam is precisely aligned in the telescope, actually hitting a lunar retroreflector array is technically challenging. At the moon's surface the beam is roughly four miles wide. Scientists liken the task of aiming the beam to using a rifle to hit a moving dime two miles away.

Once the laser beam hits a reflector, scientists at the ranging observatories use extremely sensitive filtering and amplification equipment to detect the return signal, which is far too weak to be seen with the human eye. Even under good atmospheric viewing condition, only one photon-the fundamental particle of light-will be received every few seconds.

The range accuracy of these reflectors has been improved over the lifetime of the lunar laser ranging experiments, the team noted in Science. While the earliest ranges had accuracies of several meters (or several yards), continuing improvements in the lasers and the detection electronics have led to recent measurements that are accurate to about 3 centimeters (about 1 inch).

From the ranging experiments, scientists know that the average distance between the centers of the Earth and moon is 385,000 kilometers (239,000 miles), showing that modern lunar ranges have relative accuracies of better than one part in 10 billion.

This level of accuracy represents one of the most precise distance measurements ever made," Dickey said. "The degree of accuracy is equivalent to determining the distance between Los Angeles and New York to one fiftieth of an inch."

Laser ranging has also made possible a wealth of new information about the dynamics and structure of the moon. Among many new observations, scientists now believe that the moon may harbor a liquid core. The theory has been proposed from data on the moon's rate of rotation and very slight bobbing motions caused by gravitational forces from the sun and Earth.

Other recent findings from the laser ranging experiments include:

--Verification of Einstein's theory of relativity, which states that all bodies fall with the same acceleration regardless of their mass.

--The length of an Earth day has distinct small-scale variations, changing by about one thousandth of a second over the course of a year. These changes are caused by the atmosphere, tides and the Earth's core.

--Precise positions of the laser ranging observatories on Earth are slowly drifting as the crustal plates on Earth drift. The observatory on Maui is seen to be drifting away from the observatory in Texas.

--Ocean tides on Earth have a direct influence on the moon's orbit.

Measurements show that the moon is receding from Earth at a rate of about 3.8 centimeters (1.5 inches) per year.

--Lunar ranging has greatly improved scientists' knowledge of the moon's orbit, enough to permit accurate analyses of solar eclipses as far back as 1400 BC.

Natural Law and its Influence on Science, History and Belief

Aristotle's thinking on the subject is confusing, and he has been called the Father of Natural Law. He seems in his work Rhetoric to have distinguished between particular laws that each nation has set up for itself and common law, that is according to nature. It may be that Aristotle only thought that such a principle could be invoked if the particular laws were in opposition to what the person was trying to obtain in the way of justice.

Aristotle's distinction seemed to indicate a "higher" law, a law of nature. Some people acknowledged a concept called divine positive legislation, and said that laws emanated from the gods. The Stoics believed the universe had purpose and order apart from divine or natural influences, an "eternal" law. To them the true natural law was a rational being living according to this law. Actions had to follow dictates of virtue. Stoics believed that the worth of the individual, his moral duty, and the brotherhood of men were universal ideas. Roman jurists followed these principles, and they were passed down through the development of legal theory.

Many churchmen attempted to incorporate this supposedly secular theory into Christian doctrine. It was difficult to do so without creating confusion about clear teaching on man's fallen nature after the original sin and his inability as a consequence to make or follow any natural laws. Thomas Aquinas believed that man's reason could only go so far and needed God's law to complete it.

Aquinas' beliefs became part of Roman Catholic teaching, the basis for the ideas of the unity of the body and the soul, the conscience, and the ability to perceive and choose good or evil were codified by his teachings. Aquinas believed reason could bring man closer to conformity with God's will. A sort of divine corollary to the idea of preserving life is his belief that reason will lead man to seek good and avoid evil. He believed sin could blind reason and render it ineffective.

There belongs to the natural law, first, certain most general precepts, that are known to all; and secondly, certain secondary and more detailed precepts, which are, as it were, conclusions following closely from first principles. As to those general principles, the natural law, in the abstract, can nowise be blotted out from men's hearts. But it is blotted out in the case of a particular action, insofar as reason is hindered from applying the general principle to a particular point of practice, on account of concupiscence or some other passion, as stated above (77, 2). But as to the other, i.e., the secondary precepts, the natural law can be blotted out from the human heart, either by evil persuasions, just as in speculative matters errors occur in respect of necessary conclusions; or by vicious customs and corrupt habits, as among some men, theft, and even unnatural vices, as the Apostle states (Rm. i), were not esteemed sinful. (Summa Theologica Sixth Article [I-II, Q. 94, Art. 6] Objection 3)

Application has been made to every kind of behavior, and how it relates to man's ability to live by natural law. Even motive must play a part, since doing a good deed for the wrong reason negates the good deed. Aquinas believed that even good intentions were not enough, and he formulated the Cardinal Virtues (Prudence, Justice, Temperance and Fortitude, developed by reason applied to nature). He also believed in the necessity of practicing the theological virtues (Faith, Hope and Charity, developed by spiritual application). All are necessary.

Thomas Hobbes created a massive body of works including one called Leviathan, and in his writings outlined principles that resulted in a natural law based on rational needs for survival, prosperity, and the actions that would need to result from these considerations. Hobbes believed man needed a supreme ruler as the source of law in order for natural law to work. Hobbes essentially believed that natural law forbade man to engage in self-destructive behavior. Man could not take away what preserved life and he had to give up anything that might be harmful to this key principle, that life must be preserved.

Hobbes was a philosopher, and his work led to the strengthening of the power of absolute rulers. He didn't consider whether a ruler was moral or not to be important. Divine Right, the idea that a monarch's power to rule is given by God and cannot be challenged, extends from this philosophy.

Hugo Grotius believed even an all-powerful God could not change natural law. He said that even if there were no God, or if God did not care about man (neither of which he believed was true) natural law would remain solid and unchangeable. This statement gave rise to the separation of natural law from theology. Whether Grotius intended this consequence is questionable. He believed it was impossible that God did not exist, according to his De iure belli ac pacis, Prolegomeni XI), which deals with the natural law question. It seems he only intended to say that natural law was a protective device that would not change and could be relied on, not that since it existed there was no need to consider God.

John Locke took the opposite view from Hobbes and the Divine Right theories. In works that included Two Treatises of Government, he taught that a ruler could violate natural law and his mandate to protect "life, liberty, and property." In such a case the people were obligated to depose and replace him.

Thomas Jefferson's concept of inalienable rights comes from Locke. In the declaration of Independence he refines the natural rights theory and makes it a part of American History. We hold these truths to be self-evident, that all men are created equal, that they are endowed by their Creator with certain unalienable Rights, that among these are Life, Liberty and the pursuit of Happiness.

Pierre Charron in his De la sagesse (1601), said: "The sign of a natural law must be the universal respect in which it is held, for if there was anything that nature had truly commanded us to do, we would undoubtedly obey it universally: not only would every nation respect it, but every individual. Instead there is nothing in the world that is not subject to contradiction and dispute, nothing that is not rejected, not just by one nation, but by many; equally, there is nothing that is strange and (in the opinion of many) unnatural that is not approved in many countries, and authorized by their customs."

This is an interesting contrast to all those who assume the existence of natural law. It is surprising that more secularists and even believers do not hold this view. Charron seems to put his finger on the problem of a fallen world and fallen man exactly. Whether he is himself a believer in fallen nature, he states the truth that we cannot practice obedience to any natural law because our sinful minds are in chaos and conflict.

U.S. statesman James Madison believed that some rights, such as trial by jury, are social rights. These simply develop as social interaction gives rise to a government system and develops laws it needs to exist as a unit. This idea combines the ideas of natural and concrete man-made laws and gives a key to understanding the original intention of the founders in the so-called controversy over the relationship they intended between religion and government.

The following includes excerpts from Dr. Jonathan Sarfati's article "Who's Really Pushing Bad Science?" From Creation.com, the website of Creation Ministries International, including the website's statement of the author's credentials. The quoted material is extensive because it so clearly and completely defines important aspects of natural law, materialism, Humanism, evolution and creation study. It also addresses the issues brought up by those who insist Science must rely on Natural Law and that belief in God has no part in scientific study.

The first paragraph is the website's presentation of Dr. Sarfati's credentials. Dr. Sarfati's article appears in italics, as does all quoted material. He also quotes extensively from the work Good Science, Bad Science: Teaching Evolution in the States by Lawrence S. Lerner, since Sarfati's article is written in response to that work. Both Sarfati and Lerner have outside sources quoted within their works.

Dr. Sarfati studied science at Victoria University of Wellington. He obtained a B.Sc. (Hons.) in Chemistry with two physics papers substituted (nuclear and condensed matter physics). His Ph.D. in Chemistry was awarded for a thesis entitled 'A Spectroscopic Study of some Chalcogenide Ring and Cage Molecules'. He has co-authored papers in mainstream scientific journals on high temperature superconductors and selenium-containing ring and cage-shaped molecules. He also had a co-authored paper on high-temperature superconductors published in Nature when he was 22.

The following information on Dr. Lerner is taken from the website of the California State University, Long Beach.

Dr. Lawrence S. Lerner is Professor Emeritus of Physics and Astronomy at the California State University, Long Beach. He received his B.A., M.S. and Ph.D. from the University of Chicago. His areas of Expertise are Condensed-matter physics; history of science; science education (college level and K-12); textbooks; science and the humanities; science and religion; K-12 science textbooks, evaluation of K-12 science. His books include two college-level calculus-based physics texts; translation of Giordano Bruno, The Ash Wednesday Supper (1584), An Appraisal of Science Standards in 36 States (1998), and has written more than 100 papers on the subjects listed above. He is also a consultant to several states on science standards.

A Response to Good Science, Bad Science: Teaching Evolution in the States by Lawrence S. Lerner, Thomas B. Fordham Foundation, 26 September 2000.

The theory that Lerner and other materialists are really promoting, and which creationists oppose, is the idea that particles turned into people over time, without any need for an intelligent designer. This 'General Theory of Evolution' (GTE) was defined by the evolutionist Kerkut as 'the theory that all the living forms in the world have arisen from a single source which itself came from an inorganic form.'

Lerner claims that evolution occupies a 'central place' and has a 'unifying role' in the life sciences, and the title even hints that the physical sciences are affected.

Author's Note: Dr. Sarfati refers to the two following Scripture passages in his article. They are placed here in their entirety for easy reference.

(Colossians 1:15–17: He is the image of the invisible God, the firstborn over all creation. For by him all things were created: things in heaven and on earth, visible and invisible, whether thrones or powers or rulers or authorities; all things were created by him and for him. He is before all things, and in him all things hold together.)

(Genesis 2:1–3: Thus the heavens and the earth were completed in all their vast array. By the seventh day God had finished the work he had been doing; so on the seventh day he rested from all his work. And God blessed the seventh day and made it holy, because on it he rested from all the work of creating that he had done.)

Kansas State University immunologist Scott Todd asserted:

'Even if all the data point to an intelligent designer, such an hypothesis is excluded from science because it is not naturalistic.'

That is, never mind the facts — nature is all there is. Naturalism is king! So the opposition to creation has nothing to do with the facts, but with the fact that creationists refuse to play by the self-serving rules of the game formulated by materialists. This contrasts with what most people might think, e.g. double Noble laureate Linus Pauling: 'Science is the search for the truth.'

So how do Lerner et al. try to get around the charge that evolution is really pushing the religion of humanism? After all, the first two tenets of the Humanist Manifesto II (1973), signed by many prominent evolutionists, are:

Religious humanists regard the universe as self-existing and not created.

Humanism believes that Man is a part of nature and has emerged as a result of a continuous process.

The current version, Humanist Manifesto 2000, was signed by the prominent evolutionary propagandists Richard Dawkins, E.O. Wilson, Richard Leakey, Molleen Matsumara and Daniel Dennett.

The atheistic Marxist evolutionist Stephen Jay Gould has claimed that religion and science are 'non-overlapping magisteria' (NOMA). That is, science deals with facts of the real world, while religion deals with ethics, values, morals, and what it means to be human. He expounded this thesis in his book Rocks of Ages: Science and Religion in the Fullness of Life (Ballantyne, NY, 1999).

However, this is based on the philosophically fallacious fact-value distinction, and is really an anti-Christian claim. For example, the Resurrection of Christ is an essential part of the Christian faith (1 Corinthians 15:12–19), but it is also a matter of history, it passed the 'testable' claim that the tomb would be empty on the third day, and impinges on science because it demonstrated the power of God over so-called 'natural laws' that dead bodies decay.

Lerner and others claim scientists must practise methodological naturalism, i.e. that natural causes are the only ones allowed, and God, if He exists, did nothing that can be investigated (contrary to Romans 1:18–23). They claim that doesn't necessarily imply ontological naturalism, i.e. that nature is all that really does exist, and God doesn't. The scare tactic they use to promote methodological naturalism is reasoning like:

'It is simply not possible to solve a scientific question if one is willing to invoke a supernatural answer, because supernatural answers foreclose further scientific inquiry. As we have already noted, a person who accounts for the motion of the planets by asserting that angels propel them is simply not going to be able to account for Kepler's laws of planetary motion in any kind of fruitful way.'

This fails to note the distinction between normal (operational) science, and origins or historical science. Normal (operational) science deals only with repeatable observable processes in the present, while origins science helps us to make educated guesses about origins in the past. Operational science has indeed been very successful in understanding the world, and has led to many improvements in the quality of life, e.g. putting men on the moon and curing diseases.

(Author's Note: The following is a letter Dr. Sarfati wrote to an enquirer who believed that atoms had to be held together by miraculous means.)

"'Natural laws' also help us make predictions about future events. In the case of the atom, the explanation of the electrons staying in their orbitals is the positive electric charge and large mass of the nucleus. This enables us to make predictions about how strongly a particular electron is held by a particular atom, for example, making the science of chemistry possible. While this is certainly an example of Col. 1:17, simply saying 'God upholds the electron' doesn't help us make predictions."

The difference between operational and origins science is important for seeing through silly assertions such as the following by Levitt (as quoted by Lerner): '... evolution is as thoroughly established as the picture of the solar system due to Copernicus, Galileo, Kepler, and Newton.'

We can observe the motion of the planets, but no one has ever observed an information-increasing change of one type of organism to another.

To explain further: the laws that govern the operation of a computer are not those that made the computer in the first place. Lerner's anti-creationist propaganda is like saying that if we concede that a computer had an intelligent designer, then we might not analyse a computer's workings in terms of natural laws of electron motion through semiconductors, and might think there are little intelligent beings pushing electrons around instead. Similarly, believing that the genetic code was originally designed does not preclude us from believing that it works entirely by the laws of chemistry involving DNA, RNA, proteins, etc. Conversely, the fact that the coding machinery works according to reproducible laws of chemistry does not prove that the laws of chemistry were sufficient to build such a system from a primordial soup.

The following definition and discussion of fact-value distinction comes from Wikipedia. Dr. Sarfati refers to the term in his discussion of Stephen Jay Gould's book.

The fact-value distinction is a concept used to distinguish between arguments which can be claimed through reason alone, and those where rationality is limited to describing a collective opinion. In another formulation, it is the distinction between what is (can be discovered by science, philosophy or reason) and what ought to be (a judgment which can be agreed upon by consensus). The terms positive and normative represent another manner of expressing this, as do the terms descriptive and prescriptive, respectively. Positive statements make the implicit claim to facts (e.g. water molecules are made up of two hydrogen atoms and one oxygen atom), whereas normative statements make a claim to values or to norms (e.g. water ought to be protected from environmental pollution).

The fact-value distinction emerged in philosophy during the Enlightenment; in particular, David Hume (1711-1776) argued that human beings are unable to ground normative arguments in positive arguments, that is, to derive 'ought' from 'is'. Hume was a skeptic, and although he was a complex and dedicated philosopher, he shared a political viewpoint with previous Enlightenment philosophers such as Thomas Hobbes (1588-1679) and John Locke (1632-1704). Specifically,

Hume, at least to some extent, argued that religious and national hostilities that divided European society were based on unfounded beliefs; in effect, he argued they were not found in nature, but a creation of a particular time and place, and thus unworthy of mortal conflict. Thus Hume is often cited as being the philosopher who finally debunked the idea of nature as a standard for political existence. Alternatively, the phrase "naturalistic fallacy" is used to refer to the claim that what is natural is inherently good or right, and that what is unnatural is bad or wrong (see "Appeal to nature"). It is the converse of the moralistic fallacy, or that what is good or right is natural and inherent.

Samuel Adams believed, along with many rationalists who also acknowledged and respected biblical belief, that Natural Law originated with God at Creation, and was something He had set in motion to keep things running as they should. It included God's provisions and dealings with man, an immutable law, but one that was natural, in the sense of originating with the God of Nature. "The natural liberty of man is to be free from any superior power on Earth, and not to be under the will or legislative authority of man, but only to have the law of nature for his rule."

Alfred, Lord Tennyson and Nature Red in Tooth and Claw

The phrase "nature red in tooth and claw" comes from In Memoriam, A.H.H., a long group of poems written over many years by Alfred, Lord Tennyson completed in 1849. In it Tennyson struggled with his grief over Arthur Henry Hallam, a dear friend who was engaged to Tennyson's sister but died at age 22. The section containing the often-quoted phrase appears below. The complete work is many pages in length and can be viewed in various literature textbooks or online.

*LVI*

*'So careful of the type?' but no.*

*From scarped cliff and quarried stone*
*She cries, 'A thousand types are gone:*
*I care for nothing, all shall go.'*

*Thou makest thine appeal to me:*
*I bring to life, I bring to death:*
*The spirit does but mean the breath:*
*I know no more.' And he, shall he,*

*Man, her last work, who seem'd so fair,*
*Such splendid purpose in his eyes,*
*Who roll'd the psalm to wintry skies,*
*Who built him fanes of fruitless prayer,*

*Who trusted God was love indeed*
*And love Creation's final law—*
*Tho' Nature, red in tooth and claw*
*With ravine, shriek'd against his creed—*

*Who loved, who suffer'd countless ills,*
*Who battled for the True, the Just,*
*Be blown about the desert dust,*
*Or seal'd within the iron hills?*

*No more? A monster then, a dream,*
*A discord. Dragons of the prime,*
*That tare each other in their slime,*
*Were mellow music match'd with him.*
*O life as futile, then, as frail!*
*O for thy voice to soothe and bless!*
*What hope of answer, or redress?*
*Behind the veil, behind the veil.*

These poems chronicle Tennyson's struggle to understand how death fit in with the God of life. In them he also tried to deal with philosophical questions in areas including the newly-named science of Biology.

Darwin had not yet made a name for himself, but other writers were beginning to put together theories of evolution. These were based on ideas like inheritance of acquired characteristics, spontaneous generation, and vital fluids flowing through living things that forced them to undergo evolutionary changes.

All of these ideas were disturbing to thinking men like Tennyson, trying to embrace Rationalism and rely on man's reason to solve life's great questions. They also wondered how the so-called "discoveries" of randomness and chance could co-exist with the orderly Creator and loving Sustainer of the Bible. The theories listed above have all since been discredited but more have sprung up to replace them.

Tennyson's final conclusion in the same set of poems, finished in 1849, includes the following section. It is usually placed first in the published versions but was probably written last. The emphasis is added to show what Tennyson thought of his earlier doubts about how "natural law" fit in with a loving creator God. The text comes from http://www.online-literature.com/tennyson/718/).

*For knowledge is of things we see;*
*And yet we trust it comes from thee,*
*A beam in darkness: let it grow.*
*Let knowledge grow from more to more,*

*But more of reverence in us dwell;*
*That mind and soul, according well,*
*May make one music as before,*
*But vaster.*

*We are fools and slight;*
*We mock thee when we do not fear:*
*But help thy foolish ones to bear;*
*Help thy vain worlds to bear thy light.*

*Forgive what seem'd my sin in me;*
*What seem'd my worth since I began;*
*For merit lives from man to man,*

*And not from man, O Lord, to thee.*

*Forgive my grief for one removed,*
*Thy creature, whom I found so fair.*
*I trust he lives in thee, and there*
*I find him worthier to be loved.*

*Forgive these wild and wandering cries,*
*Confusions of a wasted youth;*
*Forgive them where they fail in truth,*
*And in thy wisdom make me wise.*

## Solar Energy Source Appendix

We have condensed more information from two articles from the Institute for Creation Research website. The first one, "The Sun Is Shrinking," begins with a "disclaimer" of sorts which is included here in its entirety.

"The Sun Is Shrinking"

by Russell Akridge, Ph.D.

Since publication of this article in 1980, studies of the sun's size have yielded different results. Currently, scientists are not united enough concerning any broadscale trends to support age estimates based on the size of the sun. In his 1998 article "The Young Faint Sun Paradox and the Age of the Solar System," Dr. Danny Faulkner provided an updated perspective that is more consistent with the relevant solar data. Other studies do provide ample evidence for the youth of the solar system and earth, such as the studies cited in the Evidence section Many Earth Clocks Indicate Recent Creation.

It may seem at first that ICR is backing off its position on whether this article is accurate or not. More likely they are simply acknowledging that this article is somewhat dated, saying they do not currently have writers working in this particular field of study, and instead offering other young creation articles in support of the position. (We will also deal with Dr Faulkner's article in this review.) Our position is that the information in this article and Dr. Faulkner's are both accurate and present uniformitarians with real dilemmas which they are probably unwilling to address.

The following quotation appears near the beginning of the Akridge article.

"John A. Eddy (Harvard -Smithsonian Center for Astrophysics and High Altitude Observatory in Boulder) and Aram A. Boornazian (a mathematician with S. Ross and Co. in Boston) have found evidence that the sun has been contracting about 0.1% per century...corresponding to a shrinkage rate of about 5 feet per hour."

Dr. Akridge explains the significance of this statement.

"A creationist, who may believe that the world was created approximately 6 thousand years ago, has very little to worry about. The sun would have been only 6% larger at creation than it is now. However, if the rate of change of the solar radius remained constant, 100 thousand years ago the sun would be twice the size it is now. One could hardly imagine that any life could exist under such altered conditions. Yet 100 thousand years is a minute amount of time when dealing with evolutionary time scales."

In his article, Dr. Akridge presents a formula for calculating the size of the sun in the past based on this current shrinkage remaining consistent. His conclusion is that if uniformitarianism is true,

"It is amazing that all of this evolutionary development, except the last 20 million years, took place on a planet that was inside the sun. By 20 million B.C., all of evolution had occurred except the final stage, the evolution of the primate into man."

He points out that it is much more reasonable to simply say that at 100,000 BC the sun would have been twice its present size. Further calculations can be presented based on *"a balance of solar forces"* and assuming a constant shrinkage rate. In fact, figures indicate that the sun's rate of shrinkage would actually have been greater in the past, making the 20 million years figure still too far in the past.

Dr. Akridge's article presents calculations to explain whether a 2.5 feet per hour contraction of the solar surface would be enough to liberate all the solar energy measured as being present. His conclusion is that there is far more than sufficient contraction taking place to produce the observable energy output. He says that gravitational self-collapse certainly accounts for at least some of the sun's energy. According to Dr. Akridge, when uniformitarians calculate the evolution of the sun, *"all of those calculations attribute practically 100% of the sun's energy over the past 5 billion years to thermonuclear fusion."* We have read many articles where the uniformitarians dismiss the solar shrinkage argument simply by saying the sun is so big a little shrinkage doesn't matter. Others claim there are cyclic variations and any shrinkage would be offset. But, as Dr. Akridge points out,

*"This* (cyclic) *claim is made in spite of the evidence that the shrinkage rate of the sun has remained essentially constant over the past 100 years when very accurate measurements have been made on the size of the sun. Less accurate astronomical records spanning the past 400 years indicate the shrinkage rate has remained the same for the past 400 years."*

Dr Akridge's historical background explains that the Kelvin-Helmholtz Contraction theory was considered the most likely explanation of the sun's energy production up until the 1930's, when

*"the theory of evolution began to dominate the scientific scene. Then Helmholtz's explanation was discarded because it did not provide the vast time span demanded by the theory of organic evolution on the earth. The substitute theory was introduced by Bethe in the 1930's precisely because thermonuclear fusion was the only known energy source that would last over the vast times required by evolution."*

This second article is presented on the ICR website as being a more updated study than the previous one.

*The Young Faint Sun Paradox and the Age of the Solar System*

*by Danny Faulkner, Ph.D.*

Dr. Faulkner gives an illustration of the unique position of the Earth for sustaining life by comparing it with conditions on Venus and Mars, making the point that the Earth's position in relation to the sun assures it is neither too hot nor too cold for life. Dr. Faulkner rehearses the standard evolutionary theory about the origin of the solar system. He points out the commonly accepted belief that gravitational compression probably explains the early history of stars and their planets. Most uniformitarians even grant that this accounts for the sun's method of generating energy in its infancy. At some point,

"conditions in the center of the Sun permitted the conversion of hydrogen into helium through nuclear fusion. While theoretical and observational questions remain, it can be assumed for purposes of discussion, that this model approximates the truth."

Faulkner goes on to explain how this thermonuclear theory of the sun's energy production works. *"Calculation shows that it is capable of supplying the Sun's current luminosity for about ten billion years."* If, as evolutionists claim, the sun was formed 9.2 billion years ago, that puts the sun at its halfway point of life and energy use.

"This means that about half the hydrogen in the core of the Sun has been used up and replaced by helium. This change in chemical composition changes the structure of the core. The overall structure of the Sun would have to change as well, so that today, the Sun should be nearly 40% brighter than it was 4.6 billion years ago."

Evolutionists, however, agree that temperatures and luminosity would need to have been relatively consistent for life to evolve as it has. Faulkner suggests a theory, which he calls "naïve," that perhaps

"Earth began cooler than it is today and has been slowly warming with time. But this is not an option because geologists note that Earth's rock record insists that Earth's average temperature has not varied much over the past four billion years, and biologists require a nearly constant average temperature for the development and evolution of life."

Faulkner presents the theories evolutionists propose to explain how this paradox could be explained. The theories explain that early atmospheres of the planets were very different from today.

"Hydrogen was quite abundant. Much of the oxygen present would have been in the form of water. With time these atmospheres followed different evolutionary paths to become the current secondary atmospheres. The prime characteristic of the secondary atmospheres is that they are oxidized, that is, most of the hydrogen has escaped, which has forced the oxygen to recombine to form other compounds."

Explanations are offered for the differences between Mars and Venus and Earth, based on the effect their relative positions and gravity would have had on this evolution of atmosphere. When it comes to Earth, however, the story gets stranger, according to Faulkner's retelling of evolutionists' claims.

"Early life forms are supposed to have introduced free oxygen into the air and regulated the amount of other gases, such as nitrogen. As new forms of life evolved, the mix of gases in Earth's atmosphere gradually changed. Evolution proposes that the early atmosphere contained a greater amount of greenhouse gases (such as methane) than today. This would have produced average temperatures close to those today, even with a much fainter Sun. As the Sun gradually increased in luminosity, Earth's atmosphere is supposed to have evolved along with it, so that the amount of greenhouse gases have slowly decreased to compensate for the increasing solar luminosity."

Faulkner makes the very understandable statement that *"The precise tuning of this alleged co-evolution is nothing short of miraculous ... Thus the incredibly unlikely origin and evolution of life had to be accompanied by the evolution of Earth's atmosphere in concert with the Sun."* We have stated many times that Secular Humanism is a religion of mythology, so it is not surprising they demand we believe in their miraculous evolutionary processes. The problem is that they claim to be factually and scientifically correct but they produce no evidence to support this claim.

*"The physical principles that cause the early faint Sun paradox are well established, so astrophysicists are confident that the effect is real."* Some physicists have actually ventured theories about the biosphere being a unified, living organism capable of sustaining and adapting, though this is not a popular theory. Others try to propose a kind of symbiosis with the Sun, also unlikely. There is in some scientific circles the idea that a *"life force has directed the atmosphere's evolution through this ordeal. Most find the teleological or spiritual implications of this unpalatable, though there is a trend in this direction in physics."*

"Of course, there is a third possibility. Perhaps the Earth/Sun system is not billions of years old and so there has not been a 40% increase in solar luminosity. If Earth were recently created and designed to have the kind of atmosphere that it has now and the Sun has not changed appreciably in luminosity, then the young faint Sun paradox has been resolved. While the early faint Sun paradox does not tell us that the Solar System is only thousands of years old, it does seem to rule out the age being billions of years."

**Akridge, R. 1980. The Sun Is Shrinking.** *Acts & Facts*. **9 (4).**

Faulkner, D. 1998. The Young Faint Sun Paradox and the Age of the Solar System. Acts & Facts. 27 (6).

## Appendix Four: Recommended Reading

Websites

Heritage Foundation *askheritage.org* "To build an America where freedom, opportunity, prosperity and civil society flourish. Public policy research organization."

Cato Institute *www.cato.org* "Increase the understanding of public policies based on the principles of limited government, free markets, individual liberty, and peace."

Discovery Institute *discovery.org*. "Explore ...technology, science and culture, reform of the law, national defense, the environment and the economy, the future of democratic institutions, transportation, religion and public life, government entitlement spending, foreign affairs."

Answers in Genesis *answersingenesis.org*. "enabling Christians to defend their faith ... answers to questions surrounding the book of Genesis, ... train others to develop a biblical worldview..."

Institute for Creation Research *icr.org*. "Scientific research from a biblical perspective ...graduate-level degree program in science education, graduate-level training in biblical education and apologetics ... Publications, Events, and Media."

Ayn Rand Center for Individual Rights *aynrandcenter.org* "advance individual rights (the rights of each person to life, liberty, property, and the pursuit of happiness) as the moral basis for a fully free, laissez-faire capitalist society."

National Rifle Association *nra.org* safety and training programs for military, law enforcement, civilian, female protection and child safety, and "a major political force ... America's foremost defender of Second Amendment rights."

The Internet Sacred Text Archive *sacred-texts.com* Every kind of public-domain material remotely connected with spiritual, philosophical, and broadly religious subjects.

Creation Research Society *creationresearch.org* Education, research, journal publication, "committed to full belief in the Biblical record of creation and early history."

World Net Daily *wnd.com* Original news articles and links to outside sources for news, opinion, commentary with a conservative emphasis.

Books

James Hannam, Web site and book *God's Philosophers: How the Medieval World Laid the Foundations of Modern Science.* Icon Books, London, 2009.

Allan Bloom, *The Closing of the American Mind.* Documentation on secular humanist influence from non-Christian but conservative perspective with extensive research and proofs.

Francis Schaeffer *The God Who Is There, The Christian Manifesto, How Should We Then Live, True Spirituality, Escape from Reason, Back to Freedom and Dignity.* Schaeffer is reformed in theology, evangelical rather than fundamentalist, left America for Switzerland. He was the first evangelical to advocate political activism opposing abortion.

Aleksandr Solzhenitsyn *Gulag Archipelago* (3 volumes) Believer imprisoned under Stalin. collected stories of other prisoners massive, well-documented work on the effects of communism on its own people.

Dr. Don DeYoung, *Thousands, Not Billions: Challenging an Icon of Evolution Questioning the Age of the Earth.* Disproves uniformitarianism by collection of individual scientific studies

George W. Dollar, *A History of Fundamentalism in America.* Church history in America from founding to early 70's emphasis on the 20th century.

David O Beale, *In Pursuit of Purity.* American church history up to 1980's emphasizing conflicts between belief and unbelief, as it affects the church.

William Evans. *The Great Doctrines of the Bible.* Brief easy to read basic Bible doctrines.

John Foxe. Foxe's Book of Martyrs. History of martyrs up to Foxe's time sections added mid-16th century.

Humphreys, D. Russell, Ph.D. *Starlight and Time, Solving the Puzzle of Distant Starlight in a Young Universe.*

Josephus, *Antiquities of the Jews.* Roman General and Jewish historian. Late first century writer from Creation to his lifetime.

Josh MacDowell, *The New Evidence that Demands a Verdict.* Conservative evangelical Christian apologist, evidence in support of the Bible's truth.

G. Campbell Morgan. Commentator Baptist preacher English, lived in America.

Michael Oard. *Frozen in Time: The Wooly Mammoth, The Ice Age and the Bible.* Recent information refuting uniformitarianism.

Antonin Scalia. Supreme Court Justice, Conservative constitutional jurisprudence.

William Warren Sweet. *The Story of Religions in America*. Well-documented, honest but liberal perspective.

J.C Whitcomb and H. M. Morris. *The Genesis Flood*. Classic scientific treatise on Earth geology.

## Bibliography for Antidisestablishmentarianism

Scripture references are as follows: The Bible: The King James Version, public domain. A few verses for comparison purposes are from other translations as follows: The New International Version, from the HOLY BIBLE, NEW INTERNATIONAL VERSION Registered. NIV Registered. Copyright 1973, 1978, 1984 by International Bible Society. Used by permission of Zondervan. All rights reserved. The New American Standard Version: Scripture quotations taken from the New American Standard Bible Registered, Copyright 1960, 1962, 1963, 1968, 1971, 1972, 1973, 1975, 1977, 1995 by The Lockman Foundation Used by permission.

Antidisestablishmentarianism references hundreds of authors and works, yet one source needs special mention. The website Sacred Texts by J.B. Hare is the largest collection of public domain material of which we are aware. The entire website of over one thousand books is available for purchase on either CD ROM or DVD ROM. Most of the ancient texts used in this work are public domain books from this collection. A problem with this or any other collection is proving the validity of the primary sources. Though we do not know anything about John B. Hare, except the information posted on his website, we believe that he faithfully and accurately scanned the texts. The problem is, are the texts reliable? Since they are public domain, they are older and sometimes not the latest translations. We are confident, however, that they are acceptable. Some sources we use are books where Westerners lived among a tribe and wrote down oral traditions. Though we trust that the authors accurately recorded the oral traditions, how much 'contamination' with outside influences shaped these oral traditions? The Lore of the Whare-Wananga, a New Zealand tribe, is well documented by the translator S. Percy Smith to be older than outside influences and free of 'contamination.' Myths of the Cherokee by James Mooney, however, was published in 1900 after more than 250 years of wars and close contact with outsiders. The level of outside influence on the oral traditions of the North American Indians is impossible to measure or deny.

It should also be noted that some of the authors listed here have been accused of being pseudoarchaeologists or pseudoscientists and are largely discounted by many as scholarly sources because of the conclusions they drew from their research or the inability to substantiate some of their claims. Examples of these authors are Graham Hancock, Emmanuel Velikovsky and Thor Heyerdahl. Their conclusions are in some cases not worthy of serious consideration and some of their findings are unverifiable. However, the research they conducted and the discoveries they claim to have made, when verifiable, bear serious consideration. It is necessary to go back to verifiable evidence uncovered by archaeology, exploration and scientific discovery and to draw realistic conclusions from this evidence based on biblical understanding.

Material used from these books includes discoveries verified by repeated similar references in primary sources, documented archaeological sites which beyond question exist and testimony of ancient manuscripts accepted by scholars for hundreds of years. Some evidence cannot be substantiated because it exists in off-limits areas like the interior of China or other countries experiencing dangerous travel conditions. Presenting such claims does not attest to their truth, but in most cases these finds are part of an established pattern repeated throughout the *world.*

_____________. *"1549, 1559, 1662 Acts of Uniformity." Hanover Historical Texts Projects.* History Department, Hanover College, Hanover, IN. *history.hanover.edu.*

_____________. Access Research Network (*ARN.org*). (A scholarly website containing scientific research articles.)

_____________. *The American Heritage® Dictionary of the English Language*, Fourth Edition. ©2000 Houghton Mifflin Company. Updated in 2003.

_____________. *americanpresbyterianchurch.org*

_____________. "Ancient temple found under Lake Titicaca." *BBC News.* Wednesday, 23 August, 2000, 11:04 GMT 12:04 UK.

_____________. *answersingenesis.org.*

_____________. *Assyrian Kings' Lists.* Various translators, various public domain texts with sources including Google Books, Wikipedia, The Internet Ancient History Sourcebook, (http://www.fordham.edu halsall/ ancient/asbook.html), and various universities which have placed public domain works online.

_____________. (Atheist poster compilation) From the website *scottklarr.com.*

_____________. Bethel Lutheran Church, Cupertino, CA website.

_____________. *Biblefacts.org*

_____________. The Book of Enoch. Translated by R.H. Charles, 1917. *The Apocrypha and Pseudepigrapha of the Old Testament.* Oxford: The Clarendon Press, 1913.

_____________. *BBC online*, updated April 10, 2002.

_____________. "Bible Answers." Like the Master Ministries. (Mathematical calculation from proves that 10,000 people could have been born before Adam and Eve died.) *Never Thirsty.org* website.

___________. "Boat People, a Refugee Crisis." *cbc.ca digital archives.* Broadcast May 1, 2000.

___________. "PART I THE BUNDAHIS-BAHMAN YAST, AND SHÂYAST LÂ-SHÂYAST." *Sacred Books of the East, Volume 5,* 1860. Taken from the Internet Sacred Text Archive, www.sacred-texts.com, managed by John Bruno Hare.

___________. "Cave Reveals Southwest's Abrupt Climate Swings During Ice Age." *Science Daily.com,* January 25, 2010.

___________. Church Community Services, Elkhart, IN website.

___________. *Church of the Holy Trinity v. United States. U.S. Supreme Court:* 143 U.S. 457 (1892). *www.talkorigins.org.*

___________. *CNN.com.*

___________. "Coal, Volcanism and Noah's Flood," *TJ (Technical Journal)* 1(1):11–29, Creation Ministries International, April 1984.

___________. Committee on the Judiciary House of Representatives, Prohibiting Detention Camps, March 18, 1971.

___________. *Corpus Aristotelicum,* collected works of Aristotle preserved by Medieval manuscript transmission. They are studies of philosophy made by Aristotle's school since many of his original works have been lost. Immanuel Bekker's nineteenth-century edition (1831-1836) is based on ancient classifications of these works. *Gutenberg.org*

___________. "The Date of Christ's Birth," Bible Studies at *The Moorings.org.*

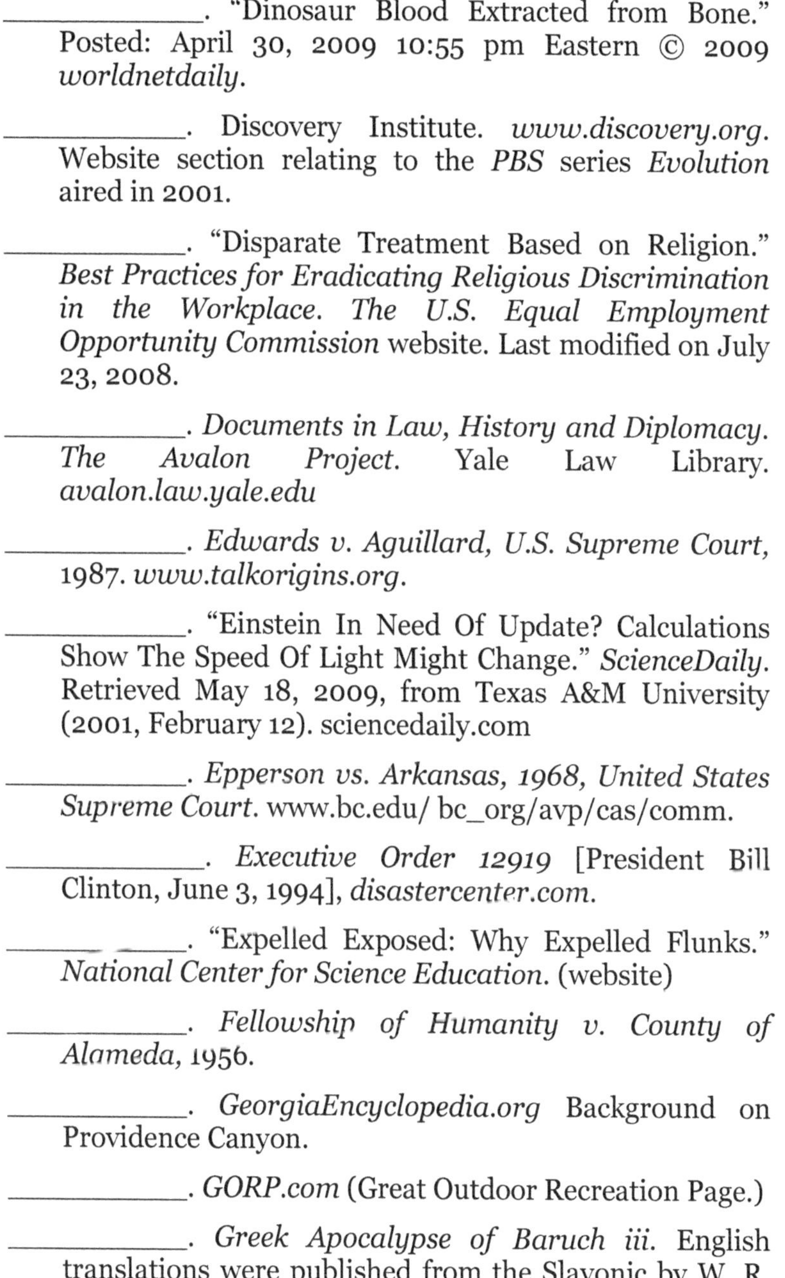

___________. "Dinosaur Blood Extracted from Bone." Posted: April 30, 2009 10:55 pm Eastern © 2009 *worldnetdaily*.

___________. Discovery Institute. *www.discovery.org*. Website section relating to the *PBS* series *Evolution* aired in 2001.

___________. "Disparate Treatment Based on Religion." *Best Practices for Eradicating Religious Discrimination in the Workplace. The U.S. Equal Employment Opportunity Commission* website. Last modified on July 23, 2008.

___________. *Documents in Law, History and Diplomacy. The Avalon Project*. Yale Law Library. *avalon.law.yale.edu*

___________. *Edwards v. Aguillard, U.S. Supreme Court*, 1987. *www.talkorigins.org*.

___________. "Einstein In Need Of Update? Calculations Show The Speed Of Light Might Change." *ScienceDaily*. Retrieved May 18, 2009, from Texas A&M University (2001, February 12). sciencedaily.com

___________. *Epperson vs. Arkansas, 1968, United States Supreme Court*. www.bc.edu/ bc_org/avp/cas/comm.

___________. *Executive Order 12919* [President Bill Clinton, June 3, 1994], *disastercenter.com*.

___________. "Expelled Exposed: Why Expelled Flunks." *National Center for Science Education*. (website)

___________. *Fellowship of Humanity v. County of Alameda*, 1956.

___________. *GeorgiaEncyclopedia.org* Background on Providence Canyon.

___________. *GORP.com* (Great Outdoor Recreation Page.)

___________. *Greek Apocalypse of Baruch iii*. English translations were published from the Slavonic by W. R.

Morfill (Apocrpyha Anecdota II, ed. M. R. James [T&S 5.1] Cambridge: CUP, 1987. Pp. 95-102) and from the Slavonic and Greek by H. M. Hughes (APOT 2. Pp. 533-41). The pseudepigraphon was composed in the beginning of the second century A.D., but it is difficult to discover whether it was written in Greek, Hebrew, or Aramaic. (Background note from Charlesworth, James H. The Pseudepigrapha and Modern Research: with a Supplement. SBLSCS 7. Chico, Ca.: Scholars Press, 1981.)M. R. James's publication of the Greek text, until then entirely unknown, in "Texts and Studies: Contributions to Biblical and Patristic Literature," edited by J. Armitage Robinson, v., No. i., pp. 84-94, Cambridge, 1897.

____________. *gulaghistory.org*.

___________. "How Old are Kimberlites and Diamonds?" *American Museum of Natural History* website.

___________. "Judge Says UC (University of California) Can Deny Religious Course Credit. "*Answers in Genesis News to Note*. From the *San Francisco Chronicle,* Aug 16, 2008.

___________. "Kim Jong Il." *BBC news online*. Asia/Pacific Profile: Page last updated at 11:14 GMT, Friday, 16 January 2009.

___________. "Letter of Oct. 7, 1801 from Danbury (CT) Baptist Assoc. to Thomas Jefferson," *Thomas Jefferson Papers*, Manuscript Division, Library of Congress, Wash. D.C.

___________. Library of Congress website.

__________. *McLean v. Arkansas Board of Education*, 1982. www.talkorigins. org/faqs/mclean-v-arkansas.

___________. *Magna Carta*, 1215 AD, from *The Avalon Project. Documents in Law, History and Diplomacy*. Yale Law Library. *avalon.law.yale.edu*.

____________. The Mahabharata. "Santiparva," cclx.20, 21, 23 and cxxiv.67, translated by Friedrich Max Müller and others *in Sacred Books of the East* (50 volumes), Oxford University Press, 1879-1910.

____________. *Mayflower* 1620.com (website).

____________. The National Archives. *archives.gov.*

____________. *National Geographic,* photo caption, March 1, 2010.

____________. National Park Services Website.

____________. National Park Service report on Wall Arch collapse August 4-5, 2008.

____________. *The New York Times.* News item published September 14, 1999.

____________. "NC State Paleontologist Discovers Soft Tissue in Dinosaur Bones." North Carolina State University News Release from *www.ncsu.edu/ news/press* /05-03/05 March 24, 2005.

____________. Novori.com. History and manufacture of synthetic diamonds.

____________. "Parents Fuming as Texas Schools Let Gideons Provide Bibles to Students." *Foxnews.com,* Tuesday, May 19, 2009.

____________. *Peloza v. Capistrano School District,* 1994. *www.talkorigins.org.*

____________. "Prohibiting Detention Camps." U. S. House of Representatives, Committee on the Judiciary, March 18, 1971.

____________. "Superbridge." *NOVA. PBS.* November 12, 1997.

____________. Public Information Office, Jet Propulsion Laboratory, California Institute of Technology, NASA, press release, July 21, 1994.

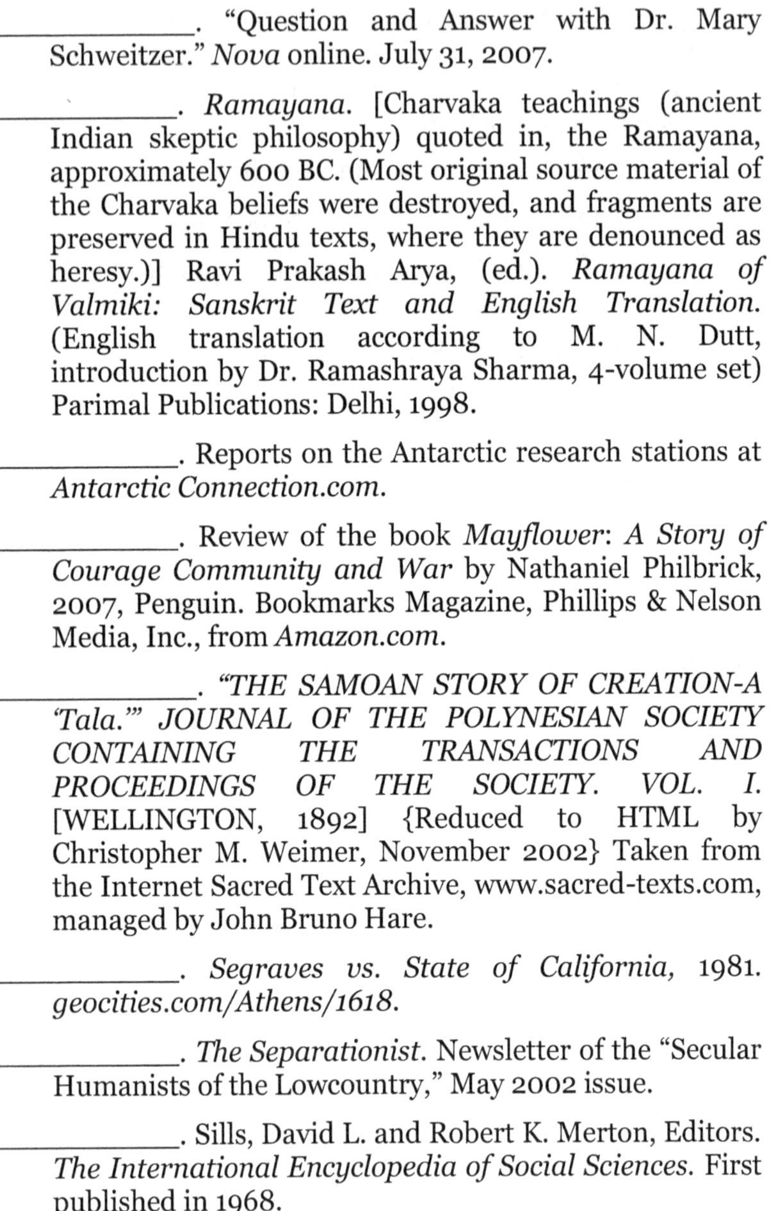


___________. "Question and Answer with Dr. Mary Schweitzer." *Nova* online. July 31, 2007.

___________. *Ramayana.* [Charvaka teachings (ancient Indian skeptic philosophy) quoted in, the Ramayana, approximately 600 BC. (Most original source material of the Charvaka beliefs were destroyed, and fragments are preserved in Hindu texts, where they are denounced as heresy.)] Ravi Prakash Arya, (ed.). *Ramayana of Valmiki: Sanskrit Text and English Translation.* (English translation according to M. N. Dutt, introduction by Dr. Ramashraya Sharma, 4-volume set) Parimal Publications: Delhi, 1998.

___________. Reports on the Antarctic research stations at *Antarctic Connection.com.*

___________. Review of the book *Mayflower: A Story of Courage Community and War* by Nathaniel Philbrick, 2007, Penguin. Bookmarks Magazine, Phillips & Nelson Media, Inc., from *Amazon.com.*

___________. *"THE SAMOAN STORY OF CREATION-A 'Tala.'" JOURNAL OF THE POLYNESIAN SOCIETY CONTAINING THE TRANSACTIONS AND PROCEEDINGS OF THE SOCIETY. VOL. I.* [WELLINGTON, 1892] {Reduced to HTML by Christopher M. Weimer, November 2002} Taken from the Internet Sacred Text Archive, www.sacred-texts.com, managed by John Bruno Hare.

___________. *Segraves vs. State of California,* 1981. *geocities.com/Athens/1618.*

___________. *The Separationist.* Newsletter of the "Secular Humanists of the Lowcountry," May 2002 issue.

___________. Sills, David L. and Robert K. Merton, Editors. *The International Encyclopedia of Social Sciences.* First published in 1968.

___________. *State v. Scopes, Scopes v. State, 152 Tenn. 424, 278 S.W. 57. Scopes vs. The State of Tennessee* (1926).

___________. "Thanksgiving Ain't No Holiday for Wimps." *Pickens County Progress,* Staff Review of the book *Mayflower: A Story of Courage Community and War* by Nathaniel Philbrick, 2007, Penguin. November 27, 2008.

___________. "Tiny Fossils reveal Warm Antarctic Past." *National Geographic.* July 26, 2008.

___________. "Titanic" article. *New World Encyclopedia.org.*

___________. *Torcaso v. Watkins. U.S. Supreme Court.*1961. *uftonline.org/* TestOath/Torcaso.htm

___________. University of Oxford, Bodleian Philosophy Faculty Library, Manuscripts and Rare Books "Medieval Manuscript Sources and Incunabula." *ox.ac.uk.*

___________. Utah Geological Survey, *Utah.gov.*

___________. *varchive.org.* A scholarly archive of Immanuel Velikovsky's unpublished works.

___________. *Voices for Evolution* (website).

___________. *Washington Ethical Society v. District of Columbia,* 249 F.2d 127 (D.C. Cir. 1957).

___________. *Web of Science* (Formerly Science Citation Index). Guillermo Gonzalez - publication record at ISU.

___________. *Webster v. New Lenox School District,* 1990, the Seventh Circuit Court of Appeals. *geocities.com/Athens/618/Webster_vs._New_Lenox.html*

___________. *Wikipedia.org*

___________. The *Wisconsin University website,* overview of the Laramide/ Yellowstone mountain ranges with aerial maps designating geologic ages.

___________. World Net Daily. *wnd.com.*

___________. Youth Ministry Entertainment (or Y-ME ministries). *y-ment.com.*

___________. Abbott, Frank Frost and Alan Chester Johnson (authors, translators and editors). *Municipal Administration in the Roman Empire [concerning the The Law of the Twelve Tables (Duodecim Tabulae), the ancient foundation of Roman law*]. Princeton University Press, Princeton, NJ, 1926.

Adams, John. "Argument in defence of the soldiers in the Boston Massacre trial." December 1770.

___________. "Letter to Abigail Adams." July 7, 1775.

___________. "Letter to the 1st Brigade of the 3rd Division of the Militia of Massachusetts." October 11, 1798.

___________. "Letter to a friend." 1805.

___________. "Letter to Benjamin Waterhouse," 29 October 1805.

Adams, Samuel. "Letter to John Pitts." 21 January 1776.

___________. "The Report of the Committee of Correspondence to the Boston Town Meeting" Nov. 20, 1772. *history.hanover. edu/texts/adamss.html.*

Ahlstrom. Sydney F. *A Religious History of the American People.* New Haven: Yale University Press, 1972.

Aquinas, Thomas. *Summa Theologica* 1265-1274 AD Sixth Article [I-II, Q. 94, Art. 6] Objection 3. Translated by Fathers of the English Dominican Province. Benziger Brothers, New York. 1947.

Archer, Gleason Leonard, Jr. *A Survey of Old Testament Introduction.* Chicago: Moody, c. 1974. Updated and revised ed., c1994.

Arndt, William F. and F. Wilbur Gingrich, trans. Bauer, Walter. *A Greek-English Lexicon of the New Testament and Other Early Christian Literature.* University of Chicago Press: Chicago, 1967.

Asimov, Isaac. *The Roving Mind.* Prometheus Books, 1997.

Athenagoras of Athens. *Legatio pro Christianis* [ "Supplication for the Christians"]. (Letter to Marcus Aurelius), 177 A.D. Translated by B. P. Pratten in "Athenagoras." *The Ante-Nicene Fathers, vol. 2*, Wm. B. Eerdmans, Grand Rapids: Michigan, 1954.

Augustine of Hippo. *City of God.* Selections. series 1, vol. 2 of the Nicene and Post-Nicene Fathers. Translated Henry Bettenson. Pelican Books, England, Clay's LTD, St. Ives Place, 1972.

Austin, Steven. Citing Hamilton Hicks. "Mineralized sodium silicate solutions for artificial petrification of wood," United States Patent Number 4,612,050, September 16, 1986, pp. 1-3. *CatastroRef*--'Catastrophe Reference Database: Catastrophes in Earth History, Geologic Evidence, Speculation and Theory', Institute for Creation Research, San Diego. Entry no. 267.

Austin, S.A. (editor). *Grand Canyon: Monument to Catastrophe.* Institute for Creation Research, Santee, California, 1994.

Ayer. A.J. (editor) *The Humanist Outlook.* Rationalist Press Association, Ltd. 1968.

Bakunin Mikhail. *God and the State.* written 1871. First published 1882 (Discovered posthumously by Carlo Cafiero and Elisée Reclus). Translated by Benjamin R. Tucker. Published by Mother Earth Publishing Association, New York, 1916.

Baldwin, James. *The Fire Next Time.* 1963 by the Dial Press. Copyright renewed 1990, 1991 by Gloria Baldwin Karefa-Smart. Published in the United States by Vintage Books, a division of Random House, first Vintage International Edition, February 1993.

Baldwin, Roger Nash. "Thirty Years Later." *Harvard Class Book of 1935.* "Baldwin's Class of 1905 on its thirtieth anniversary," Insight on the News 1997.

Balmer, Randall and John R. Fitzmier. *The Presbyterians.* Westport, CT: Praeger, 1994.

Balter, Michael. "How Human Intelligence Evolved—Is It Science or 'Paleofantasy'?" *Science* magazine, 2008.

Barnett, Randy E. "The Case for a Federalism Amendment." *Wall Street Journal,* April 23, 2009.

Bates, Mike. "Aleksandr Solzhenitsyn: The Power of One," *The National Ledger, an Eclectic Mix.* August 7, 2008. The article quotes from Aleksandr Solzhenitsyn's *The Gulag Archipelago,* 1918-1956, Volume 1, English translation by Thomas P. Whitney and Harry Willetts, Harper & Row, New York, NY, 1973.

Beale, David O. *In Pursuit of Purity.* Bob Jones University Press: Greenville, SC, 1986.

Beckford, Martin, Antony Flew, Richard Dawkins. "Flew Speaks Out: Professor Antony Flew reviews The God Delusion." (Flew's review is copyrighted as follows) Antony Flew, 2008, *bethinking.org. www.telegraph.co.uk/ science/science-news,* 9:30 PM BST 02 Aug 2008.

Bentham, Jeremy. *The Works of Jeremy Bentham,* vol. 4, Edinburgh: William Tait. 1838-1843. 11 vols, 1843.

Bhartruhari, Neeti Shatakan (spelling varies; a work of Sanskrit philosophical verse). The empire in which he lived lasted from 185 B.C. to 135 A.D. Sahu Dharanidhar published *An English Verse Translation of Three Shatakas of Bhartruhari* in 2003.

Bierce, Ambrose. *The Enlarged Devil's Dictionary*. 1906.

Billington, Ray Allen. *Westward Expansion: A History of the American Frontier,* Macmillan, New York, NY, 1974.

Blackburn, Simon. "Independent on Sunday." *National Secular Society Newsline,* 12 May 2002.

Blackstone, William. Commentaries on the Law of England, 1765–1769.

Bonomi, Patricia U. "Religious Pluralism in the Middle Colonies." *Divining America: Religion in American History,* New York University, National Humanities Center. *nationalhumanitiescenter.org* accessed May 6, 2010.

Bowden, Thomas A. "Your Child Is Not State Property," *FrontPage* Magazine, April 4, 2008. Reproduced at Ayn Rand Center for Individual Rights Website. (Thomas A. Bowden is an analyst at the Ayn Rand Institute, focusing on legal issues.)

Bradford, William. *History of Plymouth Plantation. Bradford's History of 'Plimoth Plantation' From the Original Manuscript. With a Report of the Proceedings Incident to the Return of the Manuscript to Massachusetts.* c. 1650. *Gutenberg.org*

Breasted, James Henry. *Ancient Records of Egypt: Historical Documents from the Earliest Times to the Persian Conquest,* collected, edited, and translated, with Commentary. Chicago: University of Chicago Press, 1906–1907.

Brian, Denis. Adapted from *Einstein, A Life*. John Wiley and Sons, New York, 1996.

Briggs, Charles Augustus. *American Presbyterianism.* New York, NY: Charles Scribner's Sons, 1885

Brown, Brian. *The Wisdom of the Egyptians* (1923). Taken from the Internet Sacred Text Archive, *www.sacred-texts.com,* managed by John Bruno Hare.

Budge, E. A. Wallis. "Legends of the Gods. THE HISTORY OF CREATION." *The Egyptian Texts, edited with Translation.* (Brit. Mus. Papyrus No 10,188). [1912] Taken from the Internet Sacred Text Archive, *www.sacred-texts.com,* managed by John Bruno Hare.

Butt, Kyle, M.A. "'So We Make Up Stories' About Human Evolution." Apologetics' Press. 2008. *www.apologeticspress.org.*

Byrnes, Ryan. "Private Sector Jobs Decline, Government Jobs Increase." Quoting Bill Beach, director of the Center for Data Analysis at the Heritage Foundation. *CNS News,* Monday, March 09, 2009.

Calvin, John. Commentary on Luke 24:45. *Commentary On A Harmony of the Evangelists, Matthew, Mark, and Luke.* Translator from Latin and collator with the French version Rev. William Pringle. Edinburgh, Calvin Translation Society, 1847-1850. Calvin's Commentaries, Vol. 33: Matthew, Mark and Luke, Part III, translated by John King, 1847-50.

__________. *Institutes of the Christian Religion.* Thomas Norton, Translator. 1581.

Calabresi, Guido. *A Common Law for the Age of Statutes.* Copyright by the President and Fellows of Harvard College, 1982.

Callaway, Henry. *The Religious System of the Amazulu.* Springville, Natal, 1870.

Carson, Jonathan David. "Science's Sins of the Eyes." *New Oxford Review,* November 2001.

Castillo, Bernal Diaz Del. *The Discovery And Conquest Of Mexico* 1517-1521. Edited by Genaro Garcia, Translated with an Introduction and Notes, A. P. Maudslay. first pub 1928. Taken from the Internet Sacred Text Archive, *www.sacred-texts.com*, managed by John Bruno Hare.

Catullus, Gaius Valerius (c. 84 – c. 54 BC). *Carmina.* Translated by Leonard C. Smithers. 1894.

Chamberlain, B.H. translator. [1882] *THE KOJIKI PART I.- THE BIRTH OF THE DEITIES. THE BEGINNING OF HEAVEN AND EARTH* Taken from the Internet Sacred Text Archive, www.sacred-texts.com, managed by John Bruno Hare.

Charron Pierre. *De la sagesse* ("Of Wisdom," In Three Parts). French version, 1601. Translated by Samson Lennard, Eliot's Court Press for Edward Blount and Will, Aspley, London, c.1615.

Chauceer, Geoffrey. "Prologue." *The Canterbury Tales.* 14th century. (Description of the Poor Parson). *msgr.ca/msgr-3/church_of_england.htm and the subsite msgr.ca/msgr-3/canterbury_tales_parson.htm.*

Clarke, Arthur C. *90th Birthday Reflections,* 2007.

___________. *Greetings, Carbon-Based Bipeds! : Collected Essays,* 1934-1998 including "Credo" (1991). St. Martin's Press, New York, NY, 1999

Cline, Aaron. Agnosticism/atheism columnist for ten years. *About.com.*

Clinton, Hillary. Speech. Global Business Coalition on HIV/AIDS Annual Awards for Business Excellence Gala at the Kennedy Center in Washington, D.C. Wednesday, Sept. 28, 2005.

___________. Speech in San Francisco, CA. June 28th, 2004.

Coe, R.S. and M. Prevot. "Evidence suggesting extremely rapid field variation during a geomagnetic reversal." *Earth and Planetary Science Letters,* Elsevier, Amsterdam, Netherlands. Vol. 92, pp. 296-297, 1989.

Coomaraswamy, Rama. "The Conflict Between Science and Faith," from his online archives, 2001.

Covey, Stephen. *Principle-Centered Leadership*. Fireside, Simon and Schuster, Rockefeller Center, New York, NY, 1992.

Cunningham, G., Fluckiger-Hawker, E, Robson, E., and Zólyomi, G.,*The Epic of Gilgamesh, The Electronic Text Corpus of Sumerian Literature,* Oxford 1998-.

Curtis, Adrian. *Oxford Bible Atlas*, Fourth Edition. Oxford University Press: London, 2009.

Custer, Stewart. *A Treasury of New Testament Synonyms.* Bob Jones Univ. Press: Greenville, SC, 1975.

Cyprian of Carthage (3rd century AD). Letter LXXII, *Ad Jubajanum de haereticis baptizandis.* Translated by Robert Ernest Wallis. From *Ante-Nicene Fathers, Vol. 5.* Edited by Alexander Roberts, James Donaldson, and A. Cleveland Coxe. (Buffalo, NY: Christian Literature Publishing Co., 1886.)

Dalrymple, G. Brent. *The Age of the Earth.* Stanford University Press: Stanford, CA, 1991.

Darwin, Charles. *The Correspondence of Charles Darwin. 1821-1860. Vol. 8* Cambridge University Press, 1993.

___________. *The Descent of Man.* Princeton University Press, Princeton NJ, 1981.

___________. "Charles Darwin's Natural Selection," Being the Second Part of his *Big Species Book* Written from 1856 to 1858, ed. R.C. Stauffer Cambridge, 1975.

Davidson, J. P., W. E. Reed, and P. M. Davis. "The Rise and Fall of Mountain Ranges." *Exploring Earth: An Introduction to Physical Geology,* Upper Saddle River, New Jersey, Prentice Hall, 1997.

Davies, A. Powell. *America's Real Religion.* Boston: Beacon Press, 1965.

Dawkins, Richard. *The Ancestor's Tale: A Pilgrimage to the Dawn of Evolution.* (Editorial research by Yan Wong) Boston, N.Y.: A Mariner Book, Houghton Mifflin, 2004.

___________. quoted in "The Evolutionary Future of Man." *The Economist.* 1993-09-11, vol. 328.

___________. The Extended Phenotype: The Long Reach of the Gene. London: Oxford University Press, 1982, 1999.

___________. quoted in "The Flying Spaghetti Monster." Steve Paulson. *Salon.com,* October 13, 2006.

___________. *The Greatest Show on Earth.* Free Press, Simon and Schuster, New York, NY, also by Bantam Press Transworld Publishers in Great Britain, 2009.

___________. *River Out of Eden.* Basic Books, the Perseus Book Group, New York, NY, 1995.

___________. *The Root of All Evil.* Television documentary, January 2006.

___________. "Science, Delusion and the Appetite for Wonder." *The Richard Dimbleby Lecture.* BBC1 Television, November 12,1996.

___________. *The Selfish Gene.* London: Oxford University Press, 30th Edition, 2006.

___________. "Slaves to Superstition," *The Enemies of Reason.* [1.01], timecode 00:46:47ff, aired 13 August 2007.

___________. "From Tail to Tale On the Path of Pilgrims In Life." *The Scotsman.* April 9, 2005.

___________. Speech at the Edinburgh International Science Festival, April 15, 1992.

___________. Speech following the 9/11/2001 Islamic-led terrorist attacks on targets in the United States.

__________. *Unweaving the Rainbow: Science, Delusion and the Appetite for Wonder.* Houghton-Mifflin, New York, NY, 1998.

DeYoung, Dr. Don. *Thousands, Not Billions: Challenging an Icon of Evolution Questioning the Age of the Earth.* Green Forest, AR: Master Books, Inc., 2005.

Dickens, Charles. *Bleak House.* originally published serially from March 1852 to September 1853.

__________. *A Tale of Two Cities.* 1859.

Dickinson, Emily. "The Bible Is an Antique Volume," poem # 1545, Johnson, Thomas H., editor. *Complete Poems.* Boston: Little, Brown, 1960.

Dillard, Annie. *Pilgrim at Tinker Creek.* Harper's Magazine Press, New York, NY, 1974.

Disney, Walt. Quoted on *justDisney.com.*

Dollar, George W. *A History of Fundamentalism in America.* Greenville, SC: Bob Jones University Press, 1973.

Douglass, Frederick. "What, to the Slave, is the Fourth of July?" address given to a women's anti-slavery society in Rochester, New York. July 4, 1852.

DuBois, W.E.B. essay on birth control in Margaret Sanger's *Birth Control Review.* 1932.

Dunphy, John J. Quoted in *Humanist Magazine,* January-February 1983.

Dyer, B.D. and R.A. Obar. *Tracing the History of Eukaryotic Cells.* Columbia University Press, 1994.

Edison, Thomas A. "The Philosophy of Paine," a June 7, 1925 essay from the book, *The Diary and Sundry Observations,* edited by Dagobert D. Runes (1948).

Edwards, Chris. "Federal Pay Continues Rapid Ascent." *The Cato Institute Website. Cato At Liberty.org.* The Bureau of Economic Analysis annual data on compensation levels by industry. August 24, 2009 11:57 am.

Edwards, Jonathan. "Sinners in the Hands of an Angry God." Enfield, Connecticut, July 8, 1741.

Eisenhower, Dwight David. Speech when installed as president of Columbia University in 1948.

Epicurus, from the *40 Sovran Maxims* (or "Sovereign Maxims"), 341-270 BC, as translated by Robert Drew Hicks, 1925.

__________. *Orestes*. Translated by E. P. Coleridge, 1910. Taken from the Internet Sacred Text Archive, www.sacred-texts.com, managed by John Bruno Hare.

__________. Recorded by Seneca the Younger in his *Epistle XX. From Lucius Annaeus Seneca. Moral Essays*. Translated by John W. Basore. The Loeb Classical Library. London: W. Heinemann, 1928-1935. 3 vols.

Epictetus. *The Encheiridion*. Transcribed by Flavius Arrianus. Translated by Sanderson Beck, 1911.

Eskridge, William Jr. *Dynamic Statutory Interpretation*. Copyright by the President and Fellows of Harvard College, 1994.

Eusebius of Caesarea. *Church History or Ecclesiastical History* (Hist. Ecc viii 2.) written by in the 4th century. Translated by Arthur Cushman McGiffert, From Nicene and Post-Nicene Fathers, Second Series, Vol. 1. Edited by Philip Schaff and Henry Wace. Christian Literature Publishing Co., Buffalo, NY, 1890.

Evans, William. *The Great Doctrines of the Bible*. Moody Publishers: Chicago, IL, 1995.

Fa-Hien (or Fa-Xien)). *A Record of Buddhistic Kingdoms, Being an Account by the Chinese Monk Fa-Hien of his Travels in India and Ceylon in Search of the Buddhist*

*Books of Discipline*. Written between A.D. 399 and 412. Translated by James Legge, 1886.

Fange, Erich A. Von. "Time Upside Down." *Creation Research Quarterly*. June 1974.

Farabee, M.J. *The Online Biology Book*. Estrella Mountain Community College, Avondale, Arizona. emc.maricopa.edu.1992-2002.

Faure, G. *Principles of Isotope Geology*. 2nd. edition. John Wiley and Sons: New York, NY, 1986.

Fowler, Regi (Church/ Community Vice President). "Tolerating Thoughts On Tolerance," *Texas Sings,* Volume 13, number 2, Fall 1997.

Foxe, John. *Foxe's Book of Martyrs*. Written ca. 1560, revised in the 1700s edited by William Byron Forbush. Taken from the Internet Sacred Text Archive, www.sacred-texts.com, managed by John Bruno Hare.

Franklin, Benjamin. *Autobiography*. First English version published London, 1793. (Please see the Great Awakening Appendix for publication history.)

____________. From his speech at the Constitutional Convention Philadelphia, PA. June 28, 1787.

Freud, Sigmund. *The Future of an Illusion*. 1927. Translated by W.D Robson-Scott. English translation published by Horace Liveright and the Institute of Psychoanalysis. 1928.

Gibbs, Phil (original writer, 1996) and Sugihara Hiroshi (1997 update). "Occam's (or Ockham's) razor." University of California, Riverside, *Math.ucr.edu*.

Gibson, Rebecca. "Canyon Creation." *Answers in Genesis,* September 2000.

Gilley,Gary E. *This Little Church Went to Market–Is the Modern Church Reaching Out of Selling Out?* Evangelical Press, Carlisle, PA, July 2005.

Gish, Duane T. "A Decade of Creationist Research" (Part I). *Creation Research Society Quarterly*. 12 (1): 34-46 June, 1975.

Goetz, Delia, and Sylvanus Griswold Morley. *The Book of the People: POPOL VUH*. from Adrián Recino's translation from Quiché into Spanish. 1954. Taken from the Internet Sacred Text Archive, *www.sacred-texts.com,* managed by John Bruno Hare.

Goldberg, Justice Arthur J. The Supreme Court of the United States No. 02-1574 UNITED STATES OF AMERICA, PETITIONER v. MICHAEL A. NEWDOW, ET AL. ON PETITION FOR A WRIT OF CERTIORARI TO THE UNITED STATES COURT OF APPEALS FOR THE NINTH CIRCUIT REPLY BRIEF FOR THE UNITED STATES. June 26. 2003.

Grant, Peter R. and B. Rosemary Grant. "Genetics and the origin of bird species." *The National Academy of Sciences of the USA Colloquium Paper,* 1997.

Green, Joey, editor. *Philosophy on the Go*. Joey Green and Alan Corcoran, Running Press, Philadelphia, PA, 2007.

Green, Nathan, Dr. *Course overview for GEO.101,"Introduction to Geology,"* University of Alabama. Spring 2006.

Grinspoon, Lester. *Marihuana Reconsidered*. Quick American Archives. Quick Trading Company, Oakland, CA, 1971.

Hall, Edward T. *Beyond Culture*. Anchor Books, Random House, New York, NY, 1976.

Hall, Fred. "Ice Cores Not All That Simple." *AEON II*: 1, 1989:199.

Haeckel, Ernst. *The History of Creation*. Vol. 1, 6-9. 1876. Translated by Joseph McCabe, Watts & Company, London, 1912.

Hamilton, Alexander. Letter to James Bayard. 1802.

Hamilton, Alexander and James Madison. *The Federalist Papers*. Signet Classics, Penguin, Putnam: New York, NY, 2003.

Hammond, James Henry (Senator of South Carolina) "Reply to Senator William H. Seward of New York." 1858.

Hancock, Graham. *Fingerprints of the Gods*. Three Rivers Press, New York, NY: Crown Publishing Group, Random House, 1995.

___________. *Underworld: The Mysterious Origins of Civilization,* Three Rivers Publishing, Crown, Random House, New York, NY, 2003.

Han Fei. c 200 BC. *The Five Vermin*. W. K. Liao (translator and annotator), The Complete Works of Han Fei Tzu. 2 vols, London, 1939-59.

Hannam, James. "Medieval Science and Philosophy" and "Science and Church in the Middle Ages." (From his Web site for the book.) *God's Philosophers: How the Medieval World Laid the Foundations of Modern Science*. Icon Books, London, 2009.

Hapgood, Charles H., J.B. Delair and E.F. Oppe. *The Path of the Pole*. Chilton Books, Philadelphia, PA, 1970.

Harris, Sam. *The End of Faith*. W.W. Norton & Company New York, NY, 2004.

Haught, James A. *2000 Years of Disbelief: Famous People with the Courage to Doubt*. Prometheus Books, Amherst, NY, 1998.

Hawking, Stephen. *The Illustrated A Brief History of Time*. New York, NY: Bantam Dell, a division of Random House, 1996.

Heinlein, Robert A. *The Notebooks of Lazarus Long,* 1978, Pomegranate Publications, Inc., 1999.

Herndon, William and Jesse W. Weik. *Herndon's Lincoln: The True Story of a Great Life,* a three volume edition published by Belford, Clarke & Company beginning in 1889.

Herodotus (484-ca. 425 BC). *Histories*. English translation G. C. Macaulay. Macmillan, London and NY, 1890.

Hesiod. *Theogeny*. Translated by Hugh G. Evelyn-White. 1914. Taken from the Internet Sacred Text Archive, www.sacred-texts.com, managed by John Bruno Hare.

Heyerdahl, Thor. *Kon-Tiki: Across the Pacific in a Raft* (The Kon-Tiki Expedition: By Raft Across the South Seas) F.H. Lyon, Translator. Rand McNally & Company: Skokie, IL, 1950.

____________. *Aku-Aku: The Secret of Easter Island*. 1958.

Hitler, Adolph. Speech given May 1, 1937.

____________. Speech given at Elbing, Germany. November 6, 1939.

Hoagland, Peter. American lawyer and congressman (US House of Representatives, Democrat, Nebraska), in a radio speech with Pastor Everett Silevan, 1983, documented in Bill Clinton: Friend or Foe? Ann Wilson, J. W. Publishing Company, 1993.

Hodges, Charles. *Systematic Theology*. 3 Volumes. Hendrickson Publishers: Peabody, MA, 1999.

Holmes, Oliver Wendell. "The Theory of Legal Interpretation." 12 Harvard Law Review. 417, 419 (1899).

Homer. *The Iliad*. C. 850 BC Translated by Samuel Butler, 1900. Gutenberg.org.

____________. *The Odyssey*.

Hornberger, Jacob G. "Your Children Are the Property of the State," *The Future of Freedom Foundation Website*. April 2000.

Howorth, H.H. *The Mammoth and the Flood: An Attempt to Confront the Theory of Uniformitarianism with the*

*Facts of Recent Geology*. London: Sampson Low, Marston, Searle & Livingston. 1887. Reproduced by the Sourcebook Project, Glen Arm, Maryland.

Humphreys, D. Russell, Steven A. Austin, John R. Baumgardner, and Andrew A. Snelling. "Helium Diffusion Age of 6,000 Years Supports Accelerated Nuclear Decay." *Creation Research Society Quarterly Journal*. (CRSQ) Vol 41 No 1 June 2004. Creation Research.org, Copyright © 2004 by Creation Research Society.

Humphreys, D. Russell, Ph.D. *Starlight and Time, Solving the Puzzle of Distant Starlight in a Young Universe*. Green Forest, AR: Master Books, Inc., 2004, Ninth Printing.

Huxley, Aldous. "Confessions of a Professed Atheist," Report: *Perspective on the News,* Vol. 3, June 1966, p. 19.

Huxley, Julian. "At Random," a television preview on Nov. 21, 1959.

Huxley, Thomas Henry. Letter to Charles Kingsley (23 September 1860).

Ingersoll, Robert G. *Thomas Paine*. 1892. Thomas Paine National Historical Association website, http://www.thomaspaine.org/ bio/ingersoll1892.html.

Iype, George. First press conference of Indian Prime Minister Manmohan Singh. *Rediff, India Abroad,* May 20, 2004.

Jay, William. "Charge to the Grand Jury of Ulster County" on Sept. 9, 1777. from *The Life of John Jay*. J. & J. Harper, New York, NY, 1833.

Jefferson, Thomas. *Autobiography*. 1821.

___________. "Draft for a Bill for Establishing Religious Freedom. Proposed to the Virginia Assembly," 1779. odur.let.rug.nl ~usa/P/tj3/writings/draft1779.htm

__________. "Letter to the Secretary of the Treasury, Albert Gallatin," 1802.

__________. *The Writings of Thomas Jefferson,* Albert E. Bergh, ed. (Washington, D. C.: The Thomas Jefferson Memorial Association of the United States, 1904), Vol. XVI, pp. 281-282.

__________. University of Virginia Library Collection of the letters and papers of Thomas Jefferson.

Jensen, Carl, *http://web.archive.org/web/20050831053419 /www.pbnnews.*reposted on the website *D.program.net* October 1, 2008,

Johnson, Allen H. "James Dale, the Supreme Court and fond memories of Troop 148," *News and Record I,* July 30, 2000. *Gay Straight Advocates for Education Website (gsafe.org).*

Johnson, Samuel. *The History of Rasselas, Prince of Abissinia.* 1759.

Josephus, Flavius. *Against Apion.* William Whiston, Translator, 1737. Taken from the Internet Sacred Text Archive, www.sacred-texts.com, managed by John Bruno Hare.

__________. *Antiquities of the Jews.*

__________. *Autobiography.*

__________. *Hades.*

__________. *Wars of the Jews.*

Justin Martyr. *First Apology.* Translated by Alexander Roberts and James Donaldson. 1867.

Keil, C. F. and F. Delitzsch. *Commentary on the Old Testament. 10 Volumes* Hendrickson Publishers: Peabody, MA, Updated Edition 1996.

King, Coretta Scott. Speech at the Palmer House Hilton in Chicago April 1, 1998.

King, Leonard William, translator. *ENUMA ELISH: THE EPIC OF CREATION (from The Seven Tablets of Creation,* London 1902) Public Domain. Taken from the Internet Sacred Text Archive, www.sacred-texts.com, managed by John Bruno Hare.

Kipling, Rudyard. *The Jungle Book.* originally published serially, 1893-1894.

Kurtz, Paul, Editor. *A Secular Humanist Declaration,* issued by The Council for Democratic and Secular Humanism (now the Council for Secular Humanism). Published in Free Inquiry Magazine, 1980.

LaBahn, Jeri. "Education and Parental Involvement in Secondary Schools: Problems, Solutions, and Effects," *Educational Psychology Interactive.* Valdosta, GA: Valdosta State University, 1995.

Landor, Walter Savage. "Melanchthon and Calvin," *Imaginary Conversations.* 1824-29.

Lee, Harper. *To Kill A Mocking-Bird.* Harper and Row, New York, NY, 1961 (copyright 1960 by the author, renewed 1988).

Lee, Robert E. (General Lee's son). *Recollections and Letters of General Robert E. Lee.* Rod and Black Publishers, St. Petersburg, Fl, 1904.

Leeuw, Nick De. Posting by contributor Monday, Nov. 10, 2008 on the *Right Michigan.com website,* email by Mount Hope Church in Lansing, Michigan attendee who witnessed the infiltration and actions of Bash Back (A Michigan-based pro-gay and lesbian organization) at the church November 9, 2008.

Lenin, Vladimir Ilyich. *Two Tactics of Social-Democracy in the Democratic Revolution.* Written June-July 1905, first published as a pamphlet in Geneva, July 1905, translated by Abraham Fineburg and Julius Katzer, published in Lenin's Collected Works, Volume 9, 1962, Moscow. Taken from Marxist Internet archive.

Lennon, John. "Imagine." Title song from the *Imagine album.* Ascot Sound Studios Tittenhurst Park and The Record Plant, New York, NY. Apple/EMI Label. 1971.

Lerner Lawrence S. *Good Science, Bad Science: Teaching Evolution in the States,* Thomas B. Fordham Foundation, Washington, DC, 2000.

Lewis, Charles. "Gay Altar Server Contests Firing Human Rights Tribunal asked to intervene." *National Post* (Canada). Tuesday, July 14, 2009.

Lewis, C.S. *The Abolition of Man or Reflections on education with special reference to the teaching of English in the upper forms of schools.* 1943. Available online at *www.columbia.edu/cu/augustine/arch/ lewis/abolition1.htm.*

Lewis, Joseph. *Ingersoll the Magnificent,* a compilation of Ingersoll's quotations, dedicated at a memorial address in 1954, published American Atheist Press, Austin TX, 1983.

Lewontin, Richard. Quoted in a review,"Billions and Billions of Demons," *The New York Review,* p. 31, January 9, 1997.

Lial, Margaret L., Charles David Miller and E. John Hornsby. *Beginning Algebra,* Harper-Collins College Division, New York, NY, 1992.

Liddell, H.G. and R. Scott, eds. *A Greek-English Lexicon.* Oxford University Press: London, 1982.

Lincoln, Abraham. "Response to Horace Greeley's abolitionist editorial." *New York Tribune,* August 22, 1862.

Linder, Douglas O. "Speech on the Occasion of the 25th Anniversary of the Scopes Trial," July 10, 2000. "State v. John Scopes" ( "The Monkey Trial") *http://www.law.umkc.edu/faculty/projects/ftrials/scopes/evolut.htm.*

Lisle, Jason, Ph.D. "God and Natural Law." *Answers in Genesis,* August 28, 2006.

Livingston, Dr. David P. "Nimrod: Who Was He? Was He Godly or Evil?" *Associates for Biblical Research.* Originally published in *ABR's BIBLE AND SPADE,* 2001.

Lowder, Jeffery Jay, ed. Farrell Till et. al. "The Jury Is In: The Ruling on McDowell's 'Evidence.'" 1997-2001. *www.infidels.org.*

Lubicz, Isha Schwaller, de. *Her-Bak: The Living Face of Ancient Egypt and Her-Bak: Egyptian Initiate.* Inner Traditions, Santa Fe, New Mexico, 1978.

Lucian of Samosata. c. A.D. 125 – after A.D. 180. An Assyrian rhetorician, and satirist who wrote in the Greek language, translated by A. M. Harmon, 1936.

Lucretius (Titus Lucretius Carus). *Of The Nature of Things.* (c 95-55 BC) Translator: William Ellery Leonard, 1916. Gutenberg.org.

Lundstrom, Laurel. "Students Free to Thank Anybody Except God." *Fox News.com.* Monday, November 22, 2004,

MacAuliffe, Max Arthur (Author and translator of Sikh texts). *The Sikh Religion, DIVINE SERVICES BY GURU NANAK AND OTHER GURUS THE JAPJI, Volume 1.* Oxford University Press: London, 1909. Taken from the Internet Sacred Text Archive, www.sacred-texts.com, managed by John Bruno Hare.

McCafferty, Phil. "Instant petrified wood?" *Popular Science.* October 1992.

MacDowell, Josh. *The New Evidence that Demands a Verdict.* Thomas Nelson: Nashville, TN, 1999.

MacRae, Andrew. *Radiometric Dating and the Geological Time Scale Circular Reasoning or Reliable Tools?* Copyright 1997-2004 [Text last updated: October 2, 1998] *Talk Origins.org.*

Madison, James. *Federalist No. 47,* quoting Montesquieu (Charles de Secondat, Baron de Montesquieu, 1689-1755), *The Spirit of the Laws, vol. 1,* trans. Thomas Nugent (London: J. Nourse, 1777).

__________. "Letter to Robert Walsh." March 2, 1819. *http://www.stephenjaygould. org/ ctrl/church-state.html.*

Malthus, Thomas Robert. *An Essay on the Principle of Population.* 1798.

Manning, Richard and Hans Beimler, writers. Directed By: Robert Wiemer. Executive Producer: Rick Berman. Created by Gene Roddenberry,"Who Watches the Watchers?" *Star Trek the Next Generation,* Season Three, Episode Four, first aired October 16, 1989.

Marcus Aurelius. *Meditations.* 167 AD. Translated by George Long. 1862.

Marx, Karl and Friedrich Engles. "Address of the Central Committee to the Communist League." London, 1850. Translated from German in the Soviet Union, individual translators not given. Foreign Languages Publishing House, Moscow, 1951.

__________. "Contribution to the Critique of Hegel's Philosophy of Right," 1843. Published Cambridge University 1970, editor Joseph O'Malley, translators Annette Jolin and Joseph O'Malley.

Matson, Dave E. "How Good Are Those Young-Earth Arguments?" copyright 1995.on *Infidels.org.*

Maududi, Sayeed Abdul A'la. From an address given on April 13, 1939, translation on the site *IslamistWatch.org,* no translator credited.

Merrill, Eugene H. *An Historical Survey of the Old Testament.* Baker Books: Grand Rapids, MI, 1991.

Maxwell, Bill. "Intolerance as policy." *St. Petersburg Times.* August 9, 1998.

Mill, John Stuart. *Autobiography*. 1873.

Miller, Kevin and Ben Stein, writers. *Expelled: No Intelligence Allowed*. Prod. Logan Craft, Walt Ruloff and John Sullivan. Dir. Nathan Frankowski. Assoc. Prod. Mark Mathis. Ed. Simon Tondeur. © 2008 Premise Media Corporation, Rampart Films Production.

Morgan, G. Campbell. *Acts of the Apostles*. 1924.

Morton, G.R. "Young-Earth Arguments: A Second Look," 1998. *home.entouch.net*.

Montgomery, Peter. Article on *AlterNet.org*. Feb. 10, 2010.

Mooney, Chris. "Survival of the Slickest: How Anti-Evolutionists are Mutating Their Message." *The American Prospect, Liberal Intelligence*. December 2, 2002.

Mooney, James. *MYTHS OF THE CHEROKEE. From Nineteenth Annual Report of the Bureau of American Ethnology 1897-98, Part I. COSMOGONIC MYTHS.* Taken from the Internet Sacred Text Archive, www.sacred-texts.com, managed by John Bruno Hare.

Morris, Henry M. *The Genesis Record: a Scientific and Devotional Commentary on the Book of Beginnings.* Grand Rapids, MI. Baker Book House, 1976.

Mulsow, Martin and Jan Rohls. *Socinianism And Arminianism : Antitrinitarians, Calvinists, And Cultural Exchange in Seventeenth-Century Europe,* part of the series *Brills Studies of Intellectual History,* edited by A.J. Vanderjagt, University of Gronigen, Netherlands, 2005.

Newton, Isaac. Unpublished notes for the *Preface to Opticks* (1704) quoted in *Never at Rest: A Biography of Isaac Newton* by Richard S. Westfall, Cambridge Paperback Library, 1983.

Nicholls, David. *Atheist Foundation of Australia,* undated article on the Foundation's website.

Nietzsche, Friedrich. Human, *All-Too-Human, A Book for Free Spirits.* German version 1878. Translated by Marion Faber and Stephen Lehmann. English version published by Lincoln: University of Nebraska Press, 1984.

Oard, Michael. *Frozen in Time: The Wooly Mammoth, The Ice Age and the Bible.* Green Forest, AR: Master Books, Inc., 2004.

Ovid (Publius Ovidius Naso). *Metamorphoses.* Completed in AD 8.Translated by Henry Thomas Riley, 1851.

Paine. Thomas. *The Age of Reason,* in 3 parts, 1794, 1795, 1807. *Gutenberg.org*

__________. *Agrarian Justice,* printed in English by W. Adlard in Paris, and in London for T. Williams, No. 8 Little Turnstile, Holborn, 1797.

__________. "Answer to the Bishop of Lladaff." (Concerning The Age of Reason) published in the *Theophilanthropist,* New York, NY, 1810. [Submitted posthumously by the widow of Elihu Palmer, who attended Paine during his illness in 1806, in the house of William Carver.]

__________. *Common Sense. Gutenberg.org*

__________. "Essay on Dream." Published New York, 1807. [Full title: "An Examination of the Passages in the New Testament, quoted from the Old and called Prophecies concerning Jesus Christ. To which is prefixed an Essay on Dream, showing by what operation of the mind a Dream is produced in sleep, and applying the same to the account of Dreams in the New Testament. With an Appendix containing my private thoughts of a Future State. And Remarks on the Contradictory Doctrine in the Books of Matthew and Mark."].

__________. *Examination of the Prophecies,* pamphlet published in 1807.

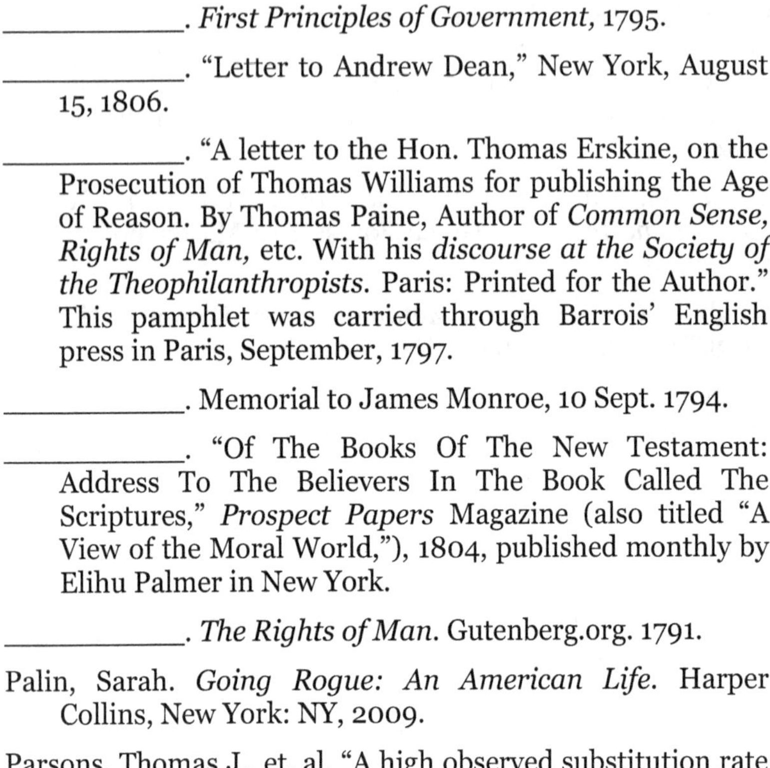

___________. *First Principles of Government,* 1795.

___________. "Letter to Andrew Dean," New York, August 15, 1806.

___________. "A letter to the Hon. Thomas Erskine, on the Prosecution of Thomas Williams for publishing the Age of Reason. By Thomas Paine, Author of *Common Sense, Rights of Man,* etc. With his *discourse at the Society of the Theophilanthropists.* Paris: Printed for the Author." This pamphlet was carried through Barrois' English press in Paris, September, 1797.

___________. Memorial to James Monroe, 10 Sept. 1794.

___________. "Of The Books Of The New Testament: Address To The Believers In The Book Called The Scriptures," *Prospect Papers* Magazine (also titled "A View of the Moral World,"), 1804, published monthly by Elihu Palmer in New York.

___________. *The Rights of Man.* Gutenberg.org. 1791.

Palin, Sarah. *Going Rogue: An American Life.* Harper Collins, New York: NY, 2009.

Parsons, Thomas J., et. al. "A high observed substitution rate in the human mitochondrial DNA control region." *Nature Genetics* 15, 363 - 368 (1997).

Pasteur, Louis. Correspondence I, p. 382-383,"To the Rector of the Academia de Douai," 15 Nov. 1855. Cuny, H., *Louis Pasteur, The Man and his Theories,* Translated P. Evans, London, The Souvenir Press, 1965.

Patten, Donald W. and Samuel R. Windsor. "Catastrophic Theory of Mountain Uplifts (A Crustal Deformation Theory)." *Catastrophism and Ancient History Vol. XIII Part 1* January 1991.

Pell, George, Cardinal. "Varieties of Intolerance: Religious and Secular," Thomas More Lecture on Religion in the Public Square, hosted by the Oxford University Newman Society, *LifesiteNews,* published March 12, 2009.

Penn, William. *THE TRYAL of WILLIAM PENN and WILLIAM MEAD*, at the Sessions held at the Old Baily in London, the 1st, 3rd, 4th, and 5th of September, 1670. *Gutenberg.org.*

Pierce, Chester M. Address at Childhood International Education Seminar, 1973.

Pitman, Sean, M.D. "Ancient Ice" (a PowerPoint presentation) created in Jan 2006. Includes testimony from a telephone interview with Bob Cardin, project manager to recover "Glacier Girl."

Plato. *The Republic.* Translated by Benjamin Jowett over a period of 30 years until his death in 1893, completed by Lewis Campbell. *Gutenberg.org.*

_________. *Critias.*

_________. *Phaedrus.*

_________. *Timmaus.*

Plutarch. *Lives.* Translated by John Dryden, 1683. Gutenberg.org.

Poincaré, Henri. "Science et méthode." ( "Science and Method"), 1908, English translation in *The Foundations of Science: Science and Hypothesis, The Value of Science, Science and Method,* The Science Press, translated by George Bruce Halstead, 1913.

Polo, Marco and Rustichello of Pisa, *The Travels of Marco Polo, Volume 1, THE COMPLETE YULE-CORDIER EDITION Including the unabridged third edition* (1903) of Henry Yule's annotated translation, as revised by Henri Cordier; together with Cordier's later volume of notes and addenda. 1920. Chapter XVII. Gutenberg.org.

Porter, Janet. "Forced Vaccines: Ready For Yours?" *Faith2action,* posted: August 18, 2009 1:00 am Eastern 2010 *World Net Daily. wnd.com.*

Prager, Dennis. "Breastfeeding as a Religion." *World Net Daily. wnd.com.* posted November 11, 2003 1:00 am Eastern.

Protagoras of Abdera (ca. 490-ca. 420 BC) Greek philosopher, agnostic, logician, believed to be from his lost work *On the Gods.* Included in the following work: *Aristophanes. Clouds.* Intro. and trans. by Carol Poster. In Aristophanes 3, ed. David Slavitt and Palmer Bovie. Philadelphia PA: University of Pennsylvania Press, 1999.

Radest, Howard B. "Are We Religious?" By Algernon David Black. Collected in *Understanding Ethical Religion.* Produced for the American Ethical Union Library, 1975.

Rand, Ayn. *Atlas Shrugged*, author's copyright 1957. Signet, New American Library, Penguin Group, New York, NY 1996.

Randerson, James. "We Know Nothing About Brain Evolution." *Guardian* (UK). Report on a 2008 Lewontin speech titled, "Why We Know Nothing About the Evolution of Cognition."

Rantoul, Robert. Fourth-of-July address. Scituate, Massachusetts, 1836.

Reese, Lizette. 1856-1935. From the poem "Truth." *American Women Poets of the Nineteenth Century.* Anthology edited by Cheryl Walker. Rutgers University, New Jersey, 1992.

Regnerus, Mark. "Sex and the Evangelical Teen." *Forbidden Fruit: Sex & Religion in the Lives of American Teenagers.* Oxford University Press, New York, NY, 2007). THOUGHTS, "Minority report," World magazine, Vol. 22, No. 29, August 11, 2007.

Rickman, Thomas Clio. *Life of Thomas Paine,* 1819.

Robertson, A.T. *Word Pictures of the New Testament.* Broadman Press: Nashville, TN: 1932, 33, Renewal 1960.

Rolston, Bruce. "Speed Of Light May Not Be Constant, Physicist Suggests." Report on an article co-authored by University of Toronto Physics professor John Moffat and former U of T researcher Michael Clayton and published in *Physics Letters* in 1999. *ScienceDaily*, October 6, 1999.

Rooney, Andy. *Sincerely, Andy Rooney*. Essay Productions, Public Affairs, by the Perseus Group, New York, NY, 1999.

Rosenhouse, Jason. *EvolutionBlog*, Posted March 5, 2010.

Roys, Ralph L, translator. *THE BOOK OF CHILAM BALAM OF CHUMAYEL* 1933. Taken from the Internet Sacred Text Archive, www.sacred-texts.com, managed by John Bruno Hare.

Rummel, R.J. STATISTICS OF DEMOCIDE Chapter 4 "Statistics Of Cambodian Democide Estimates, Calculations, And Sources." Prepublication excerpt 1997, *Hawaii.edu.*

Rushdoony, Rousas. *The Mythology of Science*. Nutley, NJ: Craig Press, 1967.

Rushdie, Salman. A 1996 speech.

Russell, Bertrand. "Why I am Not a Christian." Lecture March 6, 1927, delivered to the National Secular Society.

Sagan, Carl. *Contact*. Pocket Books, Simon and Schuster, NY: NY, 1985.

____________. *Cosmos* television series. PBS, 1980.

____________. *Cosmos: A Personal Voyage* (Updated), television series, PBS, 1989.

____________. Interview with Charlie Rose, late-night PBS talk show host, 1996.

____________. *The Demon-Haunted World: Science as a Candle in the Dark*, Ballantine Book, Random House, New York, NY, 1996.

Sand, George (Amantine Aurore Lucile Dupin). 1804-1876 Letter to Gustave Flaubert, 14 September, 1871. Translated by A.L. MacKenzie, 1921.

Sanderson, Terry. Address as president of the National Secular Society of the UK, Dec 17, 2009.

Sanger, Margaret. *Pivot of Civilization,* 1932.

___________. *The Woman Rebel, Volume I, Number 1.* Reprinted in *Woman and the New Race.* New York: Brentanos Publishers, 1922.

Sarfati, Jonathan. "Who's Really Pushing Bad Science?" *Creation.com,* Creation Ministries International, 26 September 2000.

Saxe, John Godfrey. (1816-1887). "The Blind Men and the Elephant."

Sayers, Dorothy L. "The Other Six Deadly Sins." *Creed or Chaos,* Harcourt, Brace and Company, New York: NY, 1994.

Scalia, Antonin. *Common-Law Courts in a Civil-Law System: The Role of United States Federal Courts in Interpreting the Constitution and Laws.* THE TANNER LECTURES ON HUMAN VALUES. Delivered at Princeton University, March 8 and 9, 1995.

Schaff, Phillip. *History of the Christian Church, Volumes 5, 6 and 7.* Charles Scribner's Sons, New York, 1910.

Schaeffer, Francis A. "A Christian Manifesto." An address delivered by Dr. Schaeffer in 1982 at the Coral Ridge Presbyterian Church, Fort Lauderdale, Florida. It is based on the book of the same title.

___________. *The God Who Is There.* InterVarsity Press: Downer's Grove, IL, 1998.

Schmid, Randolph E. (Associated Press). "Skull Suggests Interbreeding of Neanderthal and Modern Man." *The Denver Post,* January 15, 2007.

Schweitzer, Mary H. and Jennifer L. Wittmeyer, North Carolina State University; John R. Horner, Montana State University; Jan B. Toporski, Carnegie Institution of Washington Geophysical Laboratory. "Soft-Tissue Vessels and Cellular Preservation in Tyrannosaurus rex." *Science,* March 25, 2005. NC State, the N.C. Museum of Natural Sciences and the National Science Foundation funded the research.

__________. "Soft tissue and cellular preservation in vertebrate skeletal elements from the Cretaceous to the present." *Proceedings of the Royal Society of Biological Sciences.* vol. 274 no. 1607 183-197, 22 January 2007.

Schleiermacher, Friedrich. Letter to his father. January 1787. Martin Redeker, translator, *Schleiermacher: Life and Thought.* Fortress Press. 1973.

Sedgwick, Adam (Woodwardian Professor of Geology at Cambridge). "Letter to Charles Darwin." November 24, 1859.

Sellars, Roy Wood and Raymond Bragg. *Humanist Manifesto I draft*, 1933.

Semken, Steven, ct. al. "Trail of Time" Exhibit, Grand Canyon National Park. Associate Professor of Geoscience Education and Geological Sciences, School of Earth and Space Exploration at Arizona State University. From the *Arizona State University website.* 2008.

Seneca, Lucius Annaeus (Seneca the Younger. 4 BC to AD 65). "A letter to Serenus," as translated in *Tranquillity of Mind and Providence* by William Bell Langsdorf, 1900.

Serling, Rod. Last interview before his death, with Linda Brevelle, March 4, 1975.

Shakespeare, William. *Hamlet,* Act I Scene iii, Polonius to his son Laertes.

Shallit, Jeffrey. "Pamela Winnick's Science Envy." *Blogspot.* Monday, July 10, 2006.

Shaw, George Bernard. *Androcles and the Lion.* 1913.

Shelley, Mary Wollstonecraft. *A Vindication of the Rights of Woman With Strictures on Political and Moral Subjects,* 1792.

Shelley, Percy Bysshe. *The Necessity of Atheism* (1811), to serve as a note to the line in Queen Mab,"There is no God" (1813).

Shepherd. Jessica. "Children educated at home twice as likely to be known to social services, select committee told" and "Home pupils more likely to be known by social services and be out of work, education or training." *guardian.co.uk.* Tuesday, 13 October 2009.

Shermer, Michael. "The Fossil Fallacy: Creationists' demand for fossils that represent 'missing links' reveals a deep misunderstanding of science." *Scientific American.* 21 February 2005.

Simon, Sidney. *Values Clarification.* Originally published 1972, Warner Books. Revised edition by Grand Central Publishing, September 1, 1995.

Simpson, George Gaylord. *The Meaning of Evolution.* Revised edition. New Haven: Yale University Press, 1967.

Smith, S. Percy, trans. *The Lore of the Whare-wananga; or Teachings of the Maori College On Religion, Cosmogony, and History.* Written down by H. T. Whatahoro from the teachings of Te Matorohanga and Nepia Pohuhu, priests of the Whare-wananga of the East Coast, New Zealand. (Smith was the F.R.G.S. President of the Polynesian Society.) Part I.-Te Kauwae-runga,Or 'Things Celestial.' New Plymouth, N.Z. Printed for the Society by Thomas Avery. -- 1913. {Reduced to HTML by Christopher M. Weimer, February 2003} Taken from the Internet Sacred Text Archive, www.sacred-texts.com, managed by John Bruno Hare.

Snelling, Andrew. "Radiocarbon in Diamonds Confirmed." *Answers in Genesis,* November 7, 2007. (This study was conducted during the RATE (Radioisotopes and the Age of The Earth) research project at the Institute for Creation Research.)

___________. "The Earth's magnetic field and the age of the Earth," first published: *Creation* (Creation Ministries International), 13(4):44-48 September 1991.

___________. "The Recent Origin of Bass Strait Oil and Gas." *Creation,* 5 (2):43–46 March 1982.

Sparks, Muriel. *The Prime of Miss Jean Brodie.* Harper Collins, New York, NY, 1961.

Spence, Lewis. Excerpt from: *The Popol Vuh The Mythic and Heroic Sagas of the Kichés of Central America.* Published by David Nutt, at the Sign of the Phoenix, Long Acre, London [1908]. Taken from the Internet Sacred Text Archive, www.sacred-texts.com, managed by John Bruno Hare.

___________. *The Myths of Mexico and Peru.* (1913). Taken from the Internet Sacred Text Archive, www.sacred-texts.com, managed by John Bruno Hare.

Spurgeon, Charles Haddon. "Our Reply to Sundry Critics and Enquirers," *The Sword and Trowel,* Metropolitan Tabernacle, Elephant and Castle, London, Sept. 1887.

Steinem, Gloria. "Address to the Women of America," at the founding of the National Women's Political Caucus, 1971.

Sternberg, Dr. Richard. *RichardSternberg.org.*

Strong, James. *Strong's Exhaustive Concordance of the Bible.* Hendrickson Publishers: Peabody, MA, Updated Edition, 2007.

Suetonius (Gaius Suetonius Tranquillus). *The Twelve Caesars.* c. 117 138 AD. translation J. C. Rolfe, 1913-1914.

Sun Tzu, *The Art of War.* Estimated to have been written between 476-221 BC. Translated by Lionel Guiles, 1910. Gutenberg.org.

Swatt, Barbara (Preparer, Reference Intern). Adapted from,"Themis, Goddess of Justice," *Marian Gould Gallagher Law Library, University of Washington School of Law*. Updated Oct. 31, 2007.

Sweet, William Warren. *The Story of Religions in America.* Harper & Brothers, New York, N.Y., 1930.

Sykes, Bryan. *The Seven Daughters of Eve: The Science That Reveals Our Genetic Ancestry*. W.W. Norton: New York, N.Y., 2001.

Syrett, Harold C. editor. *The Papers of Alexander Hamilton.* NY: Columbia University Press, 1979. Vol. XXI, pp. 402-404.

Tacitus. *The Annals of Imperial Rome*. 109 AD, XIII. 32. Translated by Alfred John Church and William Jackson Brodribb, 1876.

___________. *The Histories,* 109 AD. Translated by Alfred John Church and William Jackson Brodribb, 1876.

Tamny, John. "Where Are the Supply-Side Democrats?" *National Review Online*. November 18, 2005.

Taylor, Paul (Series Editor) and Elizabeth Deane (Program Executive Producer). *American Experience, Ulysses S. Grant. PBS,* WGBH Educational Foundation, 2002.

Alfred, Lord Tennyson. *In Memoriam, AAH.* 1849. http://www.online-literature.com tennyson/718/.

Tenzin Gyatzo, 14th Dalai Lama, leader of Tibetan Buddhism,"Compassion and the Individual: the Purpose of Life." From the *Dalai Lama website.*

Thapar, Prof. Romila. *Frontline* magazine. Volume 18 - Issue 19, Sep. 15 - 28, 2001.

Thayer, Joseph Henry. *Thayer's Greek-English Lexicon of the New Testament.* Zondervan: Grand Rapids, MI, 1970.

Thiele, Edwin. *The Mysterious Numbers of the Hebrew Kings*. Zondervan Publishing House, Grand Rapids, MI, 1983.

Thiessen, Henry Clarence. *Lectures in Systematic Theology*. Wm. B. Eerdmans: Grand Rapids, MI, Revised ed., 2006.

Traufetter, Gerald. "Europe's 'Human Zoos' -- Remains of Indigenous Abductees Back Home after 130 Years." *International: Zeitgeist. Archive Der Spiegel*, 1/13/2010.

Trudeau, G.B. *Doonesbury*. Strip published in November, 1995. Universal Press Syndicate. *Doonesbury* was launched October 26, 1970.

Unruh, Bob. "Homeschooler flees state custody: Melissa Busekros surprises parents at 3 a.m." Posted: April 23, 2007 12:33 pm Eastern. *World Net Daily*.

___________. "Homeschoolers on run win U.S. asylum Judge: Teaching children 'basic right no country has right to violate.'" January 26, 2010 11:02 pm Eastern. *World Net Daily*.

Ussher, James. *Annales veteris testamenti, a prima mundi origine deducti* ( "Annals of the Old Testament, deduced from the first origins of the world"), 1650.

Ustinov, Peter. Interview with Mike Wallace. March 29, 1958.

Virgil. *The Aeneid*. c. 29 BC. Translated by John Dryden 1697. *Gutenberg.org*.

___________. *Georgics,* Book Two, published c. 29 BC. Poetic translation by John Dryden, 1697. Gutenberg.org

Vega, Garcilaso de la ( "El Inca," real name Gómez Suárez de Figueroa). *Comentarios Reales de los Incas*. Lisbon, 1609. Translated by Harold V. Livermore. 1965.

Velikovsky, Emmanuel. *Ages in Chaos*. Doubleday, New York: New York, 1952.

Voltaire (François-Marie Arouet). “Of Modern Atheists, Reasons of the Worshipers of God.” *Atheism I, Section I. C.* 1764. Selected and Translated by H.I. Woolf, Knopf, New York, NY, 1924.

Wald, George. “The Origin of Life,” *Scientific American,* 191:48, May 1954.

Walvoord, John and Roy B. Zuck. *The Bible Knowledge Commentary, Old and New Testaments.* Cook Communications: Colorodo Springs, CO, 1989.

Watts, Charles. “The Secularist’s Catechism.” complied in an undated book published by Watts & Co. entitled: *Pamphlets by Charles Watts Vol. I.* 1896.

Weinberg, Steve. “A Designer Universe?” *Address at the Conference on Cosmic Design, American Association for the Advancement of Science,* Washington, D.C. April 1999.

West, E. W., translator. 1880. *PAHLAVI TEXTS.* (Persian language works from c. 180 to 880 AD) Taken from the Internet Sacred Text Archive, *www.sacred-texts.com,* managed by John Bruno Hare.

Willebrands, Johannes Cardinal. *Response to the Boy Scouts of America official position on the admission of homosexual members and leaders,* 2000.

Willette (Site User). *Askville.Amazon.com.* posted late 2009 or early 2010.

Williams, Roger. “Mr. Cotton’s Letter Lately Printed, Examined and Answered,” (1644), and “The Hireling Ministry, None of Christ’s.” *The Complete Writings of Roger Williams.* The Narragansett Club (1652).

Wilson, Edward Osborne. *On Human Nature.* Harvard University Press, 1979.

Winthrop, John. From “A Model of Christian Charity,” 1630. *The Avalon Project. Documents in Law, History and Diplomacy.* Yale Law Library. avalon.law.yale.edu.

Whedon, Joseph Hill "Joss." Commentary on *Buffy the Vampire Slayer* series DVD, episode 5.16 ( "The Body") (Season 5, released December 9, 2003), and an interview by Tasha Robinson for *The Onion,* (an online satirical magazine) September 5, 2001.

Wheeler, Charles N. Interview with Henry Ford. *Chicago Tribune*, May 25, 1916.

Whitcomb, J.C. and H. M. Morris. *The Genesis Flood.* Grand Rapids, MI: Baker Book House, 1961.

Whitman, Walt. "Song of Myself." From *Leaves of Grass*, first published 1855. Revised and republished many times until the "deathbed" edition finished in 1892. "Definitive version" published in 1900.

Wysong, Pippa. "Dinosaur Remains Yield Soft Tissue." *Access Excellence.* Raleigh, NC April 29, 2005. (Access Excellence is an online publication of The National Health Museum, Atlanta GA.)

Xenophanes, pre-Socratic philosopher (570-475 BC). Diels, Hermann. *Die Fragmente der Vorsokratiker* ( "Pre-Socratic Fragments"). Translated by Rev. Walther Kranz. Berlin: Weidmann, 1972-1973.

Xenophon. "On Hunting." (430-354 BC). *Xenophon in Seven Volumes.* 7. Translated by E. C. Marchant, G. W. Bowersock. Constitution of the Athenians. Harvard University Press, Cambridge, MA; William Heinemann, Ltd., London. 1925.

Zahn, Drew. "Pastor waits for final word in Bible study citation: Couple ordered to get permit to host friends not out of woods yet." *WorldNetDaily* Posted: June 01, 2009 10:07 pm Eastern.

___________. "State moves to restrict Catholics in politics. Official contends church must register as 'lobbyist' to speak out." *Faith Under Fire,* Posted: June 01, 2009 9:30 pm Eastern, *World Net Daily.*

**The best gift you can give an author**

is an honest, thoughtful review. Please consider leaving one online. Help us understand what you liked and didn't like about the book and why. Help authors reach more readers and spread your influence and ours. If you liked the book, please recommend it to your spouse, friends, pastors, teachers, cashiers, employers, – anybody and everybody you see each day. If you don't know what to say, remember Proverb 16:3 – Commit thy works unto the Lord and thy thoughts shall be established. Thank you!

## OTHER BOOKS AND PRODUCTS FROM FINDLEY FAMILY VIDEO PUBLICATIONS

All our books (including Historical Fiction, SciFi, contemporary relationships short stories, and an Archaeological Mystery serial) are linked on our blog.

Elk Jerky for the Soul includes posts on current issues, excerpts from our fiction and nonfiction works, Bible teaching, travel and everyday observations, and more. http://findleyfamilyvideopublications.com/

Visit our YouTube Channel

https://www.youtube.com/channel/UCGhwNpU115ARMwgYwTIJBrA/featured. Book trailers, video excerpts, project teasers, and more. Science, History, Literature, and biblical worldview studies are the focus of our book and video projects.

**Historical Fiction**

by Michael J. Findley

The Ephron the Hittite Series (Including boxed set of all titles)

*Ephron Son of Zohar*

*Tawananna Daughter of Zohar*

*Heth Son of Canaan Son of Ham, Noah*

*Shelometh Daughter of Yovov Wife of Ephron*

*Zita Son of Ephron and Shelometh*

Adult Romantic Suspense

by Mary C. Findley

The Men of the Realmlands series

*Book One: The Baron's Ring*

*Book Two: The Captain's Blade*

*Send a White Rose*

*Chasing the Texas Wind*

*Carrie's Hired Hand* (novella)

Young Adult Historical Adventure

by Mary C. Findley

*Hope and the Knight of the Black Lion* (plus illustrated version)

The Benny and the Bank Robber Series

*Benny and the Bank Robber* (Plus homeschool editions for student and teacher with review and vocabulary)

*Doctor Dad*

*The Oregon Sentinel*

*Lines in Pleasant Places*

**Science Fiction and Fantasy**

by Michael J. Findley

*The Empire Saga* (all six of the following books in one volume)

*City on a Hill and Sojourner* (Combined Novella and Short Story)

*Nehemiah LLC* (Full-length novel available as a standalone ebook, paperback, and hardcover versions)

*Empire One: Humiliation*

*Empire Two: Repentance*

*Empire Three: Sanctification*

Steampunk

by Sophronia Belle Lyon (pen name for Mary C. Findley)

The Alexander Legacy Steampunk Literary Tribute Series

*Book One: A Dodge, a Twist, and a Tobacconist* (including illustrated version)

*Book Two: The Pinocchio Factor*

*Book Three: The Most Dangerous Game*

*Book Four: Beware the Bustle*

Fantasy/Allegory

by Mary C. Findley

Allegorical clockwork novella inspired by Little Red Riding Hood

*The Acolyte's Education*

A Paranormal Urban Fantasy serial

*His Sign: The Wait Is Over*

*His Sign 2: The Ezra Solution*

**Contemporary Fiction**

by Mary C. Findley

Romantic Suspense Novella

*Fall On Your Knees*

Relationships Short Stories

*Fifty Shades of Faithful*

*Fifty Shades of Faithful 2: In Living Color*

The Great Thirst Serial Archaeological Mystery (including boxed set of all titles)

*Part One: Prepared*

*Part Two: Purified*

*Part Three: Pursued*

*Part Four: Persecuted*

*Part Five: Persevering*

*Part Six: Protected*

*Part Seven: Prevailing*

Murder Mystery

*Mapped Out Murders*

**Nonfiction**

by Mary C. Findley

*Write for the King of Glory, 2nd Edition* (updated, with tips on indie writing and publishing)

by Michael J. and Mary C. Findley

*The Good, the Bad, and the Ugly: A Readers' and Writers' Guide for Believers*

*Biblical Studies* (Teacher and student editions plus excerpts in OT and NT Manuscript History)

*Antidisestablishmentarianism* (illustrated and plain versions)

Serial versions, illustrated and plain

*What Is an Establishment of Religion?*

*What Is Secular Humanism?*

*What Is Science?*

*What Are the Results of the Establishment of Secular Humanism?*

The Conflict of the Ages series (All have teacher and student editions plus one combined teacher edition for 1-3)

*I. The Scientific History of Origins*

*II. The Origin of Evil in the World that Was*

*III. They Deliberately Forgot: The Flood and the Ice Age*

*IV. Ice Age Civilizations*

*V. The Ancient World*

by Michael J. Findley

Short Recaps of longer nonfiction works (*Antidisestablishmentarianism* and *Conflict of the Ages)*

*Disestablish: An Overview from Creation to the Ice Age*

*Under the Sun: The Truth about History from the Beginning*

*****

Christian Books in Multiple Genres. Join Christian Indie Author ~ Readers Group on Facebook. https://www.facebook.com/groups/291215317668431/

www.ingramcontent.com/pod-product-compliance
Lightning Source LLC
LaVergne TN
LVHW050528160826
845677LV00011B/1973

* 9 7 9 8 2 3 0 9 5 5 3 1 3 *